THE
FREEDOM
PRINCIPLE

John Litweiler

THE FREEDOM PRINCIPLE

Jazz After 1958

A DA CAPO PAPERBACK

To my parents,
Ernest and Lucile Litweiler

Library of Congress Cataloging in Publication Data

Litweiler, John.
   The freedom principle: jazz after 1958 / John Litweiler.
      p.   cm. — (A Da Capo paperback)
   Reprint. Originally published: New York: W. Morrow, 1984.
   ISBN 0-306-80377-1
   1. Jazz music — History and criticism. I. Title.
ML3506.L57   1990   89-26054
781.65′5 — dc20   CIP
                                                         MN

This Da Capo Press paperback edition of *The Freedom Principle* is an unabridged republication of the first edition published in New York in 1984, here supplemented with an insert of photographs. It is reprinted by arrangement with the author.

Published by Da Capo Press, Inc.
A Subsidiary of Plenum Publishing Corporation
233 Spring Street, New York, N.Y. 10013

BOOK DESIGN BY VICTORIA HARTMAN

Grateful acknowledgment is made for permission to reprint the following.

Excerpts from *Jazz Panorama* edited by Martin Williams copyright © 1962 by Jazz Review, Inc.

Excerpt from an interview by Valerie Wilmer with Sun Ra, 1966.

Excerpt from an unpublished interview by Ted Panken with Henry Threadgill, September 1976.

Excerpts from *Down Beat* ("Coltrane on Coltrane" by John Coltrane in collaboration with Don DeMichael, and "Cecil Taylor: African Code, Black Methodology" by J. B. Figi) reprinted with permission of *Down Beat*.

Excerpt from "It's Only for Kicks Cracks and Flacks" by Roscoe Mitchell reprinted by permission of the author.

Excerpts from an interview with Joseph Jarman by John Litweiler, reprinted by permission of the Don DeMichael Archives of the Jazz Institute of Chicago.

Excerpt from the Chicago *Reader*, "Ornette Coleman: A Surviving Elder in the Universal Brotherhood of Those Who Make Music" by J. B. Figi, copyright © 1973 by Robert A. Roth, reprinted by permission of Chicago Reader, Inc.

Excerpt from the Chicago *Reader*, "An Interview with Muhal Richard Abrams, Founder and Father Figure" by John B. Litweiler, copyright © 1975 by Robert A. Roth, reprinted by permission of Chicago Reader, Inc.

Excerpt from the Chicago *Reader*, "Anthony Braxton: Music for Interplanetary Travel" by John B. Litweiler, copyright © 1979 by Chicago Reader, Inc., reprinted by permission of Chicago Reader, Inc.

Preface

The central event in post-bop jazz was the first demonstration by Ornette Coleman and his players that their music was indeed "a free thing." This book is a survey of the subsequent evolution of the jazz sensibility. For readers to whom contemporary jazz is a new experience, I hope *The Freedom Principle* will open many doors; for the other readers, may this volume help illuminate your own relationships to the music. Since the music itself is the matter of this history, little attention is given to a few individuals whose main contribution has been simply as popularizers of style; more regrettably, I've had to omit discussion of some worthy minor artists and have instead emphasized the music's main currents and major personalities. Also, post-1958 developments of the bop idiom—modal jazz, fusion music, other "inside" jazz—are for the most part discussed insofar as they're responses, direct and indirect, to the challenge of "outside" jazz. Thus a number of intriguing latter-day aspects of the art form are left to future writings or other chroniclers: this book is specifically about Free jazz and its consequences. And I've attempted to avoid duplicating the material and the methods of *Free Jazz* by Ekkehard Jost, *Four Lives in the Bebop Business* (also issued as *Black Music: Four Lives*) by A. B. Spellman, and *As Serious as Your Life* by Valerie Wilmer—these are important, original resources on the subject of musical Freedom.

This book would have been impossible to write without the interest and aid of many people from both within and without the international community of jazz musicians and listeners. In 1981, the Art Ensemble of Chicago, Derek Bailey, Ornette Coleman, Oliver Lake, Leo Smith, and Charles Tyler very kindly gave interviews, and, in particular, Charles and Kathleen Tyler provided shelter and orientation during a crucial period of study. Ron Welburn of the Institute of Jazz Studies (at Rutgers University) and Hans Lenneberg of the Chicago Jazz Archives (at the University of Chicago) were generous with their institutions' resources as well as with personal assistance. Among the others who provided important help at various stages of *The Freedom Principle*'s progress, including letters written, recordings and literature exchanged, and valuable ideas offered, were Dan Morgenstern, Ran Blake, Larayne Black, Gary Wolfe, Dick Wang, Edward Wilkerson, David Wild, Jack Maher, and the *Down Beat* staff, Chuck Nessa, J. B. Figi, and especially Terry Martin—the majority of these are associations that have been stimulating my writing for many years. Finally, my deep thanks to the National Endowment for the Humanities for the fellowship that let me begin these studies in 1981.

Contents

Preface

 1: Steps in a Search for Freedom   13

 2: Ornette Coleman: The Birth of Freedom   31

 3: Eric Dolphy   59

 4: John Coltrane: The Passion for Freedom   80

 5: Transition: Miles Davis and Modal Jazz   105

 6: The Free Jazz Underground and Sun Ra   129

 7: Albert Ayler   151

 8: Chicago, Sound in Space, and St. Louis   172

 9: Cecil Taylor   200

10: Pop-Jazz, Fusion, and Romanticism   222

11: Free Jazz in Europe:
    American, National, International   240

12: Leo Smith, Anthony Braxton, Joseph Jarman,
    and Roscoe Mitchell   265

13: Free Jazz Today   287

Appendix I: Notes   301

Appendix II: Selected Discography   307

Index   317

• I •

Steps in a
Search for Freedom

To begin, let's distinguish between freedom and Freedom; this is probably the most important distinction to be made about modern jazz. Spelled with a capital *F*, "Free jazz" is a label, the way "Dixieland" or "bop" are labels. These tags are for specific developments in jazz, and "Free jazz" comes closest to an equally standard term. At one time "avant-garde," "the new music," "the new jazz" were also commonly used to denote post-1957 developments in the jazz art, and "outside" is still frequently used. Ornette Coleman offered *Free Jazz* as the title of one of his 1960 pieces; he denies that he meant "Free jazz" to denote his new idiom, and indeed the harmonic-rhythmic features of Freedom have been anything but liberating to many musicians. But Coleman's liberation of jazz melody from traditional fetters of harmonic and rhythmic patterns certainly resulted in genuine freedom of expression for his own music and implied similar freedom to the generations that followed. So "Free jazz" is not necessarily an accurate or satisfactory label, but it's a label that has at least survived.

The quest for freedom with a small *f* appears at the very beginning of jazz and reappears at every growing point in the music's history. The earliest jazz musicians asserted their independence of melody, structure, rhythm, and expression from the turn-of-the-century musics that surrounded them; Louis Armstrong symbolized the liberation of the late twenties jazz soloist; the Count Basie band offered liberation of jazz rhythm; and Parker and Gillespie offered yet more new freedoms to jazz. Genuine freedom occurs when the artist can communicate most intimately with the materials, the language of his or her medium; each innovation in jazz, from the beginnings to the present, appears so that jazz artists can reveal what cannot be revealed in any other way. In today's jazz, if these innovations do not increase the artist's capacity for communication, then only Freedom, with a capital *F*, results.

The Free jazz idiom emerged when the developments of bop, especially hard bop, were at their height. Bop itself had appeared when the previous jazz era was largely exhausted. The purest manifestation of bop—the music of Charlie Parker, Dizzy Gillespie, Fats Navarro, Bud Powell—was a music of extremes. There were the extremes of bop's harmony, its mixtures of consonance and dissonance, its substituted harmonic structures. More extreme were bop's rhythms: the slippery accents among even tiny note values; the broken lines of eighth notes; the shock of sudden double-time runs. The fast tempos, the speed of the lines, the electrocuted leaping in the high, middle, and low ranges of the musical instruments required a coordination of nerve, muscle, and intellect that pressed human agility and creativity toward their outer limits. Bop was an exhilarated adventure; in Gillespie's dizzying trumpet heights, in Powell's hallucinated piano excitement, a deadly fall to earth is ever possible. The vividness of Parker's alto saxophone lyricism made him bop's central figure, and his rhythmic tumult is the tumult of complex, fleeting emotions. The brokenness of his phrasing, the swiftness of his passing emotions, from cruelty to tenderness, suggest a consciousness that was itself disrupted by the panic of alternating drug ingestion and withdrawal that, he said, was his life's continuity. His desperation was shared by much of his generation. Bop emerged during the national despair of World War II, when socially the art of jazz was surviving in a vicious atmosphere of racial and economic exploitation; the most readily available freedom was that of chemically induced escape. Out of the anguish of "Parker's Mood" arises a statement of faith—a generation's faith that its lyric creation redeemed its personal tragedies.

So bop was above all a romantic art. Pianist Lennie Tristano and his small circle created an even more fragile idiom out of bop's romanticism. Pure spontaneity was their objective; their materials were bop's potential ensemble unity, bop's displaced, irregular accenting, and the rhythmic effervescence of the late swing era. Harmonically Tristano's world sounded as advanced as bop, but in fact, the expressive qualities and the harmonic relationships that bop appropriated from the blues tradition had no place here; rather, the grand expansiveness of swing pianist Art Tatum was Tristano's harmonic ancestor. What the Tristano circle created was termed cool jazz for its distance from the emotional fires of bop, though in fact, it was a no less passionate quest for lyricism. A more literally detached emotionality arrived with the West Coast jazz inspired by both Tristano and Miles Davis's 1949 *Birth of the Cool* nonet, a muted, scaled-down big band. The relaxed, subdued atmosphere of West Coast jazz had a healthy acceptance of stylistic diversity and innovation, but it also accepted the emotional world of pop music at face value; even original themes are treated like more hip, more grown-up kinds of pop music. In bop's freest flights it could not escape reality, but these Californians were not aware of the conflict of values that was the source of bop.

The wide popularity of these musics prepared audiences in general for the Modern Jazz Quartet. These musicians began in bop, specifically in Dizzy Gillespie's bands, but the MJQ's narrowed range of sonorities—vibes, piano, bass, tinkling percussion—turned blues into a wicked witch that menaced structures of old-world gingerbread. For the group's pianist John Lewis liked to compose in the harmonies and forms, such as fugues, of Europe's baroque age; some of his best pieces, like the classic "Django," broke far away from the thirty-two-bar pop song harmonic structures that characterized bop. Like his friend Jimmy Giuffre, he composed some pieces in extended forms that used even classical musicians. The rhythmic movement in Giuffre's largest pieces is circumscribed; of his 1958 trio of two horn players and a guitarist, only the guitar carried pulse, and that irregularly. A self-willed asceticism characterized his work; this trio played everything *piano,* and Giuffre's own clarinet and saxes are heard only in a narrow, subtone range. The shifting rhythms and textures of his Appalachian folk variations in "The Train and the River" yield a charm that not only is new to jazz, but also contradicts the assertive expression that is jazz's birthright.

Are the largest compositions by Lewis, like "The Comedy" and "Three Little Feelings," and by Giuffre, like "Pharaoh" and "Suspensions," really jazz? If not, what are they? Gunther Schuller devised the term "third stream music" for the kind of composition that joined the streams of jazz and classical music. In Schuller's own pieces, the jazz and classical streams never do unite, but exist independently or attempt to reinforce each other; there is no real conversation in his "Conversation." He composed "Transformation" for a Brandeis University commission in 1958; among the other commissions were George Russell's important "All About Rosie," Charles Mingus's "Revelations," and two works by Schuller's fellow classical composers Harold Shapero and Milton Babbitt. In Shapero's "On Green Mountain," improvisers and orchestra cavort in a baroque dance. There's no improvisation in Babbitt's "All Set," but it is the closest these pieces come to a true hybrid idiom. Dance band sonorities and jazz phrases are extracted from context and recombined into fleeting phrases, fugues, *Klangfarbenmelodie,* stifled mutters. The jerky rhythms are founded on a percussion jungle, but the horns are modern trumpets and saxophones, so this jungle dance is urban and ominous; the implied skyscrapers are nothing more than precarious huts of earth and grass.

Many of these third stream pieces could disappear intact within the sworls of "A Trumpet," composed by Bob Graettinger in 1953. It opens with screams over throbbing drums, and the eternally upset ensemble movement resolves, midway, into Maynard Ferguson's screeching trumpet solo. "A Trumpet" is part of *This Modern World,* a cold world, cruel in the distant, pure beauty of its saxophone section, the weight of its low brass, and the nerve-racking high extremes of its trumpet ranges. The very bright colors of "Some Saxophones" blend, then quickly wilt and droop; it is only the sound of "A Cello" that conveys any warmth, for the cellist's phrases are harassed into obedient symmetry. Graettinger's constant activity and compulsive organizational virtuosity make him spiritual kin to the Free pianist Cecil Taylor; moreover, Graettinger's almost continuous state of tempo flux would not be a widespread technique for jazz improvisers before the 1970s. In *City of Glass* (1951) Graettinger adds the Antarctic shimmer of a string section; chord building mounts huge mirages in "The Structures"; the "Dance Before the Mirror" is in artificial ballroom Latin rhythms. Almost all of these two grand atonal compositions is in arpeggios or chords built up from bottom tones; this music moves sequentially, or notes are sprinkled in pointillist fashion, or moto perpetuos suggest perimeters. The vividness of every element is enhanced by the symmetry of all the moving parts, and— crucially, for this is the single constancy in Graettinger—all these beautiful instances dissolve. The city of Babbitt's "All Set" presents its primitive threat only an arm's length away," and the threat is certainly physical; the threat conveyed by Graettinger's beauty is no less dangerous for its distance and indifference, because it is a threat to our very sanity. Bob Graettinger labored at great length to create *City of Glass* and *This Modern World* for Stan Kenton's big band; he composed in poverty and seclusion and was forgotten soon after he died in 1957. Whether or not his two major works were jazz, they were prophetic. Aspects of their internal struggles would also occupy Taylor and John Coltrane, and their eventual victories would provide an alternative to Graettinger's implicit submission before the perfect shapes of his icy, iridescent metropolises.

By the mid-fifties, it was clear that the mainstream of jazz's development was hard bop. This idiom was the most direct successor to bop, since Parker, Powell, Navarro were the most direct influences on hard bop's soloists. The warmth of swing and early jazz could not survive very long in the extremes of bop, but hard bop managed to recapture some of the art's earlier range of structured feeling. Aggression and vulgarity—the vulgarity of Ellington, Lunceford, or Basie—characterize hard bop; a harder, earthier kind of blues enters the jazz repertoire. The greatest difference between bop and hard bop is in the rhythm section's role, a development of the drumming Max Roach provided Charlie Parker's groups in 1948. Players like Roach, drummer Art Blakey, pianist Horace Silver did not just accompany; they provided polyphonic interplay with their hard bop soloists. So Clifford Brown's sunlit trumpet solos are aspects of Roach's constructivist designs; the Silver quintet rides on the ongoing nervous rumble and riffing of the pianist and his drummer, and Blakey's sonic textures, dialogues, and grand swoops guide the ensemble flow of his Jazz Messengers. Inevitably, when the rhythm section became an equal partner in the ensembles, there appeared soloists like trumpeter Lee Morgan and tenorist Hank Mobley, whose improvisations depended on contrapuntal interplay as much as Kid Ory ever did.

Pianist-composer Thelonious Monk was really the inventor of bop who never played it (bop, of course, had other inventors). In place of bop's escape, he offered heightened reality, a reality that sounds surreal or abstract while it devastates the guides by which others order their musics and lives. In ensembles he withdrew support or interaction, leaving his soloists to "stroll" alone with bass and drums, only occasionally interjecting harmonic color or rhythmic opposition. A new rhythmic element enters jazz in his 1948 quartet recordings, an element scarcely understood or accepted by others until the Free era. You hear it in the unity that he creates, wholly impulsively, with a recurring low ninth interval in "Misterioso" and in the isolated, delayed, abstracted tones that are his "Evidence" theme yet seem suspended over the rhythm section's medium pace. Space is the crux of this new rhythmic tension: Pulse and line separate, and the unprecedented rests generate suspense as the listener awaits—but when?—the next fall of sound. Monk's space is a pliable element. His compression and atomization of "Carolina Moon," with measures empty of line over the furious beat, is as aggressive as a fast forte. "Bags Groove" and "I Should Care" are very different solos in which the progressive breakdown and harmonic distance of line are so concentrated that the effect is shattering. The trumpet and piano solos sound skittery in the 1957 Monk-Jazz Messengers album over the spare piano interjections, but Monk's solos create a more ominous suspense with spaces and delays over Blakey's chattering sticks. This tension of space and sound is an ancient mystery of the spirit in solitude, a mystery that was always immediate to Monk; after the quickened nerves and hasty relationships of bop, what remains is the loneliness of his dark rooms in "Round Midnight," which he composed in his youth. Perhaps it's no wonder that after confronting such darkness, he turned gradually away, toward a warmer, more nostalgic music in the 1960s.

Monk was the most dramatic of pianists in the bop era, making him the ideal teacher and partner for Sonny Rollins, whose tenor saxophone soloing became the climax of the hard bop ecology. You can hear their relationship develop from Rollins modeling himself on Monk's forms ("Think of One," 1953) through their becoming equals in terms of dramatic scope (1954) to the fascinating unities and conflicts of their 1956–57 reunions. Max Roach's rolling lines of empathy seem to have been the catalyst for Rollins's 1956–58 breakthroughs; in the sweeping tenor solos of *Max Roach + 4,* Rollins's scope suggests something of the grandeur of Louis Armstrong when *he* was also twenty-seven years old—three decades earlier. One of Rollins's favorite organizing methods was thematic restatement and reexamination ("Ee-Ah," "Blue Seven," "Sonnymoon for Two"); another was evolving excitement ("Strode Rode," his sax duels with John Coltrane and an eloquent Sonny Stitt); in ballads he chose outlines that reflected Coleman Hawkins's classicism ("You Don't Know What Love Is"). Sound, range, lyric and rhythmic effects were among his tools, and his most dramatic device was his rushing, lagging, or floating over the beat; he seemed to disengage from, expand, or contract the pulse at will. The sense of rhythmic liberation is enormous. Technically it inherits features of Parker's displacements and Monk's spaces, and in any case, Rollins's playing is a dramatic synthesis of all the best features of the swing and bop heritage.

Wilbur Ware, the colleague of Monk and Rollins, created a synthesis as close to theirs in effect as a string bassist could before Free jazz. Ware's concentration on harmonic and rhythmic fundamentals seemed revolutionary at a time when hard bop bassists sought harmonic sophistication and melodic solos. Like the unity of vocal and guitar lines in country blues, Ware's unifying effect was an earthy wisdom: simple counterpoint; tension-inspiring contrast; his pulse that throbbed atop the beat, rising and falling, and lifting ensembles. Inevitably, spontaneously every musician who played with Ware called him a natural bassist, and it was his organic fusion of the modern and the classic that made him the leading influence in a long line of Free bassists. Beginning with the first of them, Charlie Haden, this is the most important contemporary bass heritage.

Neither Herbie Nichols nor Charles Mingus had much influence on his own jazz generation. In fact, Nichols had no noticeable influence on jazz at all, even though he is one of the greatest composer-pianists and though near the end of his life he taught his songs to several young admiring New York avant-gardists—outcasts like himself. In his youth he had been house pianist at Monroe's, where he joined with Lester Young, Dizzy Gillespie, Monk, and the rest in the late thirties Harlem jam sessions out of which bop grew. He served in the army from 1941 to 1943; after that his story, as A. B. Spellman describes it in *Four Lives in the Bebop Business,* grows steadily more pathetic, until his death in 1963, at age forty-three. Ignored by the bop culture—only freaks survived, anyway, was Nichols's sad assessment—he spent the rest of his life in one grind r&b and Dixieland band after another, almost never playing his 100 unique songs for audiences. He was unaware of critic Jack Cooke's 1960 *Jazz Monthly* essay, the only article about his music in his lifetime. A prototype of the 1960s outcast musician, Nichols embodied classic and modernist jazz attitudes that bypassed bop altogether. He was a one-man tradition, less extreme but more separate than Monk.

The generous vigor of his music has not the least suggestion of his life's course of poverty and creative isolation. He led six recording sessions, in 1952, '55, '56, and '57. In the first, he improvises a pastiche of styles and a music full of disjunct phrases, substitute chord changes, unanswered calls, bar-long rests; his piano touch is strong, purposeful, even. In the rest of his recordings, we can hear that he composed not just for piano-bass-drums trios but for a pianist, himself, who was a master technically, interpretively, and emotionally. Some of his pieces had whimsical origins. "I thought a one-celled animal would be happy, too," he said, and wrote "Amoeba's Dance"; "one Saturday night I got to thinking about how the Stone Age man might have spent *his* Saturday nights," led to "Cro-Magnon Nights"; when a saxophonist asked him, "What are you playing, man? You sound like you're in a third world," it led to "The Third World," with mystery in its spare theme. He had Ellington's and James P. Johnson's gift of projecting himself into a wide variety of emotional situations; the chorus girls sweat in "Dance Line," and the meanings of "2300 Skidoo" and "Love Gloom Cash Love" are unmistakable from the opening notes. Most Nichols themes are based on call-response phrases that predict lively exchanges full of contrasts. It's no accident that all but two of his recorded pieces are in medium to fast tempos, for clarity and boldness are what he communicates.

His art of portraiture is full of fantasy, which is not the refuge for him that it was for his bop peers. Fantasy is decorative in "Spinning Song," angular and uncomfortable in "Wildflower," nutty with juxtapositions in "S'Crazy Pad." "Beyond Recall" is not an imitation of the music at a turn-of-the-century New Orleans funeral, but an event living in the glory of imagination. "Hangover Triangle" is a scary portrait: The panic is on; quick chords hit like electric shocks, followed by fleeting, grotesque visions and the twisting of exhausted nerves. He composed "Lady Sings the Blues" for Billie Holiday, but his own version is further removed from self-pity than hers; in it a phrase begins in resignation and climbs through obstacles of minor chords until it reaches resolution and simple hope.

Rhythmically he is midway between bop and Monk, with instances of stride piano. He punctuates his own lines, often with no more than an isolated chord, a tone cluster, a run swirling through space. He is unafraid of space and liked to divide his song introductions between piano and drums—nobody else did this—and to play chases with his drummers. Max Roach, especially, intuited the flow of contrasts in Nichols and developed them into sustained complement; the growing density of Roach's drumming points up Nichols's undercurrent of unease despite the happy movement in "House Party Starting"—was Nichols the guest who came alone to the party? It's important that the themes he wrote for his 1956–57 recordings stretch pop song form almost to the breaking point; the thirty-two or sixteen or twelve bars of conventional jazz become useless to him. "The Gig" is a rondo that comes apart at the seams, and the movement from certainty to dissolution over seventy-two measures introduces darkness into his world. "Query" is almost literally a query: The emphatic call rises in a question mark shape, and the response is mundane half-speed, falling notes. But when this unsatisfactory rise and fall begin a fourth time, he suddenly strikes a big, held minor chord; the reply is long, dumbfounded space. Then comes a passage of pure Nichols, for a different query in the same shape receives a less evasive reply, and the end is a perfect touch: The initial query is inverted, followed by a cadence of satisfaction.

There are two pieces in Nichols's final recording session that may be a clue to why he spent his career in obscurity. "All the Way" is a tedious pop song; he gives it a dispassionate, impersonal cocktail-piano setting. "Infatuation Eyes" is worse because it is his own composition, a lush, impenetrable maze that the clarity of his technique makes only more disagreeable. These are his only ballad performances; did this record producer ask him to play ballads? And did he sound this faceless and conventional night after night in the jive joints that provided his erratic, mediocre income? Furthermore, the mystifying "Infatuation Eyes" is the only love song he composed. It's a banal piece, the emotion is not heartfelt or remembered; for once, this composer who projects himself so thoroughly into such a range of emotions and dramas is without resources.

The richly populated world of Herbie Nichols was by no means too private for the other musicians of his generation to enter; if anything, the opposite is true. His clearly defined, fully developed dramas, without cliché or compulsion, were incomprehensible to musicians imprisoned by aesthetics of self-expression. His music advances the lines of not bop but prebop composers such as Ellington and James P. Johnson, Nichols's own heritage was not technique but sensibility, and his successors, all Free musicians, were only beginning to appear in his lifetime. A sane individual is an outcast in a mad world. Among two generations devastated by drug addictions, Nichols, too, died at an early age, but of leukemia; while he lived, only Wilbur Ware and a few others recognized his genius. Nonetheless, the animating spirit in his music also radiates outward; in this is his meaning, to set against his personal pathos.

Charles Mingus made sure he would not be obscure by roaring and thundering his way through jazz, then writing a popular, ribald autobiography. Born in 1922, in Nogales, Arizona, he was, like Nichols, older than the hard bop generation. He was a prominent Los Angeles bandleader in the 1940s; he became prominent nationally in the fifties by playing bass with vibist Red Norvo's trio. After he had settled in New York in 1951, he played with virtually every bop musician of consequence, cofounded (with Max Roach) Debut

Records, and joined the Composer's Workshop circle of experimentalists.

His own mid-fifties experiments were already revolutionary. He wrote music without foundation in pulse ("Getting Together"); he dealt in ensemble polyphony, adding layers of textural motion ("Eulogy for Rudy Williams"); he lengthened chord changes over many measures, thus predicting modal procedures; "Percussion Discussion" is wholly a duet of Mingus and Roach, unfortunately with cello overdubbed. Since these pieces are forthrightly experimental, some failures are inevitable: Despite the interest of the ever-regrouping ensembles in "Minor Intrusion," the performance on the whole suggests elephants slowly bleeding to death. While some of these works sound simply fussy, there is "Jump Monk," a *hot* piece, to predict the future course of his own composing. But in fact, the areas in which he was experimenting were ones that other musicians would explore with more success in the sixties.

Mingus's breakthrough came with "Love Chant" and "Pithecanthropus Erectus" in 1956. This breakthrough has two major components. First there's his quintet, for the blues-infused pianist Mal Waldron and the two harsh, crude saxophonists Jackie McLean and J. R. Montrose, with their heavy strong-beat accenting, were as a unit his most compatible interpreters up to then. The other, more revolutionary component is the pyramid form of these performances. "Pithecanthropus Erectus," Mingus's tragic saga of the first man to stand erect, contains the vestiges of song form in the ABAC mold of the theme. But only the curdled A is composed; B is improvised duo saxes, and C is clattering collective improvisation with tempos ajangle. Here are what would be called modal techniques: In place of chord changes, the harmonic foundation is one chord, which the band improvises on at open-end length, until the pianist's chording signals the entry of the next strain. This theme statement is the first block of

Mingus's pyramid, the next block is the tenor sax solo, the piano solo is the pyramid's apex, and the descending side of the pyramid is the alto solo and final theme statement; incidentally, the harmonic structure of the solos is again mostly modal—that is, static. This revised, longer, superior version of the older work "Love Chant" goes a step farther in renouncing song form for pyramid form: The piece is altogether themeless.

Creatively 1957 was the most important year of Mingus's career. It was when he led one of the few cohesive ensembles of his life, wholly animating a fiery group with his own intensity. Shafi Hadi (Curtis Porter) snapped off saxophone notes, growling, pecking, crying, full of bitter irony; Jimmy Knepper's dark trombone melodies flowed or slashed; on their instruments they were their generation's most expressive players, both based as much in swing as in the bop era. Drummer Dannie Richmond was a gigantic coiled spring, a Max Roach turned furious, and for most of the rest of Mingus's life Richmond would be his alter ego/rival in intensity. The theme crescendo and solos of "Haitian Fight Song" are a peak of intensity; Mingus's reputation for tempestuous music properly begins with this group. The group's necessary humanizing element arrived for a few summer weeks in trumpeter Gene (Clarence) Shaw, who glided and fluttered spontaneously, as if untouched by the other players' suppressed anger. It's the free-floating Shaw whose richly inflected, airy bop fantasies breathe warmth into the *East Coasting* routines and make the record outstanding.

In Mingus's *Tijuana* suite, the short pieces are pyramid forms packed with event, ensemble textures constantly in motion. Of the two long pyramids, "Ysabel's Table Dance" is frenzied; the dancers are not ecstatic but drunk with violence, rising in a crescendo peaked by alto sax. There's the relief of a lyrical theme, but this mood and the mad dance alternate over harmony that's static (modal) *or* mobile (chord

changes), rhythms that flow *or* pound. "Los Mariachis" is a
succession of moods, bop optimism, melancholy, stalking violence, with an innocently simple mariachi dance for relief.
The initial statement of the themes is brief, and the pyramid
mounts with longer solos, each improviser interpreting a different mood. The multiplicity of event in the *Tijuana* suite is
mind-boggling, considering that all these avant-garde ideas,
from quickly changing rhythms to collective improvisations,
were already happening in 1957. Most of all, not only was it
Mingus's ingenious forms that unified the performances, but
these interpreters were really complementary, and he would
not find such sharing among his musicians in any future ensembles.

Mingus was not getting enough engagements in jazz clubs
to keep any bands together for long in the 1950s. He did
manage to approach the 1957 sextet's intensity by way of
some improvisers who anticipated Free procedures: Tenorist
Rahsaan Roland Kirk riffs in split tones in "Hog Callin'
Blues"; altoist Jackie McLean spins a "Tensions" solo that increasingly separates from tonality; there's even a primitive
Free performance, "Passions of a Man," with no line, solos, or
development, only abstract sounds. Mingus's own advances
were in the rather more conventional, but no less inspired,
areas of creating and scoring music. The brooding of his mid-
fifties writing often comes near the maudlin, but with "Rein-
carnation of a Lovebird" in 1957 his minor seconds and his
more angular intervals are dispersed in a soft swoop of melody that retells Charlie Parker's story, ending in a long sigh
on the triumph of Parker's art. Subsequently Mingus began
writing for scaled-down big bands, and with these he finally
became accepted as the major composer that he was. He developed several series of pieces—gospel music imitations,
riffing pyramid blues, parodies of classic jazz styles—into
"Better Git It in Your Soul," "Boogie Stop Shuffle," "My Jelly
Roll Soul." These became the Mingus standards, along with

such melodies as "Goodbye Pork-pie Hat" and "Nostalgia in Times Square."

The only thing wrong with his work with these larger ensembles was that as horn sections replaced individual interpreters in his art, linear inflections disappeared and sound colors became blunted. His big band pieces gain little besides weight. "Haitian Fight Song" becomes overbearing when played by eleven musicians instead of five. "Revelations," his 1958 Brandeis composition, is stately and somber, retaining the *Tijuana* suite's method of quickly cutting from one texture to another. *The Black Saint and the Sinner Lady* (1965) is a lifetime's collection of composing devices pivoted on four grand, collectively improvised accelerandos. These last two large pieces have attractive or intense passages and little improvisation. The truth may be that Mingus was only sporadically interested in writing for big bands, for he sometimes left such matters as orchestration to lieutenants such as Jimmy Knepper, who occasionally rejoined him on trombone. When Mingus had the opportunity to present new big band music at New York's Town Hall in 1962, the result was disastrous; onstage, as the band played, copyists frantically copied his hastily composed scores for the musicians to sight-read.

Mingus's amazing autobiography, *Beneath the Underdog,* is a hilarious tale of one personal excess after another. He was an always tense individual, seemingly ever near the point of anger; when he spoke, he blurted his sentences; now and then he came to blows with his musicians, over musical as well as financial matters; he fought with others, too, and harangued audiences. His perfectionist demands on his bands were sometimes outrageous; his ambitions ranged from grand to grandiose, and as an artist he could not survive without continuously walking the line that divides extravagance from excess. There's tragedy in his gigantic egoism. He was no Ellington, who composed for the special talents of others, yet he absolutely needed other musicians' improvising to express his own intense emotionality. Down through the years his bands were a parade of musicians, only a few of whom possessed the will and the kind of dramatic intensity needed to realize his art. At times he seemed to give up: "I don't care how a guy solos, because I can't get blamed for the solos. If they get a good tone and can read . . ." And a sigh.[1]

As a harbinger of Free jazz, which Mingus despised, he had introduced most of his advanced ideas by the end of summer 1957; as we'll see, his pianoless 1960 groups with Eric Dolphy's woodwinds would become important to the emerging new music. Down through the years his most dependable value was as a bass player. He made a virtuoso art out of the Blanton-Pettiford tradition; his "Haitian Fight Song" opening solo has been studied by all subsequent bassists for its close structure and brilliant technique; he and Ware may be the only bassists of their generation to realize that the instrument could be played softly as well as strongly. Mingus's habit—or compulsion?—of spontaneously changing tempos, meters, rhythmic patterns behind his soloists was the source of an entire genealogy of modal and Free bassists, to his disgust. "I used to play avant garde bass when nobody else did. Now I play 4/4 because none of the other bassists do," he said in 1974, four years before he died.

In May 1949 Lennie Tristano and his sextet recorded "Intuition" and "Digression," performances without theme, fixed harmonic structure, or fixed tempo. Each piece begins with Tristano's piano improvising; altoist Lee Konitz begins improvising on the piano phrases; other players join to improvise on the spontaneous melodies; main and supporting roles in the collective improvisations slip from instrument to instrument. Tristano and his group sometimes included such experiments in free form in their nightclub sets, though over the subsequent years none of these musicians felt more than the rarest impulse to attempt again such innovatory ideas.

Thus the era of Free jazz does not begin with these early successes; indeed, the need for freedom was in 1949 only sensed by a nineteen-year-old saxophonist in Texas, 1,500 miles from the center of the jazz world where Tristano worked. And even when the urge to freedom grew into a self-aware need, it would be several years before that Texan, Ornette Coleman, could realize Freedom.

·2·

Ornette Coleman: The Birth of Freedom

Born in 1930, Ornette Coleman grew up in Fort Worth, Texas, hearing church music, urbanized Louis Jordan-style blues from jukeboxes in black neighborhoods, and pop music—Glenn Miller, Tommy Dorsey, "Sentimental Journey"—on the radio. When he was seven, his father died, and the boy Ornette went to work doing odd jobs. He heard a dance band play in his junior high school and became entranced with the saxophone.

> . . . I went out and worked, around 1944–45—shining shoes, busboying in hotels, doing summer jobs like scraping paint, all kinds of little jobs. Finally, after saving up my money, my mother told me to look on the couch, and there was a horn, a gold-plated Conn. . . .
>
> . . . I remember when I first got the saxophone, . . . I remember thinking, as the book said, that the first seven letters of the alphabet were the first seven letters of music, ABCDEFG.[1]

But of course, the standard concert scale reads CDEFGAB.

> So I thought my C that I was playing on the saxophone was A, like that, right? Later on I found out that it did exist thataway only because the E-flat alto, when you play C natural, it is

[the standard] A [transposed]. So I was right in one way and wrong in another—I mean, sound, I was right. *Then* I started analyzing why it exists thataway, and to this very day I realize more and more that all things that are designed with a strict logic only apply against something; it is not the only way it's done. In other words, if you take an instrument and you happen to feel it a way you can express yourself, it becomes its own law.

Ornette Coleman's special concern with his saxophone sound began "when I realized that you could play sharp or flat in tune. That came very early in my saxophone interest. I used to play one note all day, and I used to try to find how many different sounds I could get out of the mouthpiece (I'm still looking for the magic mouthpiece). That just came about from, I'd hear so many different tones and sounds. . . ."

A saxophone-playing cousin helped him with the alto and with music theory. On a 1945 visit to his aunt in New York, he first heard bop, played by Dizzy Gillespie and his pioneering big band. Coleman began playing professionally in his mid-teens: "My mother wouldn't let me go out even when I went to play; my older sister had to bring me home." A younger generation of jazz and rhythm and blues musicians was appearing on the North Texas scene when Ornette Coleman was becoming known in the area. Saxman-bandleader Red Connors, who didn't record, was probably the most advanced, but Coleman's young Texas peers included drummer Charles Moffett, trumpeter Bobby Bradford, and saxophonists John Carter, Dewey Redman, and Prince Lasha, all of whom would follow Coleman's path into the new music of the 1960s. Coleman emphasizes that in his apprentice years stylistic distinctions between jazz, r&b, bebop, dance music, pop music, meant little more to him than they did to his audiences— "I think because of being in a little city, the people never knew the difference. Once they heard the beat, they danced or they listened"—and he quite naturally incorporated the bebop solos that he learned from records into his playing.

He also began writing songs very early. As a teenager he sat in with the Stan Kenton band, playing a theme he had written over the band's arrangement of "Out of Nowhere." Coleman was playing tenor by the time he graduated from high school and left Fort Worth. He toured with a minstrel show and a blues singer, "made up" eight to nine songs for his first (and long since lost) recording date, in Natchez, Mississippi, in 1949; he then settled in New Orleans for a year and a half. Original ideas about how to improvise were already manifest in his music—"I think even bebop could have become a larger form if everyone had not taken a shortcut to the changes, instead of the line"—and he was considered something of a radical everywhere he played, by the New Orleans beboppers (a *very* underground group of musicians), by the blues band with which he toured to Los Angeles, and even by the presumably more advanced musicians in the angel city, where he settled in 1950.

Years of scuffling followed. He worked at menial day gigs, such as running an elevator, studied harmony and theory books (on the job yet), and took his alto sax around to clubs, hoping to sit in at night. A few musicians encouraged him, rehearsed with him, and Free jazz began with the small circle that studied the revolutionary ideas he was evolving: "It took me a long time to get them interested in studying with me, and staying ... because when I met Charlie [Haden] and Billy [Higgins] and Don [Cherry], they were into bebop. They got very interested in the things I was trying to write to play. So when we got together, the most interesting part is: *What do you play after you play the melody* if you don't have nothing to go with? That's where I won them over. [Italics added.]" The new challenge of this music was that Coleman didn't give his young musicians any chord changes on which to improvise. "Usually, when you play a melody, you have a set pattern to know just what you can do while the other person's doing a certain thing. But in this case, when we played the melody, no one knew where to go or what to do to show that he knew where he was going. I had already developed playing like that naturally. . . ." This is most important: "I finally got them to where they could see how to express themselves without linking up to a definite maze. . . . I think it was a case of teaching them how to feel more confident in being expressive like that for themselves." The new jazz began when Coleman and his group began playing this new music *together.*

In February 1958 Ornette Coleman recorded *Something Else!;* his quintet included Don Cherry, trumpet, and Billy Higgins, drums. In the liner notes he offers the principle that motivates his music's freedom of expression: "I think one day music will be a lot freer. Then the pattern for a tune, for instance, will be forgotten and the tune itself will be the pattern, and won't have to be forced into conventional patterns. The creation of music is just as natural as the air we breathe. I believe music is really a free thing, and any way you can enjoy it you should."[2]

Here is the Freedom principle. The era of Free jazz begins with this first document. *Something Else!* made little impact at first, and Coleman's only musical gig the rest of the year was when he, Cherry, and Higgins played for six weeks with pianist Paul Bley (Coleman almost never again performed with a pianist).

Of the seventeen Coleman and Bley quintet tracks issued from 1958, all but two are Coleman songs, usually blues or thirty-two-bar bop themes with improvised bridges. In his solos, what sounds at first like strange chord substitutions, an exotic kind of bebop, proves to be a series of changing tonalities which may be related to a single, basic center of tonality *or* to a set of changes, not necessarily based on the harmonic structure implied by the theme. Coleman's alto soloing is shot through with the adrenaline of Charlie Parker, the aggression of Parker in blues such as "Alpha" and two versions of "When Will the Blues Leave?" His broken, irregular phrasing suggests the contours of early Parker or, in the first version of "Ramblin'," a heretofore missing link between Charlie Christian and Parker; the exultant, leaping phrases and the undercurrent of loneliness in his sound fill a thirteen-chorus blues solo, a summary and summit of southwestern style. In every solo, Coleman plays phrases that turn around the beat, or accents fall asymmetrically, or phrases are spaced so that they begin irregularly within bars; this rhythmic acuteness leads to an ever-present sense of danger, of disguised, coiled accents striking at arteries. Coleman's essentially diatonic phrases also become tense with angular intervals, and his shifting tonalities add yet more tension with their apparent harmonic irresolution. In solos such as "Klactoveedsedstene" the sound of his alto moves, from phrase to phrase at times and sometimes even within phrases. He was playing an English-made plastic alto in this period, like the one Charlie Parker played in his 1953 Massey Hall recording. Coleman, searching for another plastic alto sax in 1981, said, "When I had the plastic saxophone, it was very nice because . . . you could almost see the shape of the breath of a note. Whereas with another, you can't; the breath just dissolves in the metal."

Coleman met the Modern Jazz Quartet's John Lewis in 1959, and Lewis became a most helpful friend. First, in March, MJQ bassist Percy Heath played in a Coleman recording session; then, in May, at Lewis's encouragement, Atlantic began recording Coleman. As director of the annual School of Jazz in Lenox, Massachusetts, Lewis enrolled Coleman as a student for August—the student from whom the teachers learned—introducing him to eastern listeners and leading to the Coleman Quartet's first New York gig, at the Five Spot in November. Meanwhile, Lewis placed Coleman in a show at the Monterey Jazz Festival, and the next week, in October, Coleman cut his final California record. Further dispersion of solo organization, phrase displacement, linear extension and fragmentation are among his alto style's advances in these 1959 albums. From the winter album, *Tomorrow Is the Question!*, come "Rejoicing" and "Compassion"; emotionally they are just what the titles say. In the dirge "Lorraine," bent-note phrases turn down, and upward leaps add dissonance to the harshness of loss. In his second improvised strain, an angular rise topples off into a scale with the desolation of despair; then, in the sudden bridge, his phrases careen unaccompanied until crushed into a defeated note; he repeats a hopeless phrase to conclude the tragedy.

"'Tears Inside" from this album was to be the first Coleman theme recorded by another alto saxophonist, and the differences between his solo and Art Pepper's reveal the hearts of both artists. Pepper observes blues changes strictly in "Tears Inside"; he begins pecking at a note and spins a spider web-fine rhythmic structure. The tension in this solo is almost unbearable: The brittle phrases, the edgy sound, the merciless, uncontrollable twitching of accents, the precarious chorus-by-chorus form suggest terror as much as suppressed rage. But Coleman's solo is extroverted. There is his impressive sound, bent, then increasingly strained; he brutally attacks some high notes, and others are terminally splintered; passing harmonics are heard in his cries. There are contrasts of quiet, brief phrases against longer, full-bodied ones, for now dynamic contrast becomes a conscious element of a jazz solo. There is more irresolution in Coleman's lines than in Pepper's; the difference is that Coleman accepts it, is even detached enough to dramatize it with his sound. The life of Pepper's "Tears Inside" is completely within his vibrating nervous system, and the result is a great work of art. Coleman is no less sensual, but he has a deeper awareness to offer, and despite the pain, his world is the more livable.

Before the 1958 Hilcrest Club gig Coleman began tutoring Paul Bley's twenty-one-year-old bassist, Charlie Haden. Other bassists had played on Coleman's first two albums, and Red Mitchell, by emulating Coleman's phrases, entered his world with particular sympathy, if not empathy. But empathy evolved from Haden's extensive rehearsing with Coleman, and in the 1959 Atlantic sessions you can hear how well Haden understood the general directions of Coleman's and Cherry's harmonic motions. Haden chooses bass tones that relate ambiguously or consonantly to the soloists' phrases, in lines that derive from the soloists' movement (including the times when he creates harmonic counterpoint). Haden has credited Wilbur Ware's major influence on his own style, and in amplifying the good humor of Coleman in "Music Always," Haden proves to be another virtuoso of rhythmic spontaneity. The Coleman Quartet anticipates some of the Ayler groups' independence in "Change of the Century," in which Haden arrives at an apex of spontaneous contradictions; the soloists advance despite his insults. It's the bass solo that begins the distortion of reason and emotion in "Focus on Sanity"; the unstable dissonances that rise in his solo are the suppressed form of the mad yelps and lashing trills in Coleman's.

If this quartet had played "Lonely Woman" in a slow tempo, self-pity would have resulted. But with the fast drums of Higgins and Haden's bass suspended in irregular double stops, the setting is ambiguous and the slow theme emerges as pity, sorrow, and resignation in unevenly measured strains; in Coleman's solo chorus, beginning in bar 13, the woman becomes a breathing, sexual being. Here and in "Peace" Coleman retains a vestigial feature of bop by soloing in identifiable choruses, even if his choruses are varilength. Something very new happens in his solos that break decisively away from chorus patterns. In "Mind and Time" the arching opening run "becomes the pattern" as it's tilted, curved down, then contrasted, amplified, and distorted throughout his ninety-five-bar improvisation. "Eventually" has an improvised bridge upon which Coleman plays a rising three-note lick ten times; this lick becomes a cell motive for his asymmetric solo, heard most often to begin phrases; the stabbing three notes are turned down, trapped phrases alternate with screaming arcs, squalling phrases follow, and Haden's suspensions isolate the alto. After the theme of "Free," trumpet and alto engage in a brief duo improvisation during which Coleman discovers a solo-generating cell in a rising phrase. But that initiating motive is abandoned a half minute later, when he finds a three-note motive, which then becomes a trill phrase, a long zigzag phrase, repeated rising phrases, a longer snaking phrase—and so on, in multiple disguises throughout the rest of the solo.

What's happening is thematic improvisation. It's not in the Rollins way, in which motivic recall is central among the linear and dramatic solo elements, but more like the way of Benny Carter in *Swingin' the 20s* (1958) or such earlier solos as "Crazy Rhythm" (1937), in which the essence of a motive informs every phrase of the improvisation. Coleman's motivic evolution[3] is a matter of continually reshaping the initiating cell. Even if specific intervals become approximate, the rhythmic shape remains, intact, compressed, or extended; far less commonly, the intervallic shape remains while the rhythmic shape is distorted; the cell motive is heard at the beginning, within, or at the end of phrases; it is upended, turned on its side, and viewed from different perspectives again and again; its meaning is altered and renewed. These three 1959 examples are all from fast Coleman solos, but within two years this kind of thematic improvisation would begin to dominate Coleman's soloing at all tempos.

"Focus on Sanity" offers an opposite kind of Coleman soloing, in which the unity thematic improvisation promises is deliberately cast aside in favor of discontinuity. In this instance the result is frenzy; in "Forerunner" the result is a solo as teeming with ideas as "Free," but seen through a vast kaleidoscope. Contrast in rhythmic shapes is continuous, as are dynamic contrasts unprecedented in jazz for their vividness and impulsiveness. In these solos and in his thematic improvisations Coleman reveals a new meaning to the very idea of soloing. As the faint, lingering shadow of chorus structures disappears, classic narrative form (Lester Young's "a solo should tell a story") becomes irrelevant. That's because music with a beginning, middle, and end imposes the structure of fiction on the passage of life, says Coleman implicitly. Are these solos slices of life, like the songs bluesman Sleepy John Estes draws from a well of tragedy? Certainly not in statements as closely unified as "Free," or even in "Forerunner," in which vast change is the only constant. The organization of these Coleman solos makes clear that uncertainty is the content of life, and even things that we take for certainties (such as his cell motives) are ever altering shape and character. By turns he fears or embraces this ambiguity; but he constantly faces it, and by his example, he condemns those who seek resolution or finality as timid.

The Coleman Quartet's "Ramblin' " is quite different from the 1958 "Ramblin' " by the Bley Quintet. This new performance certainly recalls Kenneth Rexroth's often-quoted remark about Coleman: that "the whole group is from the Southwest, and behind them you can hear the old bygone banjos and tack pianos, and the first hard moans of country blues." Though "Ramblin' " remains a blues, the freely substituted-upon changes stretch to irregular lengths, even in the theme; bravado begins, answered by the strummed bass; reality confronts the bravado, then another bass reply; the third theme phrase is two bars by the horns in unison, after which they separate to ride their ramshackle ways on the frontier of myth. In solo, Coleman's phrases come from Kansas City and country music, excitement and singing appear, and a growl becomes a dynamic motive. Responding to this prairie solo, Cherry is witty and personal, his jaunty lines spitting tobacco as he rides the landscape. Haden's strummed replies in the theme are a Bo Diddley vamp which then alternates with walking choruses in his accompaniments; the vamp reminds us that this frontier is vast and lonely, even if the loneliness is as stylized as a cowboy song of abandoned love. Moreover, this syncopated drone is extracted whole from folk music—Haden had been inspired by his brother, a bassist in country music bands—and the bass solo in "Ramblin' " is even a strummed bluegrass song. Even the fleeting satires of Coleman and Cherry are a feature of folk humor; like a Jimmy Yancey solo, the folk sources of "Ramblin' " are not betrayed, parodied, distorted, or otherwise set at a distance: "Ramblin' " is folk myth. It fades on trumpet and chirping alto surrounded by the Western panorama and ends by snapping out the abrupt reality phrase, and you take for granted that "Ramblin' " does not end in these final notes. (In jazz, as in history, the sequel to "Ramblin' " came seventeen years later, in Charles Tyler's *Saga of the Outlaws*.)

Success in New York has always been, for jazz musicians, national success; it's still the Big Apple. The Coleman Quartet gig at New York's Five Spot Café in November 1959 was supposed to last two weeks. Instead, it lasted two and a half months, as he became a celebrity and, for the first time in his life, his music was in demand. A. B. Spellman's *Four Lives* discusses Coleman's sudden fame and the controversy that soon resulted; here is a bit of trivia from Dorothy Kilgallen's New York *Journal-American* gossip column that captures the flavor of the period's publicity: "Leonard Bernstein took his family to the Five Spot to hear Ornette Coleman, who seems the musician most likely to affect the history of jazz this season, although many of his fellow players . . . maintain that his offbeat style won't have a lasting effect. More objective aficionados think he's fabulous."[4] The titles of Coleman's albums, like *Change of the Century* and *The Shape of Jazz to Come*, may have been accurate enough, but their immodesty raised hackles among New York's established musicians. Especially those who had trouble finding gigs—for New York has always had an oversupply of jazz talent—had reason to resent these California upstarts. Coleman himself saw no reason why any music that was as natural as his should continue to be so controversial.

The crisp, precise drummer Billy Higgins left the quartet in the spring of 1960 and was replaced by Edward Blackwell, from the New Orleans bop underground. Blackwell advances the New Orleans tradition of not just accompaniment but, as the pioneer Baby Dodds would have said, "playing for the benefit of the band." His time provided the quartet a subtle, behind the beat, and almighty swing, while his palette of sounds added new depth of color. And now an element of black humor entered their expressive capacities. The major result of their three midsummer recording sessions was *This Is Our Music*, and much of the rest is on *To Whom Who Keeps a Record*, issued only in Japan. On that album Coleman's song titles read: "Music Always" "Brings Goodness" "To Us" "All" "P.S. Unless One Has" "Some Other" "Motive for Its Use."

"Embraceable You" is the Gershwin ballad, climaxing already in its Hollywood spectacle introduction; there's mockery in Coleman's bent notes, pitch wavers, and insane little decorative phrases. But then the ballad "Some Other" is an unsentimental exposition of kindness, loss, and sadness. After Cherry's solo, a catharsis appears in an alto interlude suspended over gongs and bass ostinato. Irritation and accusation are in Coleman's complex phrases; then, as the bass climbs and moves, the alto follows into tempo and into forgiveness. Earlier there were Coleman solos shot through with fear, such as "Circle with a Hole in the Middle," and they were answered by aggressive anger in the likes of "Change of the Century." Now anger acquires depth in "Kaleidoscope": The ferocity of Rollins in "B.Swift" and "B.Quick" may be relentless, but Coleman, via diversity of phrasing, is sharper and bloodier; sensibility is sliced raw by the shattered line and the big, coarse tone. This sets the mood for "Blues Connotation," in which the concentration of his phrasing cries inevitability and intractability, power and drive, propelled by the heavy tone and speed of the bass; there's judgment in the way Haden's lines sustain as he drives downward. It is worth noting that almost all of Coleman's solos with this quartet are organized via his motivic evolution methods.

Much of "Moon Inhabitants" is in recurring collective improvisation; though inconsistently coherent, and though Cherry's lines are usually secondary, what's significant is that responsive collective playing is now a regular feature of the Coleman Quartet. "Beauty Is a Rare Thing" dominated Coleman's thinking in the final session—it supplies the cell motive for central passages in his "Poise" and "Folk Tale" solos— and the truth is that "Beauty Is a Rare Thing" advances the jazz perception of freedom in several ways. Of the performance, Coleman says, "The melodic line, the format, that has always been in jazz is two horns and a rhythm section—that's what Charlie Parker and all the guys followed—but I was never thinking about a format as much as I was thir¹˙ about a melodic line not having to be played with just thaᵗ small structure. So what I thought I was doing was to try and write a melodic line that sounded like it was structured orchestratively in small kind of context." Line and accompaniment bridge their separate identities; what pulse there is moves of communal impulse; freely moving tonality accepts atonality, and lyricism accepts *Klangfarbenmelodie.*

Over bass moans and the muffled thrust of tomtom rolls, Coleman plays the slow theme: Pain mingles with tenderness but descends to pity and resignation, subsiding to a low *piano.* In a rising phrase, hope is glimpsed; it is articulated, then vanishes. The ambiguity of the accompaniment accentuates the clarity of the melody; when bowed bass joins the alto momentarily, brotherhood in mortality appears. High, isolated trumpet tones introduce an alto phrase that hovers like a question mark before the third statement of the theme strain, and this time the sax tone becomes iron-hard, splits in the descent, and when the hope sequence rises again, it is vanquished by a held, split overtone.

The trumpeter plays fragments of alarmed innocence, echoed by the drummer's mallets, over a rumbling bass trill, but this dance in the void becomes precarious in the face of a slow crescendo on a large cymbal. The crucial development in the performance is introduced by pointillist alto and trumpet notes. Horns and bass disintegrate; the seismic movement of mallets returns to introduce Coleman's tragic soliloquy on his theme, Cherry interjecting blasts and spits of sound. Yet the weight of the sawing bass and the drumming on rims and snares—the theme's pity motive perverted into "thou shalt not"—at last dissolves Coleman's line, too: The horns play fragments and isolated tones in a desolate passage that becomes surreal in its separation of parts. But then an alto line moves out of the void into continuity; the trumpet-sax pointillist notes, even in their schizophrenic isolation, climb to a final split-toned stab. And in the end the theme appears in harmony; from the quest for beauty, the grace of compassion concludes.

Coleman says, "... I realized that if I changed the harmonic structure or the tempo structure while someone else is doing something, they couldn't stay there, they'd have to change with me. So I would bring that about myself a lot, knowing where I could take the melody. In other words, I could create a showcase for the melody and then show the distance between where I could go and still come directly back to that melody, instead of trying to show the different inversions of the same thing." Here is an orchestral work that's improvised without tempo or meter, that moves into abstract tones and tonalities, yet that develops a detailed musical conception to its conclusion. Even though "Beauty Is a Rare Thing" was recorded as early as 1960, the doors it opens would not begin to be explored in jazz for several years yet.

Haden then left the quartet. Coleman's next bassist was Scott LaFaro, who transformed Mingus's virtuosity into an art of the rococo. LaFaro's tones and rhythmic figures attracted attention to themselves by their decorative incongruity, amid the close directness of the two horns and Blackwell. Yet his line is, for a change, straightforward and integrated with the horns in this particular quartet's finest piece, "The Alchemy of Scott LaFaro," which includes no bass solo. Coleman's solo here is driving and driven; then we glimpse the edge of panic in the shattered, piercing phrases of the horns' duo improvisation. The album with LaFaro, *Ornette!*, has the three longest solos Coleman had recorded to date, all in the same medium-fast tempo, all organized via motivic evolution. These January 1961 solos may have modified the spontaneity of his earlier improvising in favor of formal unity, but in terms of rich variety of phrasing and lyricism nobody else in jazz at the time approached the quality of Coleman's playing.

It is interesting that bassist Jimmy Garrison, according to Coleman's report, actively disliked playing in the quartet's idiom. Garrison replaced LaFaro during the winter of 1961, and in *Ornette on Tenor* he sounds wholly at ease. Moreover, this quartet even does an experimental piece, "Mapa," in which the four players improvise in contrary rhythms: The bass tones are spaced, often changing to a slow waltz (Garrison playing only on beat one); percussion and other instruments speed or slow tempo so that the music's forward movement is never together. In the other pieces Garrison's swing is a contrast with the often violent charge of Haden and LaFaro. He and Coleman duet in "Harlem's Manhattan"; the tenor saxophone phrases roll with suggestions of cries, funk, and seduction, and Coleman's sound is as rich as Rollins's. In "Cross Breeding," as Coleman solos unaccompanied, his internal rhythm sounds as fluid and mobile as it ever has been in jazz. One side of *Ornette on Tenor* is again in the medium-fast tempo and the motivic evolution forms of his *Ornette!* solos, again without detracting from the variety and quality of his music.

This particular quartet—Coleman, Cherry, Garrison, Blackwell—appeared only on record, and only one record at that. Ornette Coleman accepted few engagements in 1961, and without work, Blackwell and Cherry left him. The departure of Cherry was especially significant because he had been one of Coleman's first students, and their association had been unbroken for more than four years. Cherry was born in Oklahoma City in 1936 and grew up in Los Angeles. When he met Coleman in the mid-fifties, he was already becoming known as a hard bop trumpeter; in 1957 he led a quartet (James Clay, tenor; Don Payne, bass; Billy Higgins, drums) for two weeks in Vancouver, playing many of Coleman's songs. His solos in 1958 reveal a nervous edge and an urge to play fast, many-noted phrases; without his duplicating the explorations of Bill Hardman and Lee Morgan, Cherry's kinship to them suggests that he would have become a valuable hard bopper had he not met Coleman.

Often in these early solos he fluctuates between hard bop-derived and Coleman-derived phrasing. But the discontinuity that is so often side by side with his finely realized lines demonstrates an investigative nature that is significant for the courage of his character; his rejecting the security of hard bop, with the prospect of easier idiomatic mastery (and the prospect of easier-won musical and material success) is deliberate. His turn at this musical crossroads led to rapid advances in stylistic maturity. His rhythmic ideas in solos such as "Congeniality" leave even such sophisticates as Lee Morgan and Booker Little back in the dust. He plays solos such as "Peace" in which his ideas require Haden's reinforcement, and many times his solos' points of departure are the final phrases of Coleman's preceding solos. But this willingness to incorporate the others' energies is not necessarily dependence; rather, it may be the manifestation of urges for ensemble unity as deep, if not as complex, as Coleman's.

There are pieces, such as "Una Muy Bonita" and "Poise," in which Cherry's solos are more concentrated than Coleman's. Whereas occasional fragmentary passages in some earlier solos suggested linear uncertainty in this brand-new idiom, Cherry's solo in "W.R.U." has characteristic fragmentary phrases filling out melodically, with a compelling tension of space and sound. This mastery of rhythmic and spatial tension would become one of the most distinctive features of his style, in years to come when Coleman's own rhythmic variety would appear conservative by comparison. But in this early period his solo in "Cross Breeding" is noteworthy for the way his line, initially tangled and melodic, narrows to simpler, longer phrases in increasing space. One more especially rewarding aspect of Cherry and Coleman together is their collective improvisations, which appear with increasing frequency, briefly or at length. Whereas at first Cherry's inclination was to second or comment upon the altoist, by "The Alchemy of Scott LaFaro" he refuses to flinch or be cozened by Coleman's phrases. Don Cherry's playing with Coleman is ever direct, bright, convinced of ultimate direction even in the moments when immediate intent is unclear. In contrast with Coleman and Haden, Cherry conveys less cruelty, but this should not be mistaken for innocence—not in an artist so resistant to the temptations to invent cheap or trivial music.

Certainly by the time he left Coleman, Don Cherry's sensitive marshaling of highly varied material and his mastery of rhythms make him not just Coleman's second but a major voice in jazz.

There are two more recordings to consider in this all-important first period of Ornette Coleman's music. They were taped during the week before Christmas 1960, and both were highly advanced at the time. First, Coleman plays in two Gunther Schuller third stream pieces which return to the composer's favored topic of matching seemingly incongruous styles and idioms. "Abstraction" is an atonal piece for classical string quartet and jazz musicians which halts for a fine middle section of Coleman improvising unaccompanied. In the four-movement "Variants on Monk" the juxtapositions are mostly of jazz styles, featuring bop and cool players improvising simultaneously with Coleman, LaFaro, and woodwindist Eric Dolphy. Two of the movements feature overlapping improvisations, and one of Schuller's good ideas is his inventing a niche for LaFaro's style: A second bassist is the one who advances the rhythm, so that LaFaro can be exclusively ornamental, apart from his clever rubato duet movement with Dolphy.

Free Jazz is a collective improvisation by the Ornette Coleman Double Quartet: Coleman, Cherry, LaFaro, and Higgins on the left stereo channel, and Freddie Hubbard, trumpet, Dolphy, bass clarinet, Haden, and Blackwell on the right. Each player "solos" for several minutes while the others create lines inspired by the soloist or are silent if they choose to be; also, the soloist may choose to improvise upon what he hears in the others. The objective is spontaneous ensemble structure achieved through responsive, simultaneous motivic development. Textures continually change from one to all four horns, over the rhythm. Don Cherry proves the readiest, most varied player here, and during his "solo" section the collective ideal is most nearly realized; twice Cherry permits Coleman to assume the lead voice and concludes by playing obbligato to a Coleman-Dolphy game of phrase catch. The thirty-six minute performance stays fixed at a medium tempo; moreover, one bassist plays a ceaseless shuffle beat. Though the success of *Free Jazz* is erratic, it did demonstrate that a long collective improvisation had potential for unity of form in the new music.

In June 1961 Ornette Coleman recorded another Double Quartet—another *Free Jazz?*—using his regular sidemen Bobby Bradford, trumpet; Garrison, bass; Charles Moffett, drums; and adding Cherry, soprano saxist Steve Lacy, bassist Art Davis, and Blackwell. Among the few gigs Coleman took later that year was in Cincinnati, Ohio. His Double Quartet flew to Cincinnati and rehearsed, but when the promoter refused them advance money, they refused to play. The advertisements for the performance read: "Ornette Coleman—Free Jazz Concert"; the crowd that arrived took the signs literally and protested being charged money for tickets.

In 1962 Coleman led a trio with bassist David Izenzon, who played in other jazz and classical music groups, and Moffett, who taught music in New York high schools. They needed these other jobs because Coleman hardly played in public at all that year, and after he had produced and promoted his own December 1962 concert at Town Hall, he stayed almost wholly silent for two and a half years, until he recorded a film sound track in the summer of 1965. He then scouted Europe and England for opportunities to perform. He found that the agreement between the British and American musicians' unions contained a trick clause which classified him as a "dance" musician and prohibited him from presenting a jazz concert in England, so he quickly composed a woodwind quintet, was certified a "concert artist," and, along with the classical woodwind players, presented his trio in a concert in August in the London suburb of Croydon. At this point in his career Coleman was determined to stay away from America as long as possible. For nine months the trio remained in Europe, playing clubs, concerts, festivals and recording another film sound track before returning to New York.

David Izenzon brought a major advance in jazz bass playing and in the structure of the jazz ensemble. Izenzon was born in 1932 in Pittsburgh and did not even begin to study the bass until he was twenty-three years old; he became Coleman's bassist five years later. Traditionally the bass's role in jazz had been to ground the ensemble pulse; even LaFaro, though he chafed at the role, did not find an alternative. But Izenzon was as likely to provide melodic line as pulse, avoiding direct rhythmic reference, contradicting his partners' tempos, and playing arco at least as often as he played pizzicato. The genius of Izenzon's music is that he did not become an independent voice in the trio; his fine sensitivity created ensemble tension so that in a discursive performance such as "The Ark," with shifting tempos and problematic drumming, Izenzon becomes a source of unity. When Coleman plays hard alto trills, Izenzon fiddles wildly in double stops; when drums and sax separate in fast tempos, the bass separates further with a slow, plucked line. In the middle he plays a shimmering note that begins a continuous melodic line, a characteristic solo: brief, compact, a complete statement utterly free of ornamentation. After the self-dramatizing of Mingus and LaFaro, it's a paradox that Izenzon, the most active of bass virtuosos, sounds so completely effortless. You're not overwhelmed at his speed; his music flows so naturally and lyrically, without excess, that even his blurring of pitch does not seem extreme. Izenzon was especially devoted to bass sound. At a time when electronic amplification was becoming standard for jazz bassists, he didn't use an amplifier even though he played softly; also, his experience in both jazz and contemporary classical techniques gave him a broad expressive range.

The Coleman Trio recorded strangely melancholy ballads such as "Sadness," the alto melody made stark by the Arctic winds of Izenzon's microtonal lines. Especially in the Golden Circle, Stockholm, recordings, Coleman plays brilliant, optimistic, closely unified thematic improvisations ("Dee Dee," "Faces and Places," "European Echoes"); here's evidence that thematic methods need not be any less spontaneous than the free associations of, for example, the first "Doughnuts" (1962). Despite the tensions of "Silence," with its ensemble starts and halts, space was becoming less important to Coleman; in place of phrase expansion and contraction, he was beginning to set passages of brief, fast phrases against passages of long lines and larger note values. The tension of indeterminate tonality is now often replaced by the certainty of cadential modulations; his solos contain extensive sections of sequences; much of his music conveys a modal atmosphere.

In contrast with the increasing stylization of his alto soloing, there's his violin and trumpet work of the sixties. He had no teachers or guides to playing these instruments; he purposely avoided learning standard techniques, for his objective was to play "without memory" and to create as spontaneously as possible. He had jammed with Albert Ayler in 1963; Ayler's concept of sound, especially his deliberate imprecision of pitch, certainly coincides with Coleman's point of view: "I'm very sympathetic to non-tempered instruments. They seem to be able to arouse an emotion that isn't in Western music. I mean, I think that European music is very beautiful, but the people that's playing it don't always get a chance to express it that way because they have spent most of their energy perfecting the unisons of playing together by saying, 'You're a little flat,' or '... a little sharp.' ... A tempered note is like eating with a fork, where that if you don't have a fork the food isn't going to taste any different."[5]

Despite a unique sound, Coleman's trumpet phrasing at first tends to sound like blurred, flighty abstracts of his sax phrasing; a lifetime's habit of breathing is retained on the new wind instrument. But the violin is a stringed instrument, so Coleman could create lines without the necessity to regulate phrasing and breath; his nontempered violin improvisations sound indeed like music without the distortion of will. The admiring critic Max Harrison considered them "an indeterminacy as drastic as John Cage's." In "Falling Stars" and "Snowflakes and Sunshine" Coleman and Izenzon together create thick forests of string textures, sustained by kinetic energy. The most extensive and varied example of Coleman's trumpet playing is in one of his rare appearances as a sideman on altoist Jackie McLean's *New and Old Gospel*. The trumpet phrases glitter through the many collective improvisations; Coleman sustains a delicate tension of sound and space in "Vernzone"; the trumpet lines become sober against the bronze, beautiful alto tones in "The Inevitable End." McLean's raw, powerful sound and accenting are gothic next to the airborne, mostly muted Coleman; this altoist, too, vividly and naturally plays sharp or flat "in tune."

Charles Moffett, Coleman's regular drummer, was a master of many styles and among the most sophisticated of percussion technicians. There could be no greater contrast than Coleman's ten-year-old son, Denardo, who is the drummer in *The Empty Foxhole* (1966), without style or more than rudimentary technique, but with a welcome spontaneity, a further step in the direction of indeterminacy. The *Crisis* concert (1969) is a major recording, a reunion with Don Cherry that introduces new compositions (including "Broken Shadows") into the Ornette Coleman repertoire. Is Denardo Coleman's presence, his spontaneity, in some degree an inspiration for the intense immediacy of *Crisis?* One glittering statement is unaccompanied: Ornette's powerful melodic structure that begins his "Song for Che" alto solo.

There are many more fascinating aspects to Ornette Coleman's music in this period. He's one of those jazz musicians who have sustained a high level of creative intensity year after year, even after the excitement of his 1958–60 innovations. There are his two 1968 Blue Note albums that offer the intrigue of his meeting drummer Elvin Jones; Coleman sings on alto, Jones responds with troubled complexity. There is tenorist Dewey Redman entering Coleman's music; formerly a high school bandmate, Redman is an eclectic who reinterprets Coleman in light of blues techniques, often humming through his horn to create guttural split tones. By 1971 collective improvisation had long since been common currency in jazz. While the density and speed of the ensemble are what's important in "Science Fiction," the collective passages by seven musicians in "Elizabeth" and "Happy House" are a far advance on *Free Jazz;* here is the interplay of Cherry and Bobby Bradford, while drummers Higgins and Blackwell are on each other like white on rice. There is the unity of Coleman and Haden in their 1976–77 duets, including *Soapsuds Soapsuds,* Coleman's first tenor saxophone adventure since 1961: pain, then anger in "Sex Spy," slapstick in "Mary Hartman Mary Hartman." Inevitably Coleman's trumpet playing in "The Golden Number" and "Some Day" has passed far beyond its original state of willed innocence, yet the sound and technique remain intimate.

After he had returned to America in mid-1966, he again slowed down his performing schedule. He was disgusted with the way the music business treated musicians, and he said, "I don't feel healthy about the performing world anymore at all. I think it's an egotistical world; it's about clothes and money, not about music. I'd like to get out of it, but I don't have the financial situation to do so. I have come to enjoy writing music because you don't have to have that performing image. . . . I don't want to be a puppet and be told what to do and what not to do. . . ."[6] Again he took progressively fewer and fewer gigs each year, with the goal of performing only when circumstances were right: the availability of compatible sidemen; the performance conditions; the personal need to play. His performing trio became a quartet with the addition of Haden in 1967; after that, Haden, Redman, and Blackwell were his most frequent sidemen. And as Coleman cut down his touring schedule, he presented concerts in his home, Artists House, on Prince Street in Manhattan, sometimes performing there himself, other times introducing other musicians to his audiences.

When his quartet played at a Lisbon, Portugal, jazz festival in November 1971, Charlie Haden dedicated his "Song for Che" to "the Black people's liberation movements of Mozambique, Angola, and Guinea"; the audience cheered at length, and Redman and Blackwell gave the raised-fist salute. The police canceled the day's second concert but then changed their minds and let it go on. Nonetheless, as the quartet was boarding their plane the next day, Haden was arrested and was released only upon the intercession of the American cultural attaché.

From his years in California, Ornette Coleman had been writing classical music. His string quartet *Dedication to Poets and Writers* was recorded at his 1962 Town Hall concert; his woodwind quintet *Sounds and Forms* was recorded at his 1965 Croydon, England, concert. It was during this nine-month European stay that he composed *Saints and Soldiers* and *Space Flight*. In early 1967 came two important events in his composing career: He presented *Forms and Sounds* in concert—his trumpet interludes added to the ten movements of his woodwind quintet—and he received the first

Guggenheim Fellowship ever awarded for jazz composition. *Inventions of Symphonic Poems* was composed for the fellowship; it debuted in May 1967 at the UCLA Jazz Festival, with John Carter conducting. Coleman's seven-movement *Sun Suite of San Francisco* was introduced in August 1968 at the Berkeley campus of the University of California; the performance featured trumpet soloist Bobby Bradford.

He completed his twenty-one movement *Skies of America* in 1971, and the next year conductor David Measham recorded it with the London Symphony; Coleman improvised on alto throughout much of the work's second half. These *Skies* are often clouded; movements in long, held tones turn into fast, jagged sections; "Foreigner in a Free Land" features some of his very harshest alto playing, and "The Men Who Live in the White House" includes his unaccompanied solo. His melodies are gay, or they are troubled and disturbing, and what lingers in the music is the floating feeling of light, dark, and the turning earth. Almost three months after the recording, *Skies of America* was first performed in concert, at the Newport Jazz Festival—on the Fourth of July 1972. This time Coleman's quartet played along with the symphony and also interjected improvisations on other Coleman songs; moreover, some movements were repeated out of sequence. Thus this composer who'd taught himself to play trumpet and violin "without memory" attempted to add elements of spontaneity to his classical performances; in fact, he wanted to have his own symphony orchestra, to train to vary his music from performance to performance. *Skies of America* includes orchestrations of some of his familiar combo pieces, to link further the compositional and improvisational aspects of his art; he said *Skies* is "the way I play." His subsequent orchestra compositions include both lyrics and music for a 1981 movie score, "a genetic love story," and a symphony, *The Oldest Language.*

As he improvised over his classical pieces, so he improvised over the melodies of the Berber musicians he met in Joujouka, Morocco, in January 1973. In this impoverished mountain village the performers maintain an ancient musical tradition, playing their drums and raitas (native oboes).

> And the thing that was so incredible is that they were playing instruments that wasn't in Western notes, wasn't no tempered notes, and yet they were playing in unison. It's a human music. It's about life conditions, not about losing your woman, and, you know, baby will you please come back, and you know, I can't live without you in bed. It's not that. It's a much deeper music. There is a music that has the quality to preserve life. The musicians there I'd heard had cured a white fellow of cancer with their music. I believe it. Because if you ever hear the music, man, you can understand that. . . . The thing that was very beautiful about Joujouka and the same time very sad was that all the musicians have to survive is their music. I mean, they don't have *anything* else but that.[5]

He recorded three albums' worth of his trumpet and alto improvising with the Joujouka musicians. To date, only one track, "Midnight Sunrise," has been released, and Coleman considers it a misleadingly weak performance.

In the *Skies of America* liner notes, he first mentions his "Harmolodic Theory, which uses melody, harmony, and the instrumentation of the movement of forms." Later he said harmolodics "has to do with using the melody, the harmony, and the rhythm all equal," and Don Cherry described harmolodics as "a profound system based on developing your ears along with your technical proficiency on your instrument." Just because harmolodics is a system, it can't be defined in a simple sentence or two, but the word stands for what Coleman taught his first groups back in the 1950s: a wide knowledge and experience of ways to join Free lines into an ensemble music. Needless to say, harmolodic improvising demands great skill of listening and response; Coleman says it took years to teach his system to his first band, and again it took years to train his Prime Time band.

This is the source of Ornette Coleman's Prime Time: "About 1974–75, I realized that the guitar had very wide overtones—one guitar might sound like ten violins. Like, say, in a symphony orchestra two trumpets are the equivalent of twenty-four violins; that kind of thing. When I found that out, I decided, then I'm going to see if I can orchestrate this music that I'm playing and see if it can have a larger sound—and it surely did." The result is not exactly jazz but a kind of Free jazz-rock idiom. It's as far removed from Coleman's Free jazz as from his classical music, and the term "harmolodics" has come to be associated entirely (and therefore inaccurately) with this idiom.

Coleman's first two Free jazz-rock albums were by a quintet, in December 1975; the third album, *Of Human Feelings* (1979), is by six players; and in the eighties Prime Time is a septet of Coleman, three "lead" players, and three "rhythm" players—the lead and rhythm units are each guitar, bass, and drums. The lead players don't solo but create streams of interplay with each other and with Coleman's alto lines, which ride atop the ensemble. Prime Time moves in layers of tempos: Some players double Coleman's time, some halve it, and the lead guitarist is the only one who now and then breaks away from dotted eighth-sixteenth note patterns. The foundation of the rhythm is the disco thud of the bass drum on each beat; some pieces, like "Macho Woman," use a bass drum Bo Diddley beat (compare this to the flowing Bo Diddley rhythm in "Ramblin' "). Coleman's top lines are in always changing tonalities, and therefore, the others' separate tonalities keep changing, too; everyone is constantly modulating, as in Free jazz. *Of Human Feelings* is far superior to the 1975 LPs, but James "Blood" Ulmer's (James Blood's) *Tales of Captain Black,* on which Coleman plays alto, is yet a better fusion of Free ideas with rock-pop methods. So far records haven't captured the spirit of Coleman and Prime Time in concert: an urban rhythm tribe, with a fluid alto sax dipping and curving through the merry clatter of loud rock, jerk, and bump.

Coleman's improvising with Prime Time is nonstop; his inventive stamina is amazing. In general, his playing has become simpler, with less detail, repeated phrases, accented beats, and proliferating sequences. His songs for Prime Time lack the earlier definition of emotion in his composing; his Free jazz-rock is obviously more rhythmically restricted in any case. He seldom performed in his new idiom in the 1970s, and he played Free jazz even less often; one exception was a 1977 concert in which he reunited with David Izenzon, by then a dedicated psychiatrist, working primarily with children (Izenzon died two years later). In 1981 Coleman began playing regularly in public again, always with Prime Time— "When I have them working together, it's like a beautiful kaleidoscope. The most important thing that I think of, as far as trying to keep in the music world, the music business, is doing things that stimulate other people to investigate how they can enjoy what you do. And that's the hardest part— how does someone discover they enjoy what you do?"

The wide-open spaces of Ornette Coleman's pre-Prime Time repertoire have been left to Old and New Dreams, the quartet of Cherry, Redman, Haden, and Blackwell. No great artist communicates the insights and values he or she offered twenty-five years ago, and Coleman is no longer the radical young bebopper from Texas—"The pain is still there, but it's not as detrimental as I used to think it would be." He's long since become cosmopolitan, a thorough urbanite with a big-city dweller's nerves and emotions. Now his music appeals directly to no longer the heart and mind but the nerves, reordering the congestion of life's images and emotions with infectious patterns and simple songs. What persists is the fascination of his music itself and of his urge for discovery, as he continues to transform the jazz tradition.

Eric Dolphy

Even while Ornette Coleman's first recordings were beginning to be heard, there were three other major explorers who had arrived at the edge of the Free frontier. John Coltrane was already a leading source of sound and style on the tenor saxophone; pianist Cecil Taylor had been leading his groups off and on for several years in New York; at the end of 1959 Eric Dolphy, a well-traveled, widely experienced altoist-bass clarinetist-flutist, joined this small avant-garde. Dolphy's subsequent career was a difficult one. He performed as a sideman in one group after another, joining and rejoining the groups of Mingus and Coltrane; he sometimes toured as a single—that is, traveling from city to city, soloing with one local rhythm section after another. During the jazz recording boom at the beginning of the sixties, his versatility kept him active in the studios, and he fitted with all kinds of jazz ensembles—swing and Latin bands, bop combos, experimental orchestra settings, early Free and modal combos. So Dolphy was certainly a prominent musician at the beginnings of Free jazz, but he almost never had the opportunity to do what was most essential for the growth of his art: lead his own well-rehearsed ensembles in programs of his original music. He died in mid-1964 during a characteristic circumstance of his life, traveling from one city in Europe to another, fronting pickup groups wherever he appeared.

Everyone loved Eric Dolphy. He was that rare being, a reasonable man unburdened with the weight of small vanities, cruelties, bitternesses. Again and again in his biography you read of his small kindnesses over the years; friends and fellow musicians describe him as "kind," "generous," "gentle," "compassionate," above all, "humble." Here are two examples. The ever-tempestuous Charles Mingus, who considered Dolphy "a saint," said, "I knew Eric Dolphy in California, before he played with me. He was quiet—didn't say anything hardly. Very sensitive. Very alert—his eyes were very alert. Very kind, very thoughtful of other people. I don't think he thought he was great; I don't think he was aware of how good he was."[1] From a different perspective, Harold Land, the fine bop tenor saxophonist, said:

> Eric would show such humility that he couldn't help but warm you. This coming from someone of such dazzling facility. Eric was one of the sweetest, most thoughtful people I've ever met. He was considerate of others to an extreme; always ready to do favors. He was the kind of exuberant person that everyone liked because he was constantly glowing. He loved to laugh and evidently he thought I was humorous. So when I found that out I went out of my way to crack him up. He was truly a joyous person to be around.[2]

Eric Dolphy was born in Los Angeles in 1928 and lived most of his life with his parents in central Los Angeles. As a child he went to church choir rehearsals with his mother and heard Handel's *Messiah*. He later sang in the choir himself and taught Sunday school at his family's church and at the Presbyterian church where the father of bop pianist Hampton Hawes was pastor. When Eric was six, he began playing the clarinet; by junior high school he was playing oboe. In his teens he played alto sax in a Louis Jordan-style jump band. By this time he was learning jazz solos from records; too young to enter the Central Avenue nightclubs, he stood out-side and listened to the swing bands.

The young Eric liked to play his flute in his backyard, ac-companying the songs of birds, or play the family piano very late at night when he couldn't sleep. His parents converted the family garage into a soundproof studio for him to practice his music in. After high school Eric attended Los Angeles City College for a while; more than three decades later, his father remembered: "I asked him why he didn't stick with college. I explained that he could teach music if he got his degree and then have music as a sideline on the weekends. He said, 'Dad, I want to be a musician and that's *all* I want to be.' I didn't say one more word about the matter after that."[2]

Roy Porter, who had been Charlie Parker's drummer in 1946, led a pioneering big bebop band featuring exciting ar-rangements and seventeen fire-eating young musicians, in-cluding trombonist Jimmy Knepper and trumpeter Art Farmer. Eric Dolphy joined the band when he was twenty, playing lead alto sax. Porter's main alto soloist was Leroy "Sweetpea" Robinson, and you can hear Dolphy swap fours and choruses with Robinson in "Sippin' with Cisco," both of them highly spirited, inspired by Charlie Parker. The Porter band broke up in 1950; Dolphy, facing the Korean War draft, instead signed up for the army and was stationed stateside, spending his final year in the service at the Naval School of Music in Washington, D.C. He returned home in 1953.

On the underground Los Angeles hard bop scene, Dolphy became a well-known figure. Musicians liked to drop by his backyard studio to visit and practice with him; here is where Harold Land first played for Clifford Brown and Max Roach, who then hired him for their seminal quintet. Dolphy also met John Coltrane during the tenorman's Dexter Gordon-in-spired period; stranded in the West, broke, addicted to drugs, Coltrane borrowed money from Dolphy to get home to Phila-delphia. Another young musician whom Dolphy met in this period was Ornette Coleman, already discovering the principles of Free improvising: "Ornette was playing that way in 1954. I heard about him, and when I heard him play, he asked me if I liked his pieces and I said I thought they sounded good. When he said that if someone played a chord, he heard another chord on that one, I knew what he was talking about because I had been thinking of the same thing."[3] Dolphy performed off and on throughout the midfifties. For a year, from 1956 to 1957, Eric Dolphy and his Men of Modern Jazz were the house band at the popular Club Oasis; they backed dancers and variety acts six nights a week, closing sets with their own compositions, and returned to play the club's Sunday morning jam sessions. "He seemed happy at the Oasis—deliriously happy at just being able to play professionally," wrote a friend, who described Dolphy as "an extremely affable, gentle, unassuming fellow who worshipped Bird, who was very much like a playful kitten."[4] Eric Dolphy began to receive some national attention when, in 1958, he began playing in Chico Hamilton's quintet, one of the most popular cocktail jazz groups of the day. The group's repertoire was heavy on pop songs and nonjazz material, tightly arranged for a woodwind player (Dolphy), cello, guitar, bass, and drums (Hamilton himself). Frequently in live performances Dolphy had the opportunity to solo, and critic Nat Hentoff remembered Dolphy creating intense, original alto solos even in this pre-avant-garde period. The Hamilton group disbanded after a November 1959 tour, and Dolphy settled in New York, working at first with the house band at Minton's in Harlem. In December Dolphy joined the Charles Mingus group, then beginning a long engagement in Greenwich Village.

This was during the period when Ornette Coleman was creating his first sensation, at the Five Spot Café; suddenly, with Dolphy in Mingus's band, New Yorkers were experiencing shock at all the new jazz from the West. At the beginning of April Dolphy led his first recording date; four and a half months later he taped his second album; at the end of the year, on the same day he recorded Ornette Coleman's *Free Jazz*, he also recorded his third album, the record that began his association with trumpeter Booker Little. Apart from his own albums, Eric Dolphy played on fifteen or sixteen other recording sessions in 1960, soloing on most of them; after his underground status in Los Angeles, he had become an important player in New York. This is no wonder, for his solos on the records are musical fireworks displays, dazzling in their range of shapes and colors; he explodes with ideas, delighting with the joy of his crashing, whooping lines.

There's a great sense of wonder about all his playing, a purity of scope and intention on the surface that seems almost innocent next to the emotional complexities of Coleman, Taylor, and Coltrane. His best alto solos begin with cascades of sound and are swept through with exhilarating virtuoso lines. Most amazing in these 1960 recordings is his bass clarinet work; for example, in "Serene" he displays a world of marvelous effects in his big sound, from his saxophonelike upper registers (can the instrument *really* play that high?) through the warm, reedy, vibrating lower ranges to the strange moaning and talking sounds he could make (is that *really* a bass clarinet?). In virtually all his recordings he is certainly the central figure, whoever happens to be leading the groups, and he shows no mercy in his willingness to blast away complacent,surroundings. But he also inspired fine improvising from the best of his associates, such as Mingus or, in his own first quintet, a swinging rhythm section and young trumpeter Freddie Hubbard, whose cheerfully decorated statements and brass shakes reflect Dolphy's woodwind ideas.

There's a precise description of Dolphy's music at this stage in a valuable essay by Jack Cooke.[5] To paraphrase, Dolphy's free association of ideas reconciled urgent emotional involvement with something that seemed opposite, a rare, elegant, and highly detailed sophistication of ornamentation. His most vital and personal music was his bass clarinet and alto sax work, for at this stage his flute style wasn't yet as advanced as later, and the solos are organized with the techniques of collage. This description essentially applies, I believe, to all of Dolphy's recordings; the main developments in his art to come would be in terms of opening jazz structures, with a corresponding increase of depth in his collage forms. In 1960 and 1961, though, most of his playing was a unique response to other musicians' settings, including three of the most daring individuals in jazz: Mingus, Coleman, and George Russell.

Eric Dolphy was definitely the spontaneous expressionist that Charles Mingus needed. Even more than Mingus, Dolphy projected heightened emotional states. There is the holy passion of Dolphy's swoops and trills in "Wednesday Night Prayer Meeting"; there's the high drama of his fusion of satire and agony in "Original Faubus Fables"; there's the crashing exuberance with which Dolphy opens up and animates the pyramid of collective improvisations in "Folk Forms I." All these are alto solos, and the most famous of these recordings with Mingus is a virtuoso stunt on bass clarinet. It's this horn that, in the center of "What Love," argues with the bass in the cadences and inflections of speech—and squawks, grunts, splats, blurts, mutters, and misshapen cries as well.

Dolphy left Mingus at the end of 1960. For the rest of Mingus's life he tried to re-create the surface excitement of this group with the same stock of effects—stop time, rubato, double time, contrary tempos and meters, ostinatos, chases, collective improvisations, written and improvised horn backgrounds, adding players to or subtracting them from the unit—with only occasional success, except for Dolphy's brief returns to the fold, particularly Mingus's 1964 tours.

Working with Mingus led Dolphy to a wide variety of musical and personal associations. In 1960 Mingus and others, angry at the increasing trivialization of the annual Newport Jazz Festival, held their counterfestival in Newport, Rhode Island. That was also the year of the Newport riots; when the main festival closed down, the only jazz remaining in the resort city was the Newport Rebels festival. Besides the Mingus and Ornette Coleman groups, other major jazz Rebels included Coleman Hawkins, Max Roach, Wilbur Ware, and Jo Jones. Out of this festival grew the short-lived Jazz Artists Guild, an early attempt at cooperative effort by jazz musicians.

Inevitably Dolphy's name was linked with Ornette Coleman's in the journalism of the period, even though Coleman's music happened in an entirely new world of line and forms that he created again daily, while Dolphy, for all his extremes of sound, structure, and harmony, improvised in the world of given harmonic structures: "Yes, I think of my playing as tonal. I play notes that would not ordinarily be said to be in a given key, but I hear them as proper. I don't think I 'leave the changes,' as the expression goes; every note I play has some reference to the chords of the piece."[3] Dolphy and Coleman performed together in a May 1969 concert of Gunther Schuller's music in New York; these were the Schuller pieces they recorded in December. It's Dolphy's flute that brings vitality to two movements of Schuller's John Lewis and Monk "variants," and it's interesting that both movements are organized in conservative forms of Mingus pyramids; also, the bass clarinet-bass (Scott LaFaro) duet in the "Monk Variants" is close to Mingus's "What Love" routine. In Coleman's *Free Jazz* Dolphy, on bass clarinet, creates lines that are now leading, now responsive, in unusually (for him) direct, undecorated phrasing; his experiences with Mingus's collective improvisations prepared him for Coleman's Free ensemble.

Except for the works that included Coleman and Mingus, almost all of Dolphy's recordings in this period present him surrounded with musicians more conservative than himself, but in the spring of 1961 Dolphy met his match for a brief period: composer-leader George Russell. Five years older than Dolphy, Russell grew up in Cincinnati, Ohio, where he first heard jazz on the riverboats; in his youth he played drums in a drum and bugle corps, then in a nightclub, and received a scholarship to Wilberforce University. At nineteen he entered a sanitarium with tuberculosis, and there he learned arranging from a fellow patient. In the mid-forties Russell composed and arranged for bands in Cincinnati and Chicago and also for Earl Hines and Benny Carter; he then moved to New York, where Charlie Parker asked Russell to play drums in his combo. Instead, Russell suffered a health relapse and spent another sixteen months in hospital. It was during this convalescence that he formulated the principles of his Lydian Chromatic Concept of Tonal Organization.

Upon his release he composed "Cubana Be—Cubana Bop" for Dizzy Gillespie's 1947 big band, a multiple-layered, multirhythmic showcase for the bravura conga drummer Chano Pozo. In 1949 George Russell created "A Bird in Igor's Yard," so avant-garde that it was not released until the mid-1970s. Russell composed it with Stravinsky's *Rite of Spring* rhythmic textures in mind. This "Bird" begins in a welter of lines; behind Buddy De Franco's clarinet lead, the orchestra sections rise in big, bold statements; liquid and liberated, the clarinet warbles over offbeat trombone blats, and contrary rhythms boil up in high instrument lines. Like Eric Dolphy's 1960s solos, neither of these works includes a real beginning, central climax, or end. Instead, Russell offers successions of images that enter one on another, none persisting very long; they relate, break apart, or are irrelevant to one another.

"Bird" is a three-minute work to fit on a 78 rpm record; when LP records became standard, Russell began composing longer works. "All About Rosie" is his Brandeis University commission in 1958. In "Rosie," sections of the band swap a nursery rhyme like phrase, there is a slower movement in which sections' and individuals' lines change shape or transform into one another, and the children's theme is the source of the third movement, continuously changing sound colors and a succession of solos. *New York, N.Y.* (1958–59) is a loose suite, and the title suggests the visual and emotional ways Russell perceives his music: Here are the many impressions the composer receives on a busy street corner, and more, here is the span of human interest in the way he relates, pursues, or abandons material. Nearly two decades later Russell would use almost these words to describe composing methods he later evolved, but in fact, this description is accurate for nearly all his work. Russell's cities are teeming with life; his music is extremely active with the improvisations of colorful soloists and the vitality of rich, often long melodies. With each successive work Russell offers advances in technique, and in *Jazz in the Space Age* (1960), the atmosphere of "The Lydiot" is fast-paced and harmonically open. The orchestral movements of this suite are linked by interludes of two pianists swapping irregularly shaped phrases in a distant mode and eventually improvising simultaneously. This suite is based on modal techniques instead of chord changes; it is probably inevitable that for Russell, outer space is as bright, colorful, and lively as his cities.

The avant-garde sextet that he formed in 1960 would not dare Coleman's Free adventures, but his players joined wholeheartedly in demolishing bop era conventions. Russell's objective was to sustain constant motion, as in his big band works, with his combo; he offers all of Mingus's rhythmic and textural techniques, but with an emotional range that is an opposite direction. Moreover, Russell and his sidemen shared the Lydian Chromatic Concept, which he had published in the early fifties. This unique approach to the harmonic organization of solos stems from his recognition that "Once you say that the chromatic scale contains all intervals and therefore all of music, then all music must be relative. And if all music is relative, then it can't be right or wrong."[6] For the improvising bop soloist, the real tonality of a phrase or passage is not what the key signature says, but what that soloist plays in his or her substitute chords. The Lydian Concept offers relations, scales based on the several-millennia-old Lydian mode inherited from the Greeks (who may themselves have inherited modes from more ancient people), relations which can reconcile the improviser between his or her tonality and all others, including the given key or the rhythm section's tonality. And the beauty of the Lydian Concept is that the improviser can substitute, harmonically, as freely as desired; here is the theoretical reasoning that goes with Eric Dolphy's assertion that he always improvised on chord changes, no matter how distant from these harmonic structures he sounds as if he plays.

Russell played piano in his combos, and the sextet he led briefly in spring 1961 included, besides Dolphy, two other very elegant soloists: trombonist David Baker and trumpeter Don Ellis. The group's ingenuity within new jazz techniques is consistent with Russell's own, and the satiric blues "Honesty" features the horn soloists projecting eloquent artifice over suspended time and swinging choruses in alternation. Russell's song "Ezz-Thetic" is a long, unbroken line of suggestive bop melody to which Dolphy's sharp alto lends an intoxicated edge, after which the riffs, rips, and long bent tones in his solo make the already abstract atmosphere sparkle. Russell arranged Monk's "Round Midnight" as a showpiece for Dolphy's alto, and Dolphy gives a highly dramatic reading, with long, rising decorative runs; his collage structure this time results in a stark statement, an extremely rare incident of a valuable nonthematic improvisation on what must be Monk's most forbidding piece to improvisers. It's a pity that Dolphy and Russell did not record again after this one album, for Dolphy would not again work with a group of players with such wide-ranging exploratory aims until major changes became manifest in his own music, 1963–64.

Dolphy was again busy in the recording studios in 1961, playing on at least a dozen sessions in the first six months, but the truth is that he seldom had the opportunity to perform at all except on records in this period. It was during this time that another major association, that of Dolphy and trumpeter Booker Little, developed. Little led his first recording date in 1958, when he was only twenty; he then worked often with Max Roach, and he also free-lanced like Dolphy. In describing his own approach to playing and composing, Little also unconsciously described almost the essence of Eric Dolphy's attitudes to line and harmony: ". . . I don't think anyone would deny that more emotion can be reached and expressed outside of the conventional diatonic way of playing, which consists of whole steps and half steps. There's more emotion that can be expressed by the notes that are played flat. . . . If it's a consonant sound, it's going to sound smaller. The more dissonance, the bigger the sound. . . ."[7] Little's trumpet style leads away from the broken phrasing of bop; his instinctive lyricism can even hint at the quality of peace and calm that Leo Smith would develop in the seventies. But Little's characteristic sobriety bends under strong emotion, so in "Man of Words" his careful structuring of sadness climaxes in high, distant, unfinished tones. In the modal waltz "A New Day," his phrases are so freely accented, with beats turned at will, that his rhythmic character sounds like nearly an innovation. It's a sign of shared perceptions that the hints of flamenco in his solo in "Moods in Free Time" lead Dolphy to begin his own solo with a high cry and follow with sobbing bent tones.

At last Dolphy received the chance to lead a group for two weeks in a nightclub, at the Five Spot Café, in July 1961, and fortunately Prestige Records preserved an entire evening's performance. His colleagues are Booker Little (this may have been his only public appearance with Dolphy), pianist Mal Waldron, bassist Richard Davis, and drummer Edward Blackwell. The results are Dolphy's most personal revelations to date, especially because all the soloists stretch out, and as abundant as Dolphy was with ideas, lengthy solos, you now can hear, are necessary to convey the great breadth of his playing. The pronounced vein of Charlie Parker in his phrasing is certainly evident. "Aggression," played on bass clarinet at a terrifically fast tempo, is full of Parker phrase shapes ripped from their original context and relocated, in the way of William Burroughs's cutup writing; the blues character of Parker's ideas is modified by Dolphy's wild intervallic leaps within phrases. "Status Seeking," "Fire Waltz," and especially "The Prophet" are incredible displays of alto sound and spontaneous creation. Pure virtuosity of idea and techniques are the medium, in the absence of conventional linear structure; in "The Prophet" his ties to harmonic structure appear to be as severed as possible, and it is pure brilliance of sound and idea that sustains his seven-minute solo. All the circumstances are right for these Five Spot recordings—for a change, in view of his style, his four colleagues are without flaw—resulting in a purposely, successfully astounding evening of music.

The next month Dolphy, Little, and Waldron created together for a final time in Max Roach's ambitious *Percussion Bitter Sweet*. After Abbey Lincoln sings about how "Mendacity makes the world go 'round," Dolphy plays a brief, bitter alto solo, and then Roach, without reference to meter or bar lines, asserts a series of highly detailed phrases, each followed by silence, as if to dramatize his effect. The argument, built phrase by phrase, is complex, lines emerge from colors and patterns, yet this work resists the conventions of solo building; here is a Free drum composition to stand as an ideal for the generations of drummers to come. In earlier recordings,

Dolphy had created collisions with waltz times (Oliver Nelson's "The Meetin'") and 5/4 (Waldron's "Warp and Woof"), so it's somewhat surprising that in Roach's "Man from South Africa" he accents the 7/4 beats rather more than usual. It should be noted that two months after the *Percussion Bitter Sweet* sessions Booker Little died, at age twenty-three.

It was about the time of *Percussion Bitter Sweet* that Eric Dolphy won the New Star award in *Down Beat*'s jazz critics' poll. "Does that mean I'm going to get work?" he asked, and later in August he began his first tour of Europe, which lasted through much of September. Now Dolphy was playing regularly, touring as a single and fronting rhythm sections of varying quality; though his repertoire was now his own choice, it was necessarily limited to mainly standards and originals on standard changes, for his accompanists' sakes. If part of Dolphy's attention had to be given to putting his associates at ease, it is perhaps no wonder that none of the recordings from this tour rivals his Five Spot successes or that his playing now recalls Parker phrases more specifically than usual. In each concert Dolphy offered his unaccompanied bass clarinet feature "God Bless the Child," in which the theme simply vanishes in the wonderfully lush foliage of his decorative lines. Musically the tour was a success; the audiences' warm receptions must have been gratifying, after Dolphy's difficulties in finding opportunities to perform in America.

In 1961 Dolphy joined with John Coltrane, contributing to the tenorist's spring recordings and then touring with Coltrane's ensembles in the fall. In May, three weeks after his triumph with George Russell, Dolphy played flute and alto solos in Coltrane's *Ole* album. In June Dolphy conducted his own arrangement of Coltrane's tune "Africa," featuring wild atmospheric French horn swoops and Coltrane's tenor over exotic band cries and trills. Dolphy's live recordings with

Coltrane, in November and December, show that he was almost an added attraction, standing apart from the central thrust of the music. The other players were organized magnetically by the rhythms of Coltrane's own playing, particularly the regularity of his accenting on the first beats of measures. Occasions when Dolphy truly fitted into most elements of the Coltrane context were exceptions: a long, intense duet with drummer Elvin Jones in an alternate take of "India;" lush solos in several versions of "Naima," all on bass clarinet. More typical are performances, apparently including entire concerts, in which Dolphy is near the peak of his creativity, to the complete incomprehension of Jones, who himself may be creating with great swing and equal brilliance, as in a Baden-Baden version of "Impressions." There are Dolphy solos, such as two versions of "Spiritual," in which his foreground rhythmic vivacity is so free-flashing that Jones is actually obscured, certainly an uncharacteristic situation for this highly advanced drummer. Did Dolphy influence the new ideas in Coltrane's style during this period? Hearing the first alternate take of "Impressions," with double-time Dolphy passages that move without relation to the beat, you wonder if the Freest passages in crucial Coltrane works, such as the originally released "Impressions," weren't at least partly Dolphy-inspired.

The six months with Coltrane ended in March 1962, and after that Dolphy did indeed find rather more work, though mainly as a sideman, in an unusually wide range of projects. He played in conventional pop-jazz settings and a Mingus big band, in hard bop units and again with Coltrane, and in third stream concerts conducted by John Lewis (including Lewis's Orchestra U.S.A.) and Gunther Schuller; he played Edgard Varèse's "Density 21.5" for solo flute and Schuller's "Night Music" for solo bass clarinet in concert. Dolphy's recording activity leveled off drastically after 1961, and there's no evidence that he advanced beyond his revelations in "The

Prophet" for the next twenty months (not even in his travels with Coltrane). But on occasion he did get to lead his own groups in public, and the reports are tantalizing. In one performance an artist created an abstract painting on a large backdrop while a ten-member dance troupe and Dolphy's combo (with trumpet, vibes, bass, and drums) improvised; another Dolphy quintet accompanied a poet in her readings; he led at least one nightclub gig with an advanced quintet that included Woody Shaw, trumpet; Bobby Hutcherson, vibes; Eddie Khan or the loyal Richard Davis, bass; J. C. Moses, drums.

These four join him in, at last, his own next recording sessions, for producer Alan Douglas, spread over five days in May or June 1963. The recording quality of this music emphasizes the distinctness and variety of Dolphy's sound, and the cruelty in his attack is often especially explicit. "Love Me" is an unaccompanied alto solo, cautiously reminiscent of his "God Bless the Child" successes on bass clarinet. "Alone Together" is one of three duets with Davis; this one is carefully structured, with a long introduction featuring sudden cadenzas and held split tones, then a medium tempo improvisation with phrases separated by space, in such tension that his sounds seem to draw blood; here, if ever, is demonstration that the bass clarinet is an instrument of jazz power.

Moreover, in "Alone Together" Dolphy has discovered a way to organize a performance so as to display all his prodigious creativity of idea and virtuoso techniques of sound production. This heretofore unanticipated mastery of performance organization extends to his composing for quintet. The modal "Mandrake" is in two meters, three and four; both the rhythmic and harmonic features exaggerate the disjunct qualities in his splintered alto solo. "Iron Man" includes a long modal bridge; in his alto solo a characteristic figure from this bridge becomes the cell motive of a thematic improvisation so that virtually all his lines either repeat or vary that original rhythmic pattern; his pitches achieve a personal apex of angularity in their unrelation to standard scales. "Burning Spear" is scored for trumpet, four woodwinds, vibes, two basses, and drums; again there's a harmonic pedal in the theme. Dolphy's bass clarinet solo is nothing less than an attempt to revise his 1960 *Free Jazz* "solo"; thus space (instead of explosions of sound) is an element of vitality as he extends his characteristic moment-to-moment contrasts of character into a large form. As if to emphasize the link to *Free Jazz,* he repeats, inverts, and varies a six-note motive in entering a brief collective improvisation. Most of the performances from his spring 1963 sessions are daring advances on his 1961 ideas; even in passages that appear rhythmically conservative—in "Jitterbug Waltz," the forceful lines of sixteenth notes that, for a change, do not collide with the three beat—you can hear ongoing reevaluation of his art.

He continues to advance his conception in his next album, *Out to Lunch,* nine months later. Vibist Hutcherson had made great strides in his music in the interim; more important are the young master drummer Tony Williams and his medium of rhythmic dislocation. Williams leads the rhythm section with his ingenious disruptions and contrary rhythms, and his innovatory nonaccompaniments encourage Davis's freedom of line, while Hutcherson dislocates rhythm, harmony, and dynamics, all three. This rhythm section provides a sharp counterpoint of broken, disjunct, often arhythmic line in place of a standard rhythm section's function for Dolphy and trumpeter Freddie Hubbard. The most important advance is in Dolphy's conception of overall performance. "Something Sweet Something Tender" is in five parts of equal length, with Dolphy on bass clarinet. He plays an introduction that concludes in a drawn-out harmonic, followed by a theme statement; his fast solo, with lines shooting up high and low, is over virtually no pulse at all despite the rhythm section's high activity, then, after the theme reprise, bass clarinet and bass, in a lovely low unison, play the theme a final time, in dark hues and without hardness or harshness. "Gazzelloni" is a jaunty, elegant theme, a perfect portrait of the real Severino Gazzelloni's stage personality; Gazzelloni is Dolphy's counterpart in modern classical music, a flute virtuoso who investigates sound modification and variation, and Dolphy's solo here is given over to sound abstraction and harmonic distance. The theme of "Hat and Beard" is in walking tones, bass clarinet and bass together, but this meter is 9/4; the line dissipates to faint vibes walking, but then comes a slash of band melody, and Dolphy is off with a convoluted solo which plays off the theme and against Williams in fantastic knots and gnarls.

Dolphy plays his alto in two tracks here that attempt to extend his powers of organization dramatically. "Straight Up and Down," a portrait of a drunk attempting to walk, has a stop-start theme; Dolphy's solo has a minimum of very fast phrases but many fragments and broken tones, his agonized sound featuring upward slurs and phrases extended into overtones. And his alto solo in "Out to Lunch," specifically the recurring extremes of broken phrasing in his crashing solo, appears the source of the rhythm section's disassociation, for the independence of its playing increases. There should be no doubt that with the Alan Douglas sessions and *Out to Lunch* Eric Dolphy has finally and fully broken his last remaining links to bop and hard bop. Now that he is playing with other musicians as advanced as he, especially the innovatory Williams, his style advances in clarity and impact, with increases in both subtlety and scope. In fact, his art seems to have advanced in every possible way; here are the breakthroughs to freedom that must have been implicit from his 1960 New York recordings, when those strange sounds and sweeping revisions of Charlie Parker first appeared.

And what was Dolphy's career like during this period of crucial creativity? In the summer after the Alan Douglas sessions, Dolphy depended on income from private lessons for his livelihood; of his three regular private students, he taught at least one for free because the student was as financially impoverished as he. He appeared on occasion as sideman, including more gigs with Schuller, Mingus, Coltrane, and Orchestra U.S.A. It was during this period that, according to Richard Davis, "Once I saw Eric with an armful of groceries and I asked him where he was going. He replied that he was on his way to deliver the groceries to some musicians who had just gotten into town and didn't have anything to eat. I knew he didn't have any money (no work) but he did have a twenty dollar gig the night before."[4] Dolphy's biographers note four appearances by him fronting his own groups in this period between his own recording dates. It is no wonder that in the liner notes to *Out to Lunch* Dolphy says, "I'm on my way to Europe to live for a while. Why? Because I can get more work there playing my own music, and because if you try to do anything different in this country, people put you down for it." It was Charles Mingus who provided the means for Dolphy's move to Europe, with an April 1964 tour.

Among his last performances in the United States were his recording with Andrew Hill and the Mingus Sextet's farewell concert at Town Hall, New York. Pianist Hill was by 1964 solid demonstration that the revolution that Dolphy had helped lead was a success; though the soloists in Hill's *Point of Departure* receive less solo space than Dolphy was accustomed to, he gets off a freewheeling alto solo in "Refuge," with no chord changes to deter him. Dolphy's playing in the Mingus concert did not look back from his *Out to Lunch* advances. Mingus's *Meditations* was a major new composition:

> This next number was written when Eric Dolphy explained to me that there was something similar to the concentration camps once in Germany, now down South, where they separate the prisoners ... prisons for darker skinned people with

barbed wire and electric fences . . . and the only difference . . .
is that they don't have gas chambers and hot stoves to cook us
in yet—so I wrote a piece called *Meditations* as to how to get
some wire cutters before someone else gets some guns to
us. . . .[8]

Dolphy achieves a uniquely harsh flute sound in the first
theme and ends the ballad section by bending long flute tones
back and forth; in fact, in this performance his flute achieves
a strong, raw-edged sound that's simply unprecedented on
the instrument. He also plays a bass clarinet solo in this long
piece, a solo that approximates a classic form and ends in a
definite resolution.

Throughout Mingus's tour of Europe his late appearances,
onstage tirades, and stageside tantrums were widely reported
in the press; his music was undergoing progressive disorien-
tation in this period, and in the Stuttgart concert it is Dolphy
who repeatedly saves the "Fables of Faubus" medley from
total chaos. After telling Mingus that he intended to live in
Europe no longer than a year, Dolphy settled in Paris and
began offering concerts on his own; his Hilversum, Holland,
concert of June 2, 1964, was released as *Last Date*. The
Dutch rhythm section has no problems with his music, not
even with the alternating three and four meters of "Mandrake" (retitled "The Madrig Speaks, the Panther Walks").
"You Don't Know What Love Is" is a flute solo with his
shimmering decoration in the intro and then a long improvisation in which the lowly flute, heretofore almost the most
unjazzworthy of instruments because of its expressive limita-
tions, achieves expression, line, and detail to equal his best
music on his other instruments. Elsewhere the recently acquired organizational qualities of his music are evident, as in
his "Miss Ann" alto solo, with a six-note phrase that's a mag-
net to the jagged ornamentation and twisting lines. The conclusion of the album is widely quoted, for after the final notes

of "Miss Ann" fade, Eric Dolphy speaks: "When you hear music, after it's over, it's gone in the air. You can never capture it again."

In June there were radio broadcast tapings in Paris; there later that summer he was going to marry his fiancée, who was to fly in from her home in New York. But on June 27 he arrived in Berlin seriously ill and was able to play in only two sets that night. The next day he asked friends to take him home; instead, he died on June 29, 1964, of a circulatory collapse caused by too much sugar in his bloodstream (Dolphy was diabetic).

There are two areas in which Dolphy's innovations are crucial to the emerging Free jazz. First is his instrumental virtuosity. No alto saxophonist before him could play so fleetly, with such control, and with such dramatic expression, and moreover, he not only created jazz on the flute (a handful of others had been doing it, less successfully, throughout the fifties) but also discovered, indeed, virtually invented, the bass clarinet, eventually offering on both instruments the fascination with sound and virtuoso expression that he brought to the more traditional alto sax. There was another reedman in this period, a bop stylist named Rahsaan Roland Kirk, who seconded Dolphy in making the new generation of musicians aware of the possibilities of multi-instrumental doubling; often he even played two of his strange saxophones at once. One of Kirk's most intense recordings is "Rip Rig and Panic," a shrewd satire of Free techniques in general and John Coltrane in particular. More generous and expansive, Dolphy's work convinced the new musicians that there was a world of unexplored possibilities on their instruments and that each new instrument which they could play multiplied their potential for creation and communication.

The other, probably more essential Dolphy innovation was his exploration of jazz form, an adventure that, for all his achievements, starting with his first recordings in 1960, was far from finished at the time of his death. The structure of his improvisations was from the beginning the most radical of jazz conceptions, a step into abstraction even beyond Coleman. The materials of Dolphy's free-association solos are so clearly delineated that the purport of each feature is without ambiguity; each solo element contrasts vitally with all other elements; if his emotionality is ever extreme and intense, it is also clearly defined from instant to instant; the effect of his vivid instants as they accumulate is overwhelming, not just in grand displays such as "The Prophet" and "Round Midnight," but in a multitude of other solos as well. Like the visual artists of his day, like poetry and fiction after the surrealists and Joyce, the world that Dolphy perceives is so vibrant and unbounded that expository or representational or other inherited forms are completely inadequate to reveal it.

The moves to newer ways of organizing his art in 1963 and 1964 suggest that Dolphy's may be among the great unfinished careers in art. Not only are his growing powers as a composer important here, but his work with Richard Davis and especially the *Out to Lunch* rhythm section suggest that Dolphy was developing a concept of improvising ensemble interaction that would provide an alternative to the eventually faltering and fumbling modal movement of which he had become a part. His death prevented the realization of these possibilities, of course. Worse, the limitation of his choices by plain financial necessity and his general lack of opportunity to create music in the most promising circumstances deprived him and us of the development of his powers in his lifetime.

John Coltrane: The Passion for Freedom

Ornette Coleman may have been the most revolutionary jazz artist of all, but he did not personify
the 1960s revolution in jazz. Eric Dolphy, doomed to working as a sideman, could not have led the revolution; Cecil
Taylor, doomed to scarcely working, couldn't have either.
The new music might have stayed longer on the periphery of
the jazz scene except for the personality, energy, and integ-
rity of John Coltrane. Unlike Coleman, Coltrane thrived on
endless public activity, and he willingly became the leading
jazz revolutionary. Back in the fifties he'd played tenor sax
with Miles Davis, the decade's most popular straight-ahead
jazz bandleader by far. Even then, all the young hard bop
saxophonists began incorporating his ideas, and Cecil Taylor
pointed out what it was about Coltrane that communicated:
"He has great insight, a feeling for the hysteria of the times,
and a conception that goes beyond that of his own horn."[1] In
the next decade, then, Coltrane led probably the most popular of all jazz groups, and it seemed that every young saxophonist, not just in America but throughout the world,
imitated him as best he or she could. It was Coltrane's exhaustive self-inquisitions that came to characterize avant-
garde jazz, as his followers united in the ceremonies of energy

music. And his extramusical concerns, especially his quest for spiritual principles amid "the hysteria of the times," became the preoccupation of his peers, too.

Earlier, Louis Armstrong and Charles Parker had been the other improvisers with influence as widespread as Coltrane's. Back in the swing era, not only did virtually every wind instrumentalist, on whatever horn, base his style on Armstrong, but the best trumpeters, creators such as Henry "Red" Allen and Roy Eldridge, stayed close to Armstrong's insights even in their most personal work. Parker's discoveries were similarly enlightening; much of the best saxophone music by the hard boppers, including Rollins, is in Parker phrases. Little of the best post-Coltrane saxophone playing is similarly influenced by Coltrane, and there's the best of reasons for this: He was the most passionate of musicians; his passion was too intimate to be shared or even duplicated for very long. You can play the notes he played if you have the facility—over the years scholars have transcribed every Coltrane solo they could find on record—but the passion that makes the notes necessary is too much a part of the man.

And Coltrane's passion evoked passionate responses. The intrigued or bemused audiences who heard him with the Miles Davis groups in the fifties may or may not have accepted his later adventures, but they listened, and they multiplied; surely no other jazz soloist has been so extensively documented over seventeen and a half years of recording. Twenty years after the Coltrane controversy and accusations of "antijazz," he is even worshiped; recently a San Francisco church with an altar photo of Coltrane, which plays Coltrane recordings during its services, was described in the newspapers. Has any other jazz artist been such an overwhelming cultural phenomenon?

He was born in 1926 and spent his childhood and teen years in High Point, North Carolina. His father played ukulele and violin, his mother played piano in church, and both parents sang; the Coltrane family lived with John's grandfather, a prominent minister, and the boy grew up in an atmosphere of books, music, and constant church-oriented social activity. John was a fine student in school right up to the time he received a gift clarinet, at age twelve. He played in his scoutmaster's community band; in high school he played alto saxophone. After his father and grandfather had died in 1939, his mother moved north to find work; after graduating from high school in 1944, John, too, moved north, joining her in Philadelphia.

Coltrane studied at a music school and spent two years in a navy band in the Pacific; back in Philadelphia in 1947, he began working with blues and jazz bands. This was a period when he worked some unrewarding gigs, too, such as the time he was hired as a honking tenor saxophonist and told to walk through the audience while soloing, in the fashion of the day. Coltrane declined, patting his gut and saying, "I got ulcers," to the merriment of his fellow musicians. He played tenor with singer-altoist Eddie Vinson through much of 1947 and 1948; he first recorded in 1949, playing alto in Dizzy Gillespie's big band. When Gillespie reduced his group to a sextet the next year, Coltrane stayed, playing both alto and tenor. His tenor soloing in this period is in the extroverted Dexter Gordon style, and already you can hear his distinctive sax sound, big and iron-hard, on recordings.

He stayed with Gillespie until 1951; by now he was addicted to narcotics, and Gillespie, tired of his erratic behavior, fired him. Then came a year with the very popular altoist Earl Bostic; it was in this year that Eric Dolphy rescued him in California. Coltrane had no solos with the Bostic band, but in his year with Johnny Hodges he was featured on ballads such as "Don't Blame Me" and "Smoke Gets in Your Eyes." In autumn 1955 Coltrane married his first wife, Naima, and began playing regularly with Miles Davis.

The Davis Quintet featured contrasts. The leader's own

trumpet solos were simply stated, basically in quarter notes, often muted, and mainly in his middle register; inflection was at the heart of his style, and he was inclined to tongue every note he played; poise and intimacy characterize his music. Against this style, Coltrane was exuberant, inclined to grace notes and fast filigree runs, with a large, unvarying sound in all registers. Especially in medium tempo pieces, after muted trumpet solos over the rhythm section's two beat, Coltrane conceived stunning on-the-beat phrases to set off the group in a swinging four meter. The famous Davis version of "Round Midnight," which was basically the same arrangement Coltrane had played with Gillespie, is one of the best examples of the introvert-extrovert Davis-Coltrane relationship. The trumpet solo is a statement of concentrated, finely extended pathos; Coltrane's solo is florid, but for all his loquacious activity, the lostness revealed in his many lines that wander off is as pathetic as the trumpeter's stylized brooding. Part of this lostness is a matter of stylistic inconsistency, though at best Coltrane could suggest Dexter Gordon's pure enthusiasm for the act of improvisation itself, as well as the styles of Gordon and Charlie Parker. Coltrane recorded three dozen titles with Davis in 1955 and 1956, and as the months pass, the roles of the two change. By "In Your Own Sweet Way," seven months after their first session together, Coltrane plays a clever solo, but it's the pirouettes of Davis that are more extroverted. Finally, the quintet's fast, boppish pieces derive the greatest share of their momentum from Davis's drive and widened dynamic and technical range. Coltrane solos such as "Salt Peanuts" are exciting, but such fast tempos deprive him of double time and filigree, his only means of linear relief, so that his straight-ahead playing sounds stolid.

Coltrane became enormously popular in recording sessions in this period, almost always in combinations with two or more of his partners in the Davis Quintet. Those were the days when three independent jazz labels recorded weekly at the Van Gelder studio in suburban New Jersey. Visiting his Davis bandmates at a Sonny Rollins session, he accepted the leader's invitation to record a two-tenor blues chase, issued as "Tenor Madness." Breakfasting at a cafeteria, he met tenorist Johnny Griffin's sextet awaiting their ride to New Jersey and was invited to join the session; he did, stimulating Griffin to one of his most exuberant performances. The quality of the many Coltrane recordings in mid-1955 to mid-1957 varies widely, with a fumbled solo for every valuable one. His style was unsettled as late as May 1957; in "From This Moment On" he plays like Gene Ammons, and in "Straight Street" he imitates Hank Mobley. (The younger, more rhythmically sophisticated Mobley often recorded tenor chases with Coltrane; perhaps "Straight Street" was done to show that Coltrane, too, could play in a rhythmically versatile style if he chose.) The rhythmic shape of Coltrane's phrasing very often reflected the pre-Parker saxophonists' comparative simplicity, though Coltrane had not yet settled into his rhythmically symmetrical style.

The most personal element of his mid-fifties music is his tenor sound, full and pure in all but the very highest notes, for his objective was sonic consistency in all registers. As opposed to the rich tenor sound that, for example, Rollins inherited from Hawkins, Coltrane's sound was vibratoless and legato, the human sound of Lester Young transformed into the weight of the hardest iron and the surface of brightly polished metal. The weight gave force to his attack; his sonic consistency was needed for the kind of fast, technically difficult playing he chose even in this period of stylistic casting about. It's a sound that he could vary while avoiding richness; he sounds thin on some recordings, yet his sound is simultaneously grainy and petal-soft as he breathes the affectionate theme of "On a Misty Night." The ascetic spareness of line that best reveals the beauty of his sound is heard on his first major ballad recording, "Monk's Mood." Here the arranger,

Thelonious Monk, has him simply playing the theme, but the rubato statement and Coltrane, especially the suppressed cry in his higher tones, reveal the depths of the song's melancholy.

Even in his earliest sessions with Miles Davis, the grace notes, filigree, and double time in Coltrane's playing would sometimes acquire a life of their own, however briefly. Late in 1956 the linear qualities of the mature Coltrane style came together in a Tadd Dameron Quartet session. After the affection of the "Misty Night" theme, Coltrane solos in short scalar or arpeggio phrases comprised of sixteenth notes, and the solo is wholly straight-ahead; double-time though they are, these lines are not for decorative or structural relief purposes. Although he achieves rococo excess in Dameron's "Soultrane," here and in "Gnid" he obviously seeks forms for his arpeggio configurations and runs that zoom upward. A few months later, with Mal Waldron, you can hear an improvising system beginning to appear in "The Way You Look Tonight" and "One by One"; note the quick arpeggios that rise to target notes which land hard on the beat (sixteenth-note lines ending in a quarter note on beat one), for this would become one of his favorite devices. Of historical interest is the three-note chord that ends "While My Lady Sleeps": One note is played by the trumpeter, and the other two by Coltrane on tenor sax—the first time he played two notes at once.

The great changes in his art began to appear in mid-1957, and they followed a major personal change. During the previous autumn Miles Davis had fired him when he showed up for work drunk; for some months thereafter addiction to narcotics and alcohol continued to be the main force in his life. Coltrane bottomed out in the spring, and like some other addicts who emerge from a final agony of withdrawal, "I experienced, by the grace of God, a spiritual awakening which was to lead me to a richer, fuller, more productive life." Coltrane wrote these words seven years later and added that at the time, "in gratitude, I humbly asked to be given the means and privilege to make others happy through music."[2] In the summer came a stroke of good fortune: Thelonious Monk took on a six-month gig at the Five Spot Café and hired Coltrane. "If a guy needs a little spark, a boost, he can just be around Monk and Monk will give it to him," Coltrane later said.[3] This became a period of self-discovery, as Monk gave him room to stretch out with his new ideas of harmony and rhythm that he'd been testing off and on. The choices Coltrane made in the second half of 1957 set the course from which he would not deviate for the ten years of music left to him.

"Traneing In" (August 1957) is a themeless blues-with-a-bridge, opening with Red Garland's long, lyrical piano solo. Then Coltrane begins improvising with the power of the great blues tenormen, establishing authority immediately with broad whole notes and riffing. After the first bridge, he begins double-timing, and from this point on the developments in his solo occur in sixteenth notes. Here are his "sheets of sound"—broken scales or arpeggios played so fast that he seems to be trying to give the impression of chords. Again and again the top notes of these sound sheets escape the gravity of tonality, fluttering momentarily or, as "Traneing In" progresses, for a few bars at a time. But these flutterings are between accents: Coltrane's course is defined by accents on the strong beats, one and three, as weighty as in rhythm and blues; earthbound man can achieve flight only momentarily. Three weeks later came the *Blue Train* session, which confirmed his discoveries of "Traneing In"; particularly, there's his power in the title track, arising out of his angularity of phrase and symmetry of outline.

In the Monk Quartet recording, Coltrane's scales and long arpeggios soar or plunge; Monk's own tumble up or downhill, he can't resist embellishing his own line with a Coltrane run in "Nutty," and after the Coltrane holocaust in "Trinkle Tinkle" the utter calm of Monk's solo is cherished. Moreover, the heavy labor of Coltrane's vertical lines occurs over the dancing bass of Wilbur Ware, who by contrast touches on equal harmonic obliqueness with a complete absence of strain. Like the Davis Quintet, Monk's quartet dealt in contrasts; in place of the nervous tension that Davis featured, Monk's music placed Coltrane in a setting of calm intensity. But this was a period when Monk refused to work anywhere but in New York, and when the Five Spot gig ended at the end of 1957, the quartet broke up.

"Good Bait" (February 1958) teems with life like a drop of Mississippi water under a microscope. Coltrane begins with long, heavily embellished lines that snake down into swallowed low notes, but then in general his phrases are short and in angular arpeggios. With the euphoria of fast phrases his line recedes progressively from the chord changes until, by his fourth and fifth choruses, his solo is clearly modal, bothering only occasionally to refer to the changes via an occasional phrase at the end of a strain. Early in the solo his sequences modulate downward; by the final chorus they tend to move upward—again, the optimism of Coltrane's style in this period. The same recording session produced his original version of "I Want to Talk About You," the most charming of Coltrane solos. Gaiety peeps through the occasional inflection or accent, the swing is jaunty, and the generous affection of this performance is a more active emotion than the tenderness or reflection that before long would become his main lines of ballad thought.

Coltrane rejoined Miles Davis in 1958; Davis was now leading a sextet that featured altoist Julian "Cannonball" Adderley, himself inclined to incorporate Coltrane harmonic ideas. The sense of chord changes in this group's music was obliterated by the fast tempos they preferred and by the increasing dominance of blues in their repertoire. So the blues "Straight No Chaser" is given three successively faster performances that year; in the third (retitled "Jazz at the Plaza") most of Coltrane's solo contains only a few tones, and he expends his energy on lengthy reshaping of arpeggios. In general Coltrane played solos loaded with sheets of sound, lengthy sequences, and sixteenth-note phrases that attack, zooming, in packs. He described his thinking in this period in an article he dictated two years later to *Down Beat*'s Don DeMicheal: Miles Davis, in 1958, was moving

> to the use of fewer and fewer chord changes in songs. He used tunes with free-flowing lines and chordal direction. This approach allowed the soloist the choice of playing chordally (vertically) or melodically (horizontally).
>
> In fact, due to the direct and free-flowing lines in his music, I found it easy to apply the harmonic ideas that I had. I could stack up chords—say, on a C7, I sometimes superimposed an E^b7, up to an $F^\#7$, down to an F. That way I could play three chords on one. But on the other hand, if I wanted to, I could play melodically. Miles' music gave me plenty of freedom. It's a beautiful approach.
>
> About this time I was trying for a sweeping sound . . . at the time the tendency was to play the entire scale of each chord. Therefore, they were usually played fast and sometimes sounded like glisses. . . . I thought in groups of notes, not of one note at a time. I tried to place these groups on the accents and emphasize the strong beats. . . . I would set up the line and drop groups of notes—a long line with accents dropped as I moved along. . . .
>
> I haven't completely abandoned this approach, but it wasn't broad enough. I'm trying to play these progressions in a more flexible manner now.[3]

Since this sextet was for all practical purposes playing modally anyway, Davis began to offer modal harmonic structures, first in "Miles" (1958), then in *Kind of Blue* (1959). After the loneliness and reflection of the trumpet solo in "So What," the stately, symmetrical lines that Coltrane plays turn the mood to near despair. In a spring 1960 concert in which they reunited, the long tones of the trumpet solos, with their harmonic secrets closed in Davis's heart, suggest vast, lonely flamenco plains. Coltrane assaults his simplicity with volley after volley of triplet choruses, sheets of sound, incantations, lurching playing, and contempt for the lingering traces of harmonic structure. By now Coltrane's involvement with hard bop was definitely at an end.

This first stage of his career defined his musical character and the nature of his quest; there would be changes as great in the years to come, but none more important. For John Coltrane, the rhythmic inner life of bop—its unending restlessness, its nervous multiplicity of phrase shape and character (and of harmonic suggestion, too); in sum, the idiom's rich, abundant, neurotic emotionality—was becoming irrelevant. In its place Coltrane discovered harmonic insecurity at times so vast that the only security in his music was in symmetry and rhythmic insistence; reiteration is his defense against utter dislocation, as in the several "So What" solos or the three Wilbur Harden albums (1958). Coltrane's reevaluation of resources resulted in a music of extremes, for he seemed to have bypassed the mainstream of hard bop to arrive at a more perilous music; henceforth his art would exist in an unending condition of jeopardy.

The great exception to this is his *Giant Steps* project, most of which was recorded in May 1959, two weeks after the Davis Sextet had completed *Kind of Blue*. In *Giant Steps* Coltrane's achievement overshadows his quest for a change. Now that he is not obsessed, melody flows in a stream, his phrases are rhythmically dispersed, and his music acquires new power. A rising four-note motive gives happy character to "Giant Steps"; "Syeeda's Song Flute" takes flight from a long, sinuous line. The dogged simplicity that usually rushed in violent symmetrical lines now appears in spare form in the long-toned theme of "Naima" as the purest of lyricism; embellishment, activity would violate this precious fragility. His tone is soft, and the setting is as simple as possible, over a one-note bass pedal; the melody of "Naima"—quiet, sun-filled—is worthy of Coltrane's reverence, the unsuspected calm in the midst of his storms. Like "Traneing In," a new blues, "Mr. P.C.," has the effect of prophecy, but now harmonic exploration and rhythmic certainty are no longer at opposite poles; instead, they merge as the burden of symmetry is abandoned. The sound sheets, downbeat accents, repetitions, great speed, and the other features of his most single-minded works are part of his *Giant Steps* solos; but now they are distributed throughout his solos, and the variety of his phrase shapes is unique in all of Coltrane's career. The freedom of line suggests liberation from the cave of self; life is deeply enriched by this great creativity.

It wasn't long until Coltrane left the Miles Davis Sextet. The tenorman's physical neglect during his drugging and drinking years had left him in pain that only extensive dental surgery could correct; in May 1959 he had an upper bridge put in, and subsequently he had to redevelop his embouchure. Late in the autumn he recorded a quartet date, *Coltrane Jazz*, in which he tests his embouchure to its limits with harmonics. For example, split tone chords, wherein he plays two or three tones simultaneously, conclude two tracks and decorate the theme and improvisation of the blues waltz "Harmonique." At this point in his career John Coltrane had composed (or improvised themes for) thirty songs and led sixteen recording sessions. Coltrane was now mentally pitched to form his own working group, though the areas he would investigate were not at all certain. He became friends with Ornette Coleman, then creating his first New York sensation, and cut a tentative Free album, co-led by Don Cherry, with the other members of the Coleman Quartet, using six of their themes. He reunited with Miles Davis now and again in 1960; he also played at the Monday night jam sessions at Birdland, trying out various players there. Five years earlier, in Philadelphia, he'd met McCoy Tyner, a sixteen-year-old pianist who played in trumpeter Cal Massey's big band; he'd conversed with Tyner on the Coltrane front porch, and they'd anticipated future collaborations. In 1960 Coltrane used at least two other drummers before he chose Elvin Jones to work with him; it was Jones, then, who became his crucial collaborator.

The weight of John Coltrane's tenor sax sound was so necessary to his style that in 1960 it came as a surprise that he began to double regularly on the soprano saxophone, with its high, piping sound. In fact, Coltrane became interested in the soprano by accident: "Three of us were driving back from a date in Washington in 1959. Two of us were in the front seat and the other guy, a sax player, in the back. He was being very quiet. At Baltimore we made a rest stop, then got back in the car, and 30 minutes later realized that the guy in the back wasn't there. We hoped he had some money with him and drove on. I took his horn and suitcase to my apartment in New York. I opened the case and found a soprano sax. I started fooling around with it and was fascinated. That is how I discovered the instrument."[4] He admitted the instrument's problems—"I like the sound of it, but I'm not playing with the body, the bigness of tone that I want yet. I haven't had too much trouble playing it in tune, but I've had a lot of trouble getting a good quality of tone in the upper register"[3]—but three weeks after saying this, he recorded his first and most famous soprano sax solo.

This solo is "My Favorite Things," a Broadway waltz whose changes Coltrane and pianist Tyner abandon as they play. Instead, they improvise on the minor scale that concludes the theme and the major scale of a bridge interlude. The shifting between scales and the restatements of the theme give a cyclic structure to the happy performance. With the soprano's piping sound, the ideas that sounded so dark and brooding in his fast solos of 1958—erupting up-down runs, melismatic rises, extended repetitions of small motives—now acquire a feeling of giddy fantasy; the innocent playfulness is emphasized by the stern piano vamp beneath Coltrane's solo. "My Favorite Things" was recorded at the first of four sessions which occurred over six October days; he recorded several more soprano solos at the time, as well as tenor solos that included a particularly harsh, gnarled "Liberia."

It would be six significant months before he would record again. At the end of 1960 he won his first *Down Beat* popularity poll for his tenor playing (he would win five more, plus two for his soprano playing). He began collaborating with Eric Dolphy in this period. The long solos that he'd gotten in the habit of playing with Miles Davis were becoming longer now that he led his own group, and it's interesting that at the time he expressed considerably mixed feelings about his direction in jazz:

> . . . I ran across a funny thing. We went into the Apollo and the guy said, "You're playing too long, you got to play 20 minutes." Now, sometimes we get up and play a song and I play a solo maybe 30, or at least 20, minutes. Well, at the Apollo we ended up playing three songs in 20 minutes! I played all the highlights of the solos that I had been playing in hours, in that length of time. . . . It seems like it does me a lot of good to play until I don't feel like playing any more, though I've found out that I don't *say* that much more! . . . [It] seems like we are into this thing where we want to solo on a modal perspective more or less, and therefore we end up playing a lot of vamps within a tune. I don't know how long we're going to be in that, but that's the way it's been.[5]

What's most important in these remarks is the release that Coltrane felt in playing long solos. Coleman and Dolphy were also beginning to play long solos in 1961; nowadays, when extended improvisations have been standard procedure

for so many years, it's easy to forget that Coltrane's twenty-
to thirty-minute tunes were at first considered revolutionary.

Eric Dolphy first appears in Coltrane's music under the
pseudonym "George Lane" in *Ole* (May 1961). This septet
album was recorded about the time of Coltrane's big band
project for which McCoy Tyner arranged "Greensleeves" as
a modal setting for Coltrane's soprano and Coltrane arranged
a spiritual with rare historical significance—its words were a
code for escaping slaves' route to freedom—as "Song of the
Underground Railroad." Cal Massey's "The Damned Don't
Cry" has a theme in slow and medium tempos, and Coltrane
solos on both his saxophones here; for a change, this is a composition featuring chord progressions, and these inspire particularly rich contrasts of phrasing in the tenor solo. Dolphy
plays no solos with the big band, but "Africa" in his orchestration. This piece is in six beat, with a slow bass drone and
piano and band chords in the same tempo; drummer Elvin
Jones plays a medium-up high-life tempo, and Coltrane's
tenor lines double and triple the tempo. The tension of the
multiple rhythms leads Coltrane to progressive darkness;
multiphonics cries appear out of the strangling desperation of
his phrase reiterations—all the difference in the world from
the multiphonics that decorated "Harmonique."

His soloing had not necessarily grown more intense since
"Liberia" and "The Night Has a Thousand Eyes" of the previous October—how *could* it be more intense?—but he had
advanced into an art of ever more dangerous extremes, emphasized by the seventeen pieces released from his November
1961 Village Vanguard performances. The misgivings about
his style that he'd expressed earlier in the year are now irrelevant; most of these tracks are long, and much the longest
parts of each are Coltrane's solo extravaganzas. Only the
three fast blues are not modal songs. The structure of his solos
initially emphasizes the free play of lyricism, but then he
ventures warily into harmonic Freedom as the psychological

restraints of symmetry determine the solos' movement. Yet these new boundaries of harmonic distance and sonic extremes become a prison as Coltrane thrashes at arpeggios without end, turning each in every possible direction, unable to abandon them or to separate his accents from the first beats of each bar. Sometimes the arpeggios separate at last from the tyranny of the downbeat, but these passages of "Freedom" are only nominal, as the now-savaged ego finds no lyric release, but only closer, more threatening mazes of symmetry. Each section of these solos is a lengthy passage, at best in cycles of styles to which he advances progressively, retreats, advances further, retreats, and so on. Riffing abounds; triplet motives are repeated at length without rests, in powerful gusts; five- and seven-note sheets of sound are reexamined *ad infinitum,* with inevitable one-beat rests and downbeat accents. Phrases conclude outside their harmonic boundaries, and compulsive repetition leads to exasperation, resulting in honking, high and low multiphonics, and squalling passages in which tempered pitch is abandoned.

"Impressions" (third version) is especially valuable for sustaining creative momentum throughout a fifteen-minute tenor solo, full of this turbulence, accompanied only by bass and drums. In the third version of "Spiritual" Coltrane begins with lyrical melody, but then the beautiful, dignified phrases are distorted by isolated blue notes and harsh tones, a distant signal of the forthcoming savaging of the psyche. "India" (second version) is elaborately orchestrated; the marvelous throb of the oud and the diamondlike oboe statement give way to low, reedy drone chords. But the fast, rampaging drum rhythms and Coltrane's dervish soprano cast off the stately mood; the Far East survives in Dolphy's bass clarinet solo, and as he concludes in trills, the soprano rises in trills like the moon over an exotic festival.

This is the world that Coltrane perceived. Value resides not in discovery but in the quest and in the struggles of the explorer. Dissatisfaction is eternal; the beauty of "Spiritual" cannot be developed in its own terms but must be violated and then abandoned; "India," too, depends on the establishment, then abolition of beauty. The reflexes cannot tolerate the pause that beauty affords, and the nobility of these themes is beyond the capacity of modern man to cultivate. So the subsequent improvisations are fragmented and at last brutalized, as consciousness, glimpsing freedom in harmonic Freedom, battles the unconscious, with its downbeats and symmetries, for release.

In his 1961 recordings with Coltrane, drummer Elvin Jones at last comes into his own. Born in 1927, he grew up in the Detroit area and after his late-forties army duty, he gigged around Detroit for six years before moving to New York in 1955. His natural arhythms were at odds with the mainstream of bop, and even such imaginative performances as he offered in Sonny Rollins's 1957 Village Vanguard sessions appear to be restrained by his wariness of clashing with the soloist. With Coltrane, such restraints vanish; on the contrary, Coltrane's exhaustive forms inspire the freest possible interplay from Jones. Unlike his direct stylistic predecessors such as Roach or Philly Joe Jones, Elvin Jones finds no need to make his cymbal line precise—don't Coltrane's own downbeats organize the metric divisions?—and instead, Jones concentrates on exploration. Against Coltrane's symmetries, Jones is asymmetric; the heavy résonance of his drum kit, including very large cymbals, offers additional weight to balance the tenor sax's weight; the density of his accents and polyrhythms contrasts with Coltrane's straightforward rhythmic movement.

Within his rich textures Jones can nonetheless respond quickly to Coltrane and Tyner, as in "Underground Railroad"; he might also maintain three separate, simultaneous rhythms (the third version of "Impressions" is an example) or rise to cataclysmic heights behind Tyner's block chord

vamping ("Untitled Original"). Typically Coltrane performances were largely tenor-drum duets, whether or not the bass
and piano also played (often they dropped out). The three
takes of "Africa" feature central drum solos. In the second
take his opening solo passages bear no relation at all to the
song's tempos and meters; in the third take his solo moves
away from the song's rhythms as he constructs a forest of
sound around a repeated two-note motive. Possibly no other
drummer in jazz combined such vast resources with such
quick responses; with these 1961 performances, with his
great dexterity and instantaneous command of multirhythms,
jazz percussion interplay reached its outer limits. The only
advance possible after Jones would be for the drummer to
abandon timekeeping altogether—as Sunny Murray would
indeed do in the next two years.

John Coltrane was used to being controversial. Even before his adventures of 1961 the charge that he "plays his
tenor as if he were determined to blow it apart, but his des-
perate attacks almost invariably lead nowhere" was typical
of one category of critical response. With Dolphy touring in
the Coltrane Quintet, a *Down Beat* reviewer wrote, ". . . a
horrifying demonstration of what appears to be a growing
anti-jazz trend exemplified by these foremost proponents of
what is termed avant garde music . . . nihilistic exercises of
the two horns. . . . Coltrane and Dolphy seem intent on deliberately destroying [swing]. . . . They seem bent on pursuing
an anarchistic course in their music. . . ."[6] Some established
critics advanced the antijazz attacks in several publications.
Of course, there's no possible reply to such accusations,
though it's characteristic of Dolphy's and Coltrane's con-
scientious attitudes that they published a *Down Beat* appeal
to their accusers' higher natures. Four years later Coltrane
recalled the 1961–62 attacks: "Oh, that was terrible, I
couldn't believe it, you know, it just seemed so preposterous.
It was so ridiculous, man, that's what bugs me. It was

absolutely ridiculous, because they made it appear that we didn't even know the first thing about music—the first thing. And there we were really trying to push things off. . . . Eric, man, as sweet as this cat was and the musician that he was—it hurt me to see him get hurt in this thing." Were his attackers motivated by the urge to exercise power? If so, Coltrane said, "Then you lose your true power, which is to be part of all, and the only way you can be part of all is to understand it. And when there's something you don't understand, you have to go humbly to it. You don't go to school and sit down and say, 'I know what you're getting ready to teach me.' You sit there and you learn. You open your mind. You absorb. But you have to be quiet, you have to be still to do all of this."[7]

The controversy over Coltrane certainly helped attract audiences, not all of whom were partisans. In America and Europe the Coltrane unit was one of the leading attractions on the club and concert circuit; moreover, Impulse Records was recording the quartet every couple of months and releasing Coltrane LPs at three-month intervals. One of its most influential recordings was "Out of This World" (1962), in which Coltrane perfects his cyclic solo form against an accompaniment of complex tensions. The 6/4 meter is one source of tension, amplified by Tyner's rhythmic suspension; against this is the multirhythmic Afro-Latin swing of Jones's boiling percussion. Coltrane's tenor solo surges and subsides, falls momentarily into an interlude key change at times, then restates the theme before he spills further into multiphonics and more distant harmonic relationships. Each cycle is illuminated by contrast, culminating in ever more stormy eruptions; the power of this ritual is orgiastic, endless.

There was no single direction that Coltrane's music took in 1962 and 1963. A fine album of collaborations with Duke Ellington includes "The Feeling of Jazz," and this and a long concert performance of "Bye Bye Blackbird" advance Coltrane's willingness to articulate expressive and harmonic extremes over chord changes. He returned to two of his major 1950s pieces, and the dark power of the new "Traneing In" is the bitterness of experience to set aside the enthusiasm of his 1957 performance. And the affection of the 1958 "I Want to Talk About You" becomes obscured by fantastic webs of notes in 1962 and 1963; he ends each of these later performances by playing, unaccompanied, minute after minute of gushing scales and chord permutations. "Alabama" is a prayerful melody over pedal tones and Jones's somber mallets; the unvarying weight of his tone is the perfect medium for the simple beauty of the theme (Coltrane composed it as a memorial to the children murdered in the racist bombing of a church). The beauty of Coltrane's tenor sound is all that survives a number of pop ballads he played with little improvisation or embellishment in this period. These are aesthetic mistakes. Trivia such as "Too Young to Go Steady" does not acquire value by way of being stated in the ʻclean, austere tones of John Coltrane; on the contrary, he reduces himself by respecting unworthy material. Affirmation and reflection return in the original works of *Crescent* (1964); this lyrical program ends in "The Drum Thing," a Jones solo in which the throb of tropical undercurrents rises to a long, unbroken tidal wave of fast polyrhythms.

A *Love Supreme* (December 1964) is a suite of reflections. Coltrane's liner notes begin: "Dear Listener: All Praise Be to God to Whom All Praise Is Due," and the subject of the suite's program is his 1957 spiritual awakening. Yearning—for transcendence?—underlies the suite and in fact is specific through most of the music. The line of triplets in the opening "Acknowledgement" has little relief; without succumbing to compulsion, this solo at least presents the characteristics of obsession. The "Resolution" of the second movement's theme begins in temporary resignation that is penetrated by a yearning blue note in measure 4, but acceptance arrives in the consonant conclusion of the next phrase. Tyner plays big 3/4 chords on the 4/4 rhythm to mount grand tension for Coltrane's improvisation, and now, for one of the few times in a long modal solo, the tenorist's phrasing is varied so that the patterns are not compulsive but distributed; the powerful movement of "Resolution" is of the full heart and mind. "Pursuance" begins in an extroversion that is quickly cast away: Suddenly yearning becomes overwhelming with shrieks and lurching, while in "Psalm" Coltrane's spiritual odyssey becomes disheartened. At last the overwhelming yearning appears in multiphonics lines that turn upward, mingling with downturning phrases that recall the pause afforded by acceptance in "Resolution"—however fleeting and faint that acceptance has finally become. The grand sweep of the "Resolution" movement is only a temporary abatement of his yearning, then, and the listener turns away, saddened by the troubled materials of the other movements.

By now Coltrane was friends with the rising New York generation of outside musicians who struggled for opportunities to present their art to audiences. Albert Ayler's discoveries especially intrigued him because "I think what he's doing, it seems to be moving music into even higher frequencies ... he filled an area it seems I hadn't gotten to,"[7] and Coltrane lent Ayler money and found him places on concert programs. The Coltrane group recorded a lost version of *A Love Supreme* with second tenor saxophonist Archie Shepp, whose ideas of solo form at the time were to a large extent derived from Coltrane's most exhaustive pieces. Coltrane urged his record producer Bob Theile to record the new music—he recommended 400 musicians, by Theile's count—and subsequently Shepp and Ayler were among the several avant-garde musicians whom Theile recorded. Partly because he was the most popular jazz bandleader of the mid-sixties (in fact, virtually the only popular success in the new music), Coltrane had become a father figure to the second wave of

Freedom. Archie Shepp wrote about Coltrane: "He was a bridge, the most accomplished of the so-called post-bebop musicians to make an extension into what is called the avant garde. . . . He was one of the few older men to demonstrate a sense of responsibility to those coming behind him. He provided a positive image that was greatly needed and stood against the destructive forces that have claimed so many. Having suffered and seen so much himself, he tried to see that others coming along wouldn't have to go through all that."[8]

In 1965 the younger generation then became a bridge for Coltrane as he sought release from rhythmic and harmonic constraints. Initially a rush to violent statement typifies his thought. The Coleman Quartet's "Mapa" in 1961 attempted unified exploration despite incongruent tempos and rhythms; Coltrane's "Brazilia" in 1965 finds chaos and obsession in such incongruities. He devastates the umbilical downbeat and mode in two versions of "Nature Boy" and reaches a climax of violence in the June "Transition," which begins as a majestic rising blues and continues almost wholly in the overtone and multiphonics range of Albert Ayler—and not in Ayler's defined phrases and forms but in long cries and electrocuted squeals. On the record, this squalling performance is followed by "Dear Lord," which may be a coda to *A Love Supreme.* If there is yearning in the upward movement of the chord changes, there is now unclouded grace in the acceptance phrases that resolve the line. With "Dear Lord" Coltrane's spiritual self-examination now concludes not in travail but in sweetness.

Ascension is a massive project in every way. Coltrane's band improvisation is without the latitude of the Ayler groups or Coleman's linear interplay in *Free Jazz*, but with the vast exhilaration of seven horns and four rhythm (including two basses). The modal substructure and theme material are hardly important in the face of the masses of players gathering in simultaneous lines, parting for brief solos, and rejoining in heavy wailing (the five saxophonists play in their extreme ranges). Despite the music's turbulence, the crowd of voices remains fixed by its weight; *Ascension* sounds like a thirty-eight-minute centrifuge of fire. Four days later, at the Newport Jazz Festival, Coltrane improvised "One Up One Down" in held overtone squeals divorced from tempo and pitch. He added Archie Shepp to his quartet for the Down Beat Festival in Chicago in August; as the two tenors collectively improvised, half the audience (of 5,000) screamed in ecstasy and the other half yelled in anger. In September the Coltrane group added tenorist Pharaoh Sanders, multi-instrumentalist Rafael (Donald) Garrett, and a flutist for *Om*, with massed collective improvisations and a passage of clarinet and panpipes that suggests an animate rain forest. Two weeks later came *Kulu Se Mama*, with two Afro-Latin percussionists joining their tone colors and rhythms to the already dense, massy Coltrane unit (again with Sanders and Garrett).

By *Meditations* (November) Sanders had become Coltrane's regular second saxophonist, and now the emphatic Elvin Jones rhythms are clouded by an added drummer, Rashied Ali, with his higher resonances and free dispersal of movement. Jones left Coltrane shortly thereafter, and in 1966 pianist McCoy Tyner, the most loyal of Coltrane's players, at last left him also. The heavy chording and complex modes-based harmonies of Tyner were replaced by the lighter touch and ambiguous harmonic and rhythmic relationship of Alice Coltrane. (Long a professional pianist, she was now also Mrs. John Coltrane.) Jimmy Garrison had been Coltrane's regular, and usually only, bassist after 1961; often he had been a secondary player in the ensemble, dropping out during long Coltrane solos, but now he was willing to follow Coltrane in exploring the harmonic uncertainties of a new territory. Thus Coltrane was working with a new unit—Sanders, Alice Coltrane, Garrison, and Ali—and a repertoire which increasingly abandoned even modal frameworks: Coltrane was now no longer restrained by even the last lingering traces of harmonic structures or measured time.

What, then, did John Coltrane communicate in this new world of Freedom? With the tension of his titanic struggles against structural restraints now gone, turbulence remained, turbulence reinforced by the added mass of Sanders's tenor sax. Moreover, Sanders was a sure solo voice. His long solos are in sustained growls or overtone ranges, and given the narrowness of register range and techniques within which he works, his playing is remarkable for its variety of phrase shape and definition; from this point of view his soloing with the group tends to be more varied than Coltrane's. Much of the simple beauty of the original "Naima" was retained in the several 1961 Coltrane-Dolphy versions, but in 1966 Coltrane consciously destroys the song with dissipated floridity and downward plunges. In fact, much of Coltrane's music in this new Free territory sounds anything but free; rather, he dissolves into furious symmetries, wildly, randomly, perhaps vindictively. He also added new instruments, to expand his assaults, so in "To Be" he and Sanders improvise on flute and piccolo in a diminution of their tenor styles.

Yet this last, unfinished stage of Coltrane's music is no period of unrelieved disintegration; you can hear just the opposite in *Interstellar Space* (February 1967), one of his last recordings. Here is Coltrane alone on tenor sax, joined only by the wonderful percussionist Rashied Ali. The resulting clarity of dialogue suggests that his post-1964 ensembles had obscured his real advances. These tenor solos are longer and more reckless than anything he had previously recorded, with associations sometimes so free that only the kinetic energy he generates sustains his momentum. There is the immense power of his music in the very fast "Mars"; in "Saturn" and "Leo," amid long, compulsive fire storms, Coltrane sings in longer note values, disassociated and unperturbed. You can hear, in "Venus" and "Jupiter," his familiar static kinds of phrase reiteration; you can also hear motivic reorganization, using the methods of, variously, Coleman, Ayler, and Rollins. The implications of this are enormous, for Coltrane now internalizes responsibility for structure; it's possible that future developments of his capacities of organization might have resulted in the major advances of his music. Such speculation is purely academic, of course, since he stopped playing altogether three months later and died of liver cancer in July. It was at his request that Ornette Coleman and Albert Ayler played at his funeral.

For those who respect puritanism, the occasionally expressed critical idea that John Coltrane was a kind of musical puritan is a reasonable conclusion. The rigor and determination of his music are puritan qualities; so is his abandonment of sonic richness for tenor sax power, control, and often beauty. Some puritan virtues are absent here—for example, his music is not an ennobling experience—but most obviously present throughout his recordings is the primary virtue of courage. His music was a spiritual quest long before he explicitly said so in *A Love Supreme*. His cyclic structures of the 1960s are the cycles of his inner life; that is why he needed to play long solos. They move us so urgently because in hearing him, we recognize our own struggles against complacency, against fears, ever into life's unknowns. Surely the Freest of his recordings, *Interstellar Space*, makes clear for all time what sustains his creative spirit: Now without obstacles of any kind, he nonetheless continues in conflict, endless and exalted. And the conflicts in John Coltrane's music, the inner turmoil that's ongoing in life, are what have communicated more than any other statements in the Free jazz era.

After John Coltrane's death, his most remarkable partners, Pharoah Sanders, Alice Coltrane, McCoy Tyner, Elvin Jones, and Rashied Ali, have remained musically active. Ali's polyrhythms in *Interstellar Space* eliminate specific timekeeping, yet tempo arises from his varicolored activity, and he (amazingly) accents Coltrane's lush lines as the tenor moves in and out of pulse in "Venus." Ali himself became important in stimulating the most avant-garde kinds of jazz activities in the seventies, as his art progressed in skill and sensitivity. And we'll see how McCoy Tyner, as composer and pianist, himself became one of the most influential jazz musicians in the years after he left John Coltrane.

·5·

Transition: Miles Davis and Modal Jazz

The first transitional generation in jazz appeared in the early 1940s, when young musicians who were inspired by the fresh winds that blew from the West, especially from Lester Young, subjected swing music to the romantic perceptions that soon generated bebop. These Gene Ammonses and Don Byases and Dexter Gordons and the rest really did bridge the swing and bop eras, and they then spent most of their careers completely at home with the various aspects of bop. The second transitional generation appeared twenty years later, when young musicians followed the lead of Miles Davis into modes. They subjected Free discoveries to the perceptions of hard bop and at times almost managed to bridge the two idioms. But modes were only a step toward something new and different, whereas the Free directions of Coleman, Dolphy, Cecil Taylor, and Coltrane were a leap into the unknown. So modal musicians and Free musicians did not, as a rule, perform each other's music.

Instead, in the sixties modes became a parallel idiom. To some extent it was a reaction against Freedom; Miles Davis was among the many who initially rejected Ornette Coleman's music ("The man is all screwed up inside"). Davis is the uncompromising, single-minded artist whose music is the source of modes; his own modal adventures traverse the idiom's range, and his conclusions—since 1969 he's played other musics—symbolize the failure of modal jazz.

Davis acquired his characteristic resoluteness early in life. He was born in Alton, Illinois, in 1926, and grew up in East St. Louis, the son of a prominent dental surgeon and local landowner. According to his father, Miles as a boy liked long walks in the country, hunting, and fishing; "he was an excellent horseman, and if he was ever thrown he'd remount immediately and master his mount." Dr. Davis gave his son a trumpet for his thirteenth birthday, and he learned to play it in school and from a chord book; he also had a teacher who taught him to play without vibrato. In school music competitions, according to his father, Miles "was always the best, but the blue-eyed boys always won first and second prizes. Miles always had to settle for third. The officials, Miles and everybody else knew he should have had first prize. You can't treat a kid like that and tell him to come out and say the water wasn't dirty."[1]

St. Louis was a good city for music, and at sixteen Miles was playing in a prominent local band when singer Tiny Bradshaw passed through town needing a trumpeter. Sonny Stitt, one of Bradshaw's saxophonists, recommended that he hire young Davis, but Miles's mother insisted that he stay in high school; "I didn't talk to her for two weeks. And I didn't go with the band, either." But in 1944 Billy Eckstine formed his first big band and spent a crucial period in St. Louis that summer; Miles became friendly with Dizzy Gillespie and Charlie Parker and sat in with the band (Eckstine thought he sounded "terrible . . . awful . . . he couldn't play at all"). Miles's mother wanted him to attend Fisk University ("She always used to look as if she'd hit me every time I played my horn"), but he had a scholarship to the Juilliard School of Music in New York and enrolled in 1945. Arriving there, he spent his first week, along with his first month's allowance, hunting for Charlie Parker. He learned to play the piano, at Dizzy Gillespie's suggestion, in the Juilliard practice rooms, where he also studied bop harmony by analyzing the chord progressions and substitutions he'd heard Charlie Parker improvise in nightclubs; the conservatory curriculum was obviously irrelevant to his musical education, and he abandoned it after a semester. For a year he shared an apartment with Charlie Parker and played in Parker's quintet.

Miles Davis is the trumpeter on the first recordings Parker led, and at age nineteen he did not seem to copy Gillespie or anyone else. He plays what might be called a laid-back bravura solo in "Now's the Time"; his solos with Parker are mainly in his middle register, and they're distinguished by harmonic sophistication, a warm, dry tone, and rhythmic content that's certainly simpler than the bop phrasing of the day. In fact, he doggedly resists the fabulous techniques of Gillespie and Navarro; by 1948 Miles Davis's soloing is fairly consistent in quality, and he creates intimate moods in solos such as "Marmaduke" and "Steeplechase." For the most part he formed his music in Parker's quintets—"I used to quit every night"—though there were also periods when he studied with Thelonious Monk and played for other leaders, including (1946–47) Billy Eckstine's last big band, in which he was the trumpet soloist. He led his own first recording session in 1947, upon which Charlie Parker played tenor sax.

In 1948, after Miles Davis had quit the Parker group for good, he was asked to lead the nine-man *Birth of the Cool* band, for which Gil Evans and young arrangers such as Johnny Carisi, John Lewis, and Gerry Mulligan were writing music. Davis secured a contract to record twelve sides, including Carisi's great "Israel." The nonet had a distinctive sound, with its brass-heavy, bass clef-weighted instrumentation and subdued dynamics. The group's repertoire was quite diverse, but Davis's soloing and his leadership gave the music a style. In "Godchild" his solo is so poised and unhurried that it hardly seems to come from the same world that produced bop and swing.

The Cool idiom began with this short-lived group and Lennie Tristano's sextet of the time. One of Miles Davis's many early 1950s activities was playing in a Los Angeles Cool band; he also led combos in eastern cities and, in New York, played often at Birdland on Monday nights, joined by Sonny Rollins and trombonist J. J. Johnson. There were also periods when he seldom performed in public, but he did record often, usually with hot boppers rather than Cool musicians. The recordings are erratic in quality, and Davis's technique is erratic, too. His musical personality becomes more complex, as he develops his distance from the beat, from high linear detail, from bebop, so that his solos are a series of direct statements, without adornment.

It's a style in which lightheartedness and loneliness mingle, as in his innocently lilting solo in the first "Serpent's Tooth" (1953); there's strength in his loneliness, as in his construction from the sparest of beginnings in "C.T.A." (1953). He adds distance by contrasting his relaxation with the hard driving of his partners. The 1952 "Dear Old Stockholm" is a good demonstration of his instinct to create distance by way of his attack: He plays well behind the beat, his accents never coming closer than the beat's decay. A heroin addict, Davis withdrew for the final time in early 1954, and after that his trumpet technique improved; the great period of his career, lasting around a decade, begins with his 1954 all-star recordings, including the session with Rollins that introduced "Airegin" and "Oleo" to the jazz repertoire. Both of his blues masterpieces, "Walkin'" and "Bags Groove," are long performances organized around central statements. The trumpet improvisations in these blues are marvelously poised between tension and relaxation. He creates in four-bar phrases; he forms these solos in separated choruses but creates a climactic statement in "Bags Groove."

There was a crucial event in Miles Davis's career when he joined a staged jam session at the 1955 Newport Jazz Festival. The others in the group were at least equally renowned, and they had been the trumpeter's sidemen on various recordings (they included Monk, tenorist Zoot Sims, Gerry Mulligan on baritone sax); Davis's solos were the hit of the show, and journalists assumed that he'd led the ensemble. Along with ensuing publicity there followed his recording contract with Columbia, one of the three record industry giants of the period. He made his first Columbia session in October 1955. It was around this time that Davis had a minor throat operation, after which he was under doctor's orders to avoid speaking out loud. He made the mistake of raising his voice once; his vocal cords were permanently damaged, and since then he's been unable to speak above a gravelly whisper.

Over a year's time all but one of Davis's recordings were by the same quintet, with Coltrane playing tenor and a uniquely strong yet brittle rhythm section. Pianist Red Garland left plenty of space for the drummer's interplay with the soloists; Paul Chambers was a harmonically daring young bassist; the exciting drummer Philly Joe Jones presented knife-edged interplay, sudden outbursts, and a crisp, precise sound, and gave the entire group an edge of raw nerves. Especially at fast tempos Jones played ever atop or even minutely ahead of the beat while Chambers played minutely behind the beat, yet this strangely stated beat was in synchronization. Add to this precarious rhythm section the edgy solos of Davis, with his inclination to understatement and laid-back phrasing, and of the searching Coltrane, and the result is a precarious music, ever with a threat of disintegration. All of this quintet's records were popular hits; this music's tensions extended swing into anxiety that audiences identified with.

Miles Davis sounds isolated in this group, often a private individual amid glaringly aggressive activity. Rhythmically his phrasing is based in quarter notes; his warm tone (now dry, now lightly singing), his attack, and his stream of inflection make the others' dynamics seem hard and unvarying; though their instrumental ranges seem wider, their swing seems more potent. His approach can be mistaken for shyness, but in the fastest pieces from the marathon 1956 Prestige sessions he plays driving lines that include daring high notes.

The next year, 1957, was the year of his first album accompanied by Gil Evans's colorist big band arrangements, *Miles Ahead,* which is the real beginning of Davis's adventures with modes. The slow tempos of the *Miles Ahead* suite movements assure that musical tensions are harmonic, and in fact, the rhythmic development is almost nonexistent. Evans has a favorite device of opposing Davis and the orchestra as one plays in simplified chord changes and the other in static harmony. Static harmony is, of course, the modal harmonic structure. By *Porgy and Bess* (1958) Davis's solos are on, at most, a minimum of chord changes: "When Gil wrote the arrangement of 'I Loves You Porgy,' he only wrote a scale for me to play. No chords. And that other passage with just two chords gives you a lot more freedom and space to hear things. . . . All chords, after all, are relative to scales and certain chords make certain scales. . . ."[2] This was George Russell's view also; Davis then added,

> When you go this way, you can go on forever. You don't have to worry about the changes and you can do more with the line. It becomes a challenge to see how melodically inventive you are. When you're based on chords, you know that at the end of 32 bars that the chords have run out and there's nothing to do but repeat what you've just done—with variations.
>
> I think a movement in jazz is beginning away from the conventional string of chords, and a return to emphasis on melodic rather than harmonic variations. There will be fewer

chords but infinite possibilities as to what to do with them....[2]

This is close to the principle of freedom that Ornette Coleman introduced. Davis concludes, "The music has gotten thick. Guys give me tunes and they're full of chords. I can't play them. You know, we play 'My Funny Valentine' like with a scale all the way through."[2] In the Miles Davis-Gil Evans *Sketches of Spain* (1959), too, almost all the music is modal.

As early as the 1954 *Bags Groove* session, Miles Davis had begun exploring modal structures, in "Swing Spring." Davis's thinking with his 1958–59 sextet revolved around his urge to obliterate chord changes, so that not only are the three "Straight No Chasers" progressively faster, but his distance from chord changes progressively increases and he dares to play in his highest and lowest ranges. "Miles" (1958) and two performances from *Kind of Blue* (1959) are important modal structures. "So What" uses the Dorian mode, at a slower tempo than "Miles" and with greater care for inflection, and now the loneliness of his lines bridges the cities of America's hard bop and the vast, clouded plains of Spain. "Flamenco Sketches" is a series of five scales (in the Ionian, Phrygian, and Aeolian modes) upon which each improviser, in the way of a flamenco musician, improvises as long as he wishes.

With the popularity of his sextet and especially of his Columbia records, Miles Davis became an international celebrity. His activities and silk suits were reported on in fashion and gossip columns, and when a New York cop assaulted him between sets at a club, the story made headlines. This was a period when John Lewis refused to play in nightclubs unless they turned off the cash registers during his performances and when Charles Mingus berated inattentive audiences, yet it was Miles Davis who became particularly characterized as temperamental, though he was not unique in his refusal to announce his song titles or his walking offstage when his other players soloed. After Adderley and Coltrane had left his group in 1969, he used a succession of hornmen in his group before finally settling on melodic tenorist Hank Mobley in a quintet that stayed intact for more than two years, until winter 1963. By now he was fairly often producing live recordings, in which his trumpet soloing is consistently rich and alive. He prefers faster tempos in concerts, and he plays in his horn's high and low, as well as middle, ranges. He stuck to a limited repertoire that usually included only two modal tunes, "So What" and "Neo." But specific references to chord changes were no longer needed in his music anyway; the lyricism he was discovering now required only location within a key or scale for his self-confidence.

Wayne Shorter (born in 1933 in Newark, New Jersey) played tenor sax in Newark bands at the turn of the fifties, received his music education degree at New York University, and spent most of the 1950s playing in jazz combos (including a tour with the progressive pianist Horace Silver's hard bop quintet in 1956). He spent two years in an army band, and then, "As soon as I was released from the Army, I would spend a lot of time at Trane's house, and we would analyze one another's harmonic ideas. He would play, I would listen, then vice versa."[3] In 1959 Shorter joined Art Blakey's Jazz Messengers, which also included Lee Morgan, then only twenty-one but already a trumpeter who had expanded upon hard bop's basic Clifford Brown style. Morgan's music gained depth through his ingenious explorations of expression, his brilliant interaction with Blakey's percussion lines, and immense rhythmic sophistication and responsiveness. Along with the complexities in Morgan's playing, the vulgarity and aggression, the arrogance of Shorter's own music came to characterize the group.

His tenor sound in this period is as full and weighty as Coltrane's, and with an added crying edge. Even more Coltrane-like are his tendencies to accent strong beats heavily, to construct symmetrical lines, and to play consonant phrases that end in increasingly distant chromatic intervals. His phrasing is essentially rhythmic, his syntax based in blues and prebop transitional jazz ideas; Shorter solos such as the studio "Arabia" (1961) are all riffing, far from the lyricism of the other leading hard bop tenormen. Most personal are his methods of organization in this period. Like Sonny Rollins of "Blue Seven," he creates thematic improvisations in which his initial phrases determine his entire solos' contents; his solo forms perfect the classic jazz outline of building, climax, anticlimax, and conclusion.

Above all, Shorter's music is dramatic. The insolent crudity of his music's surface makes a vivid contrast with Morgan's elegance, inspiring the trumpeter's constructivism, as in the 1960 "Lester Left Town" and "Dat Dere." Generally the emotionality that the tenorist expresses so forthrightly is also in the trumpeter, but subtly stated, cruel with ironic twists; in the slang of the period, they are killers, Shorter with a bazooka, Morgan with a switchblade knife. Shorter's humor in particular tends to the bawdy: After the exciting polyphony of the "Afrique" theme, he begins his solo with a stupendous low blat. He likes to phrase as simply as Miles Davis, so half notes, whole notes, and tied whole notes add great visceral power to a solo such as "High Modes," as mass accumulates from his form's symmetry. By "Children of the Night" (late 1961) Blakey's Messengers were a different group, but if the radical concepts of Lee Morgan were now gone, modal songs still dominated the band's repertoire, and Shorter was still composing many of them. Characteristically these songs have sections, usually opening strains or half strains, built on static harmony and also sections on chord changes.

"Wayning Moments" introduces a new lyricism to his

music; despite the boldness of his statement, this chorus is as intimate as Miles Davis, especially in its relative distance from the (static) harmonic base. Previously his improvising had not been indebted to any single saxophonist, but by 1964 he was incorporating direct features of John Coltrane's music in every solo, sometimes in wholesale quantities. In 1964 he left Blakey to join Miles Davis and also began regularly leading his Blue Note recording sessions. It's no surprise that the first three Shorter Blue Notes have drummer Elvin Jones: The completely extroverted Shorter has now turned to an inner quest, and when original kinds of phrasing no longer suffice, borrowings from Coltrane come in handy.

So Shorter's revision of style, a revision that has continued for the rest of his career, has often been a painful process. *Adam's Apple* (1966) reveals crisis in his music, as he disappears into Coltrane phrases in "Footprints" and "Chief Crazy Horse." "Adam's Apple" and "502 Blues (Drinking and Driving)" lack the overbearing sense of Coltrane, but they're equally impersonal—they could have been played by Sam Rivers or Joe Henderson or any of a dozen other gifted, sophisticated mid-sixties tenorists. The *Adam's Apple* session included "The Collector," a piece so frightening that it was not issued until more than a decade later. A distant harmonic world leaves the quartet shaken, the vague atmosphere includes a discontinuous bass line in this tempo, and Shorter's solo is disassociated, his fragmented phrases separated by space. The order that emerges from "The Collector" is a most personal statement of questing amid chaos—and this is not his only, or even his most important breakthrough in this period.

The subject of *The All-Seeing Eye* (1965) is the creation of the earth. Alan Shorter, Wayne's trumpeter brother, contributes a fine composition, "Mephistopheles," and the other major events are Wayne Shorter's sensitive and original tenor solos in "Genesis," "Face of the Deep," "Chaos." The swirls of Shorter's rhythmic tides provide a compelling undertow throughout *Etcetera* (1964); the powerful waves of his cyclic forms "Barracudas" and "Indian Song" rise and break around monumental assertions. The easy surface and optimism of "Toy Tune" result from his unusual phrase spacing and equally unusual accent distribution; unsettled harshness pervades "Etcetera," with its broken theme and motion; as in "The Collector," this performance is an organized development of unspecificity. In another 1964 solo, "Gnostic," mystery results from the rubato setting and the accompanists' distant electronic imitations. Shorter responds with lovely, drawn-out tones and long lines; a jarring forte tails into a pianissimo phrase; volume contrasts provide definition of form. From the ongoing narrative realism of his 1959–61 solos with Blakey, it's a turn in the opposite direction for Shorter to find abstraction so provocative. But the freer forms of jazz fused with this classic sense of order in the sixties, and at best, the result is a new, no less personal quality of revelation.

Of course, even to dare the modal abstractions of *Etcetera,* Wayne Shorter needed like-minded and like-skilled musicians to play with. Fortunately, by the mid-sixties he had any number of gifted, usually slightly younger musicians to choose from, players who straddled the frontier line between hard bop and Free jazz. Much of the most important activity occurred within the rhythm section, but the bass posed a real problem because as jazz drumming moved away from the timekeeping function, the bass was left as the major source of pulse. And if you're a bassist who rejects this traditional role, how do you create vital music within the ensemble? Like it or not, the decorative results of Scott LaFaro's urge for Freedom seemed to be the way for much of the modal bass playing of the sixties. Whereas the context of Freedom left David Izenzon and his successors with no problems of integration, among bassists committed to hard bop and modes the most successful avant-garde unions of their instruments with others comes in exceptional circumstances—such as Richard Davis in his 1963 duets with Eric Dolphy or in the 1964 *Out to Lunch* rhythm section.

The next advance in jazz drumming after Elvin Jones, just before Sonny Murray's total abandonment of functional percussion, came from Tony Williams, who at age seventeen left home in Boston to play a 1962 Christmas week gig with Jackie McLean in New York, and stayed. In "Frankenstein" Williams's cross rhythms and cymbal crashes have no evident relation to McLean's solo, yet because of the freedom of the altoist's form, the busy, erratic drumming line is entirely appropriate. In 1963 he began his long tenure with Miles Davis, refining the most abstract qualities of his style, resulting in contrary meters and tempos, linear disruption, and, in general, lines in which opposition follows apposition. For all the nervous tension of the 1950s Davis rhythm section in which Philly Joe Jones played, Williams elevated the instability level of the jazz rhythm section. Davis used him specifically to assault the nerves, though as we've seen, Williams was chosen for Dolphy's *Out to Lunch* to reflect and enhance Dolphy's own structural dislocations and to inspire the Dolphy group's innovatory rhythm section.

Another drummer, Joe Chambers, ventured into complex interactions of the Elvin Jones and Art Blakey kinds, combining their power with the explosive dislocations of Williams. Rolling and splashing violently against Shorter's tenor forms, he exerts a second gravitational pull in *Etcetera;* the opposing tides of tenor and drums lead pianist Herbie Hancock to play skittery responses and one-handed, electrocuted solos that add a sense of fearful tension, entrapment to the ensemble. Chambers is also one of the guiding forces, along with pianist Andrew Hill, in Bobby Hutcherson's *Dialogue* (1965), which ventures very far from hard bop and modal territory. For example, "Les Noires Marchent" and "Dialogue" not only are sololess but move through bright rain forests of sound without clear linear direction; the music is pure color, as the instruments continuously recombine. In fact, "Dialogue" doesn't even have a theme; its structure is marked by interludes of piano and bass (Richard Davis).

Like Tony Williams, vibist Bobby Hutcherson debuted in McLean's *One Step Beyond* (1963), in which the drummer's spontaneous surrealism enhances the mysterious abstraction of the vibraharp sounds; it's the sound and spacing of Hutcherson that casts the spell of foreboding throughout McLean's *Destination Out*, then. In these, in Dolphy's *Out to Lunch*, and in Grachan Moncur III's *Evolution*, vibes replace the customary piano in the rhythm trio. Hutcherson plays a poisonous accompaniment in "Air Raid," drops of pure acid between the spaces of the horn solos, but he would not develop the abstract promise in this and other early works such as "Evolution" in the years to come. Rather, he chose to perform accompanied by pianists and to replace the dramatic mystery of his most radical ideas with romantic, even-tempered lyricism.

The three individualistic pieces that Andrew Hill contributed to Hutcherson's *Dialogue* are as unlike each other as they're unlike anything else this prolific, tirelessly experimental composer was writing at the time. Hill was a piano virtuoso not only of technique but of styles. From moment to moment in his solos you can detect traces of virtually every avant-garde pianist from Art Tatum to Cecil Taylor, often with the quirkiness of Horace Silver or the phrasing of Thelonious Monk. Such extraordinary eclecticism becomes original in the context of Hill's sense of solo organization, which is as drastically abstract as Dolphy's: He creates mosaics of sound in which his light, even (Cool?) touch is the flowing element in otherwise discontinuous music.

He loves indirection, so "Pumpkin" is a series of false resolutions; among the disorienting elements of "Siete Ocho" is its 7/8 meter. In pieces like "Black Fire" his rhythmic virtuosity is especially rewarding, as his accents are distributed with what seems like chance sponaneity and the piano tempos and meters float over his accompanists' fixed (even if highly accented) pulse. The subtle "Reconciliation," with Hutcherson and Elvin Jones, is among Hill's successes in terms of his sidemen's realizing his abstract structures. Hill's art is fragile; it depends on the simultaneous virtuosic creativity of so many different elements of technique, intellect, broken line, broken emotion that the failure of any one can turn the whole into vague romantic atmospheres. It's not surprising that after these mid-sixties albums so many of Hill's subsequent performances have been solo piano or trio works, though his *Spiral* (1974) offers interesting soloists, including altoist Lee Konitz.

The young modal musicians who emerged in the late 1960s were, like Tony Williams, players without a history of performing bop, and they at least dared to experiment with Free jazz features—not just with certain outside sounds such as Coltrane's and Ayler's multiphonics but with passages or even entire works in free forms. There's a 1969 LP by pianist Stanley Cowell, *Brilliant Circles,* which attempts to advance on Hutcherson's *Dialogue* (and Hutcherson plays in Cowell's sextet here). One piece is long and entirely composed; two longer pieces move freely with tempo and meter alterations, collective improvisations, spontaneous crescendos, resulting in some academic events. But other events are as delightful as the groupings of instruments around Tyrone Washington's clarinet in "Bobby's Tune." This is music on the brink of Freedom, yet these musicians must have been more aware of their failures than of their successes here, because I believe only Woody Shaw, the trumpeter, ever again attempted such a daring program. It's pertinent that the most emotionally and structurally liberated track in *Brilliant Circles* is the fast modal swinger "Boo-Ann's Grand."

Tyrone Washington and Joe Henderson played tenor sax in various editions of Horace Silver's quintet; whether or not Silver's later pieces actually use chord changes, they reflect the opening of song forms that the modal idiom inspired. Washington's fine solos with Silver and in his own *Natural Essence* are melodramas full of honking, screaming climaxes and anticlimaxes, intended for absolutely spectacular effect. Yet his antilyricism and his inevitably symmetric, simple forms mark a native austerity as severe as Coltrane's. For the most part Washington has been retired from the national jazz scene in the seventies and eighties. Henderson, Joe Farrell, and Sam Rivers are three more gifted tenormen to arrive at modal idiom popularity in the mid-1960s. Rivers, the most experienced of the three, subsequently moved further away from the territory of chord changes and into Free jazz. Farrell went from modes to Chick Corea's Return to Forever, stars of seventies pop jazz; only Henderson continues to play in the post-hard bop modal idiom. In California, tenorist Charles Lloyd and ex-Mingus altoist John Handy III became quite the most popular of modal musicians. Like the others in this list, they are eclectics; Lloyd, whose records were the biggest hits of all, was probably the most dependent on Coltrane. Three other prominent modal altoists are Gary Bartz, Robin Kenyatta, and Sonny Fortune.

Perhaps Woody Shaw was speaking for his whole generation of modal players when he said, "I don't like to stay outside too long and I don't like to stay inside too long. I like the music I play to go in many different directions and take on many different colors."[4] Shaw, too, is an eclectic whose trumpet sources are Booker Little, Lee Morgan, and Freddie Hubbard; his many flourishes and decorative details suggest close attention to Eric Dolphy as well. Woody Shaw's solos tend toward elaborate abstraction that demands his total ongoing coordination of many different elements. The most personal element is his angular lyricism, which provides distinctive relief in the exacerbated sweeps and slashes of "Natural Essence." His 1970 version of "Boo-Ann's Grand" is a bright-sounding, carefully evolved thematic improvisation; in "Blackstone Legacy" his flourishes and fanfares materialize into a long, linear structure. Shaw is a complex player whose music over the years is alternately warm and introverted. His adventures include later recordings with Free musicians such as Muhal Richard Abrams and Anthony Braxton. Perhaps it's his willingness for adventure and his taste for a varied repertoire that have sustained Shaw's creativity over the years. Few other modal musicians have remained so consistently rewarding, right up to the present.

After Miles Davis, the second leading modal musician was Jackie McLean, who, like Davis, began his career in bebop. A year older than Wayne Shorter, McLean grew up in New York and was introduced to the new forms of jazz in his teens: "I remember when I was a kid, my uncle gave me an alto. I didn't like it, it had a syrupy sound. He played me some records of alto players and I didn't like any of them. Then he played some Lester Young, and I said I wanted to play like that. 'You're not supposed to,' he said. 'That's a tenor, and you play alto.' Then I heard a Charlie Parker record, and I said, 'that's an alto.' "[5] One of A. B. Spellman's *Four Lives in the Bebop Business* is Jackie McLean's; you can read how the young saxophonist was tutored in improvisation by Bud Powell, Parker, and Monk. Maybe Miles Davis recognized something of himself in the nineteen-year-old Jackie, who recorded with him in 1951: There are some awkward moments in the "Bluing" and "Dig" alto solos, along with personal features such as broken, free association phrasing that would remain important throughout McLean's life. The remarkable aspect of McLean's work in the fifties is his early maturity. He is already absolutely certain of what he wants to communicate; his model is Charlie Parker, specifically the blues qualities of Parker's music, the broken, blunt cry at the source of Parker's lyricism. In "Confirmation" (1956) he's now playing with Parker-like freedom of accent and he's arrived at his characteristic alto sound, marvelously bent, dramatically inconsistent, generally sharp in his highest tones, flat in his middle and lower ranges.

New Soil in 1958 breaks through to a fully realized art. The principal new quality is McLean's authority here, for his lines are big and bold. His phrases are chosen for their dramatic worth, and although his structural breadth usually extends to no more than four-bar units, a solo such as "Greasy" nonetheless turns out to be a vivid narrative. His alternation of strong and offbeat phrasing magnifies his intensity, and by now stark power is his sustaining force, however varied his structures; the surface of Parker sophistication does not shield the raw emotion in McLean's essential simple phrasing. It is McLean's sound that communicates most urgently: His broken lines are played with an unvarying resonance, almost a tenor sax weight, with consistent volume and control in all registers yet, too, with his beautiful bent-tone cry of the heart.

All of McLean's highly sophisticated techniques are refined to enhance his primary quality of expression. All emotions are experienced so deeply and articulated so exactly that his music is a magnifying glass through which you find your own strong feelings heightened. McLean began playing modal material in *Let Freedom Ring* (March 1962), and he wrote: "The new breed on the jazz scene are searching for new ways of expressing themselves. Many have cast aside the old and much overused chord progressions. We find scales and modes more outstanding in solos. The extended form (first introduced to me by Charles Mingus) is but another way of composing and blowing. . . . The new breed has inspired me all over again. The search is on. Let freedom ring."[6] In the minor-key "Melody for Melonae" he improvises six minutes of violence that rises several times from gasping notes to long, uncontrolled overtone squeals, a violence encompassing both cruelty and ecstasy. Here and in "Rene" and "Omega" the very extremeness of passion glorifies McLean's playing. "I'll Keep Loving You," a Bud Powell ballad, is a fluent solo, and the music's beauty is in rich, dark blue tones that seem wrenched from his horn; the climactic squeals in the rubato section strip away flesh and reveal raw passion; the work ends in pure, Lee Konitz-like alto sounds.

In 1963 McLean began working with young musicians, including Bobby Hutcherson, Tony Williams, and trombonist-composer Grachan Moncur III. This was the period of mysterious, threatening alto solos like "Frankenstein" and "Air Raid" and also up-tempo solos like "Kahlil the Prophet" and "Saturday and Sunday," with the immediate power of his playing stimulated by rising key changes. Somehow his moods of narrow organizational breadth go hand in hand with modes' freedom from ongoing webs of chord changes; the vividness of McLean's emotions and the drama of his phrase relationships sustain his art whatever the settings. "Moonscape" (1966) appears in sparkling notes that arise among long tones over atmospheric cymbal rolls. The overtone squeals of *Let Freedom Ring* return in "Old Gospel," from the 1967 session with Ornette Coleman on trumpet. In "The Inevitable End" long tones split and then fall, with, at last, Coleman and McLean bending pitches together as the music fades into the unknown. In the seventies McLean led a talented young modal sextet, The Cosmic Brotherhood, which included his own son, Rene, a saxophonist whose alto and tenor styles were modeled on his father's work. *Antiquity* (1974) is one of Jackie McLean's most varied albums, a collection of high-spirited duets with percussionist Michael Carvin. McLean sings, chants, plays flute, piano, and percussion and also creates alto solos, such as the sculptured one in "De I Comahlee Ah."

In all the years that McLean has been playing on modes, he's also continued to play in earlier bop styles, sometimes on records (few of his post-*Let Freedom Ring* unmodal discs were issued before the mid-seventies) but perhaps more often than not in public. He has taught in colleges for more than a decade by now; that means his live appearances have been infrequent. It's interesting that his jazz history students research the music of, among others, early composers such as James Reese Europe and Ford Dabney, whose late ragtime works are the threshold of jazz. (McLean's Cosmic Brotherhood was comprised of his students and associates from Hartt College in Hartford, Connecticut.)

When Miles Davis formed a new quintet in 1963, his rhythm section was Herbie Hancock, a young, popular pianist in hard bop bands; bassist Ron Carter; and drummer Tony Williams. The tenor sax chair was held by George Coleman and then Sam Rivers. There's no diminution of Davis's own improvising intensity. Although he continued to sound most liberated in concert LPs, there's a fresh sense of freedom in studio recordings such as "Joshua" or the modal piece "Seven Steps to Heaven." In the Antibes Festival "Autumn Leaves" (1963) Davis opens with a rip, and his first chorus is seven phrases, none of which refers to the standard theme. The spaces between his phrases become a medium of tension as fluid as in Ornette Coleman; his lines refer to nostalgic sorrow and to childlike, dancing moods, and he sometimes shifts course in mid-phrase.

Young drummer Williams now becomes the central figure in Miles Davis's music. In the 1950s Davis had created while balanced on the tightwire of Philly Joe Jones's drumming, but however precarious the music seemed, the tension was sustained. Williams made the mid-1960s Davis group unstable, not only by his own impetuosity and independence of line but by drawing Carter and Hancock into activity—crescendos, pedals, alternate meters, doubled or halved time—that opposed the soloists and left them suspended or contradicted. After Wayne Shorter had become Davis's regular tenorman in September 1964, the unit became committed to modes and instability as a way of life. This quintet's first LP, *E.S.P.*, created a sensation when it was released. For one thing, all the material was new themes by members of the group (for years, Davis had been playing standards or returning to his fifties repertoire). In "Agitation" the nervous, nattering muted trumpet solo is in fast lines, closely muted; the "accompaniment" opposes with vamps and half time upon impulse, creating a rash, ever-uncertain environment. Agitation indeed—and the rest of *E.S.P.* is almost this high-strung.

In 1965 Miles Davis was largely inactive: first hip surgery; then a broken leg. In December the re-formed quintet played an engagement at Chicago's Plugged Nickel, and the recordings are a revelation. Half the tracks begin with the same very fast tempo, but this tempo simply establishes a reference for all kinds of tempo variations without notice or motivation. Again and again solos are disrupted, usually by Williams's impetuosity and shattering crescendos; the drumming is brilliant, even if no train of thought is sustained for very long. This time Davis plays "Agitation" without his mute, over rushing, slowing, or stopping tempos; the rest of the material is his familiar 1950s repertoire, but now the tunes are distorted almost beyond recognition. Davis's opening trumpet solo in "Round Midnight" avoids not only the classic theme but also the original chord changes and strain lengths. In the initially very fast pieces Davis's solos are diffuse, often regrouping to alter emotion and linear direction. After two abrupt choruses, the waltz "All Blues" turns into four meter, and amid highly sensitive improvising he turns inexplicably whimsical; his "Walkin' " solo becomes frustrated and dissipates into spits of sound.

Constantly changing direction is this quintet's medium of communication. Davis begins "Yesterdays" as a themeless ballad, and the piece soon shifts into double time, abandoning the chord changes; after five minutes of melodic musing, he switches to his fast theme song; Wayne Shorter then plays a freewheeling solo that Davis joins, to make a collective improvisation. And since "Round Midnight" is a successor to "Ramblin' " and "Lonely Woman"—at least, it has no ancestors in Davis's own recorded history—the Free vistas of Ornette Coleman and Don Cherry become possibilities for this quintet. For Miles Davis, concentrated, sustained emotion is now out of the question. His quintet's reorganization of techniques serve not to integrate but to accentuate the increasingly disparate emotional qualities of his music.

In *Miles Smiles* (1966), "Circle" is a ballad in which Davis creates a sweet melodic line with a marvelous range of tones and inflections—playing a tightly muted trumpet! The album includes other trumpet solos of nearly the quality and character of his Plugged Nickel works, yet there's no denying that the level of energy and adventure has slipped, and the group's dislocation is resisting direction as well as resolution. In fact, the modal idiom begins to disintegrate with *Miles Smiles,* and the major reason is the rhythm section that had in 1963 and 1964 seemed to be such an advance. Pianist Herbie Hancock's harmonic ambiguity and extreme spareness of accompaniment may point in the direction of Freedom, but ambiguity is not the same as the simple vagueness of his wilted solo melodies and sequences. Bassist Ron Carter plays facile lines of cross rhythms and contrary motion; he not only abandons the bass's traditional pulse-marking role, he also tends to sound jaded, with continual world-weary glisses. Tony Williams's drumming in "Limbo" is brilliant, and what's special about this brilliance is its irrelevance. By "Vonetta" (1967) he is accompanying Davis's ballad solo with military drum rolls; it's a sign of the times that this is not amazing.

The rhythm trio sustains unity in expertly refined pieces of business: metric ambiguity ("Freedom Jazz Dance"), understated chaos ("Limbo"), fades to rubato and sudden tempo resumptions ("Madness"), and so on. But the unit is primarily interested in creation of atmosphere, and the atmospheres are so indistinct as to propose the absolute interchangeability of emotion—or else dispassion. Amid this precious decadence Wayne Shorter's contribution does not approach the quality of his own best albums of the period; moreover, somehow his tenor sax is recorded so that it lacks the force of his live performances. Clearly Miles Davis doesn't choose to pursue the freedom he glimpsed in the Plugged Nickel recordings. But since he cannot relive his earlier styles either, his late sixties music exists in an ongoing state of uncertainty. His solos become fragmented, or he plays exhausted memories (hear "Masqualero" after *Sketches of Spain*); he chooses repetitious material that avoids emotional commitment ("Nefertiti," with no improvisation); adding guitarists to the band helps diminish what remains of emotion. In "Circle in the Round," the guitar drone and the up and down Davis phrases are lulling; the next logical step is silence, the silence of sleep.

In a Silent Way (February 1969) has Davis and Shorter (now playing soprano sax) with a rhythm section of organ, two electric pianos, guitar, bass, and drums. The solos are dissipated; the understated rock ostinato of the title piece turns at times into an enervated Chicago blues line. "Shh/ Peaceful" is even more precious, with electric pianos tinkling in and out. The impersonality of the guitarist is the finishing touch on a performance with all the enduring, debilitated stimulation of a three-day drunk on white port wine: sickly sweet and effective.

Initially there had been a spirit of adventure about modes, as most bop and hard bop musicians began to play modal tunes or at least pieces with "advanced" chord changes. By the late 1970s, though, prettiness and impressionism generally characterized modal playing: Herbie Hancock's hit tune "Maiden Voyage" is, in a way, the tune that typifies the end of the modal decade, with its languid, drifting changes and near absence of melody. Modes had been mainly a final, decadent development of bop, a terrain for conservative explorers. One musician from the bop era discovered an alternative to modal methods as a means of growth, of breaking through the barriers of conventional bop structures. But that musician was Sonny Rollins, and a musician would have to be Rollins himself—grand, masterful, authoritative, brilliantly creative—for this new way of playing jazz to work.

In 1959 Rollins retired from public performance altogether and spent much time reorganizing his ideas about music and practicing his tenor sax on the Williamsburg Bridge between Manhattan and Brooklyn. He returned to public activity in 1961 and, for possibly the first time in his career, began leading a regular, well-rehearsed working group (as opposed to the pickup combos that he'd formerly led). The next year his group included Ornette Coleman's former cohorts Billy Higgins and Don Cherry. In place of his former close dramatic organization, Rollins was now inclined to very long, free-form fancies, swaggering and impetuous. "Oleo" begins very fast, and as Rollins solos, Cherry engages in passing duet with or commentary on his lines; Rollins's sense of chord changes is eventually obliterated until he turns the performance into a blues. There are solos by Higgins, bassist Bob Cranshaw, and a lyric, rhythmically free and open solo by Cherry; the rhythm section accompanies in four, drops out, breaks rhythm, halves and doubles time, as the outside groups of the day were beginning to do. If Rollins's playing with this group seems dry, staccato to an extreme, the lyricism of Cherry's soloing provides fine relief; he certainly attains the freedom of motion, rhythmically and harmonically, that Rollins finds fleeting.

What developed from Rollins's ideas with this quartet was not Coleman-like Freedom but the free-association medley form that he continues to offer right to the present. On record, the finest example is his 1965 *There Will Never Be Another You* concert, a wonderful exhibition of the great-hearted Rollins in an expansive mood, creating long, elaborate solos out of some tunes, tossing off others like sly jokes, playing unaccompanied cadenzas, and altogether being charming, witty, generous. While his later recordings are variable, in much of *Don't Stop the Carnival* (1978) he approaches this success; in this, there's also satire and cruelty in his viewpoint. In the seventies he began adding simple rock and modal tunes to his repertoire; though his music has become somewhat less dramatic and more decorative by now, power and spontaneity continue in his freewheeling improvising forms.

Charles Mingus   photo by Herb Nolan

Ornette Coleman   photo © Lauren Deutsch

Eric Dolphy   photo by Ton van Wageningen

John Coltrane (left), Rashied Ali (right)   photo by Bill Smith

Miles Davis   by permission of Fantasy Records

Sun Ra   photo by Herb Nolan

Albert Ayler   photo by Bill Smith

Cecil Taylor

photo © Lauren Deutsch

Roscoe Mitchell (left), Muhal Richard Abrams (right)

photo by Herb Nolan

McCoy Tyner (left), Sonny Rollins (right)   photo by Herb Nolan

Anthony Braxton

photo © Lauren Deutsch

·6·

The Free Jazz
Underground and Sun Ra

Jazz nightclub and recording activity was abundant throughout the hard bop period, reaching a peak about 1960. The subsequent decline in jazz commerce was abrupt, in the face of the explosion of rock music popularity, and in America the decline continued steadily for the rest of the decade. However much bop and hard bop musicians competed with each other for employment, they were united in hostility toward the jazz artists who began to manifest avant-garde attitudes.

And one by one, more avant-garde musicians, players who were liberated by the revolutionary concepts of Coleman and the advances of the other pioneers, were beginning to appear. For this second wave of outside musicians, the prospects could hardly have been less promising. Courage and commitment enough are required of anyone who chooses a life of art. With the certainty of poverty and of minimal opportunity to play for audiences, these players faced multiplied demands on their most basic internal resources. With the nightclub and recording studio doors closed to them, where could the new musicians play?

This was the time when America was becoming, if not just or integrated, at least less tightly closed to equal opportunity.

For the alternative society that grew up in the late fifties and the early and mid-sixties, the molding social forces were the antiwar movement, which became directed mainly against the orgy of slaughter and lies in Vietnam, and especially—because it was closest to home—the awakening of African-Americans' awareness that the cycles of poverty, discrimination, and segregation need not be irrevocable. The progress of the nonviolent movement was slow, painful at every step; after the violence of police and politicians, long-dormant philosophies of revolutionary violence were revived and became widespread.

All this had two meanings for the second Free wave. First, the new black self-awareness became a strong undercurrent in the jazz revolution. The demand for justice entered the musical programs of leading musicians, led by ambitious projects such as Max Roach's *We Insist: Freedom Now Suite* and his *Percussion Bitter Sweet,* with its dedications to Marcus Garvey and to the "Tender Warriors" of the freedom rides and civil rights battles, the real catalysts of the period's social changes. There's no mistaking the shared awareness that not only music but society as well was being transformed. Archie Shepp wrote: "This is where the avant garde begins. *It is not a movement, but a state of mind.* It is a thorough denial of technological precision and a reaffirmation of *das Volk.*"[1]

Second, a new young audience that was uninterested in assembly-line rock and roll or in the nightclub milieu was emerging. As bop had taken jazz out of the ballrooms and into nightclubs—listening rooms—the new jazz settled into coffeehouses, small theaters, art galleries, settlement houses, churches, bookstores, neighborhood bars, and wherever else Free jazz fans and musicians could initiate some activity. Following Ornette Coleman's lead (his 1962 Town Hall concert was self-produced), musicians began producing their own shows, renting performing spaces, hanging posters on light poles, placing small ads in the underground newspapers that were beginning to appear, and absorbing financial losses. Some people who had apartments or studios large enough presented outside jazz events in their homes, more or less reviving the rent parties of 1920s and '30s lore. At first the second wave musicians could not support their families on the New York new music scene, but what's important is that there *was* an active underground jazz scene. Artists and audience shared in an intimate creative community, though the crowds that thronged some events, like the 1964 October Revolution in Jazz, were anything but intimate.

Composer-arranger-tenor saxophonist-actor-playwright Archie Shepp (born 1937 in Fort Lauderdale, Florida) began playing sax as a teenager in Philadelphia. When he was fifteen, he got his first paying gig, playing clarinet—"at least I owned a clarinet and I'd learned how to hold a note, a B-flat concert or high C, which was my 'ride,' as they said at the time."[2] Shepp studied drama at Goddard College in Vermont, was graduated in 1959, and went to New York to seek work as an actor. He got no acting jobs; instead, he went on welfare, played with a Latin sextet, and also played with Cecil Taylor's 1960 quartet. For Shepp, some musical direction is already evident in "Air": His sound is large, rich with a hoarse, split-tongued edge; his harmonic territory is ambiguous, and he has a taste for the dramatic phrase. Otherwise his questing tenor solos in Taylor's three 1960–61 LPs sound fragmentary or seem decorative ("Lazy Afternoon") against the constant piano activity and the high purposefulness of Taylor's improvising structures.

So the 1962 *Archie Shepp-Bill Dixon Quartet* LP is a revelation in that Shepp's playing is powerful, excitable, at times charming. There's nothing of Ornette Coleman's quest for serenity in this version of "Peace." On the contrary, Shepp is loquacious, his double-time solo is a tumult of inner dialogue; his corrosive harmonies blister the Broadway sentimentality of "Somewhere," and his sound and ideas satirize pop emotion. This is high-spirited playing, matched with good humor in his LP of standards the next year. The nine-minute Shepp solo "The House I Live In" begins with elegant syncopations in the trilling theme statement, then careens through fast lines, sheets of sound, and, at last, multiphonics lines that in their unspecificity of pitch predict Albert Ayler.

"The House I Live In" was one of the forgotten pop songs that Sonny Rollins brought to jazz, back in 1956. In Shepp's "Cisum" solo he quotes "Sonny Boy" as if to emphasize his kinship with Rollins; the Shepp style of the period seemed built from the Rollins drama and phrase contrast of "Ee-Ah" and "Sonny Boy." "Cisum" is from a 1963 album by the New York Contemporary Five, in which Shepp reveals advances on his previous year's playing. After the trumpet (Don Cherry) and alto (John Tchicai) solo in broken phrases in "Consequences," Shepp's solo offers contrast by way of longer lines with melodic weight and characteristic propulsive rhythmic energy. Especially in contrast with the others in this group, Shepp's soloing features a compelling linear naturalness derived from heavily accented rhythms. The tenor sax tradition that begins with Ben Webster and that features climactic contrasts of coarse tone, register, and volume makes a major advance in these Shepp solos.

The three horn players of the New York Contemporary Five had very different styles, so the arrangements had to serve as a unifying element; there are the bop riffing behind solos in two Ornette Coleman blues and the respectful interpretation of "Crepescule with Nellie," the most beautiful of Thelonious Monk melodies. Shepp's elaborate composing for the group is revealing. In "The Funeral" Shepp's setting recalls Miles Davis's "Solea," but the sorrowing trumpet and alto solos (over distantly pulsing drums) draw out brief, angry drum responses and momentary collective mourning. The simple conclusion—tenor tones alternating with the other horns' trills—speaks of tragedy as unending as the composition is unfinished. "The Funeral" is dedicated to Medgar Evers, the Mississippi NAACP worker murdered in a racist attack, and the dedication is the beginning of a program in Shepp's music. Like Rollins, Roach, and Mingus, he was becoming interested in musical subject matter that related directly to black experiences and the rising African-American self-awareness. "I don't believe in the word 'art,' " Shepp said. "It's, to me, not functional, it's passive. It's bourgeois in the sense that art develops at a point when people have leisure time. That's like the Platonic ideal, something that can be observed as art, something outside experience."[2]

In 1964 he shyly approached John Coltrane and asked if he would recommend Shepp to his own record producer, Bob Theile. Coltrane did, and Theile asked Shepp to record *Four for Trane,* an LP of Coltrane's songs. On Coltrane's recommendation, the Shepp piece "Rufus (swung his face at last to the wind then his neck snapped)" was included in the album. The next Shepp album was comprised of his own compositions. "Hambone" is made of folk themes and riffs transformed into art song, in the way of Paul Robeson or Béla Bartók; the cheer and simplicity of the folk themes rub against the coarse, sometimes mocking soloists, and the 5/4 and 7/4 rhythms create anxious complexity. "Los Olvidados" (the forgotten ones) does not recall the famous Luis Buñuel film of that name, though the subject matter is almost the same: Shepp's piece reflects on the hopelessness of the youths he met when he worked as a counselor to juvenile delinquents. Shepp liked to divide his four horns into brass and sax sections, with sax scoring as rich as Benny Carter's; tempos rise and fall, with choppy slow melodies and yearning in the fast melodies. Ted Curson's sensitive trumpet and the gnarled, aching alto saxophone of Marion Brown join Shepp in making the meaning of "Los Olvidados" clear.

While his powers as composer increased, his tenor playing

developed, too. A few solos such as "Consequences" are exceptions to the rule that he conceives in short, broken phrases with great rhythmic propulsion, though less lyrical ingenuity. The 1965 trio of Shepp, David Izenzon (bass), and J. C. Moses (drums) offers closely attuned realizations, among which "Malcolm, Malcolm, Semper Malcolm" is especially dramatic, with both Shepp's poem and his tenor solo. "Le Matin des Noirs" is from the 1965 Newport Jazz Festival. Over Bobby Hutcherson's minor vibes vamp, Shepp drifts in softly, the notes barely escaping his horn; he then slams hard on the beat with brief phrases that begin delicately and rise to forte accusation; fragmentary phrases become self-dialogue; the drama of Rollins is turned to melodrama by Shepp's high contrast, especially of attack and volume level.

Yet Shepp's is a precarious style; his balance of elements is fragile. In more extroverted surroundings, such as collective improvisations with trombonist Roswell Rudd, the balance is vanquished by the melodramatic features and by the Coltrane-ish turbulence that often becomes the main line. "Portrait of Robert Thompson," though only nineteen minutes long, is typical of his nightclub medleys (Shepp credits Rollins with the medley idea). Here are brooding original themes, lengthy collective improvisations broken by Ellington's "Prelude to a Kiss," ending with a Sousa march. The music is driven to frenzy by the polyrhythms of drummer Beaver Harris; it's also largely static, the collective babble (including Shepp's raging, embroiled tenor) negating individual voices and most qualities of expressive and linear differentiation. The unending shock statements and release of anger accumulate in futility and exhaustion.

One of Shepp's plays, *Junebug Graduates Tonight,* is definitely verbose, as well as wistful, comic, bitter, affectionate by turns; its characters have names such as America, Cowboy, Muslim, Uncle Sam, and the hero Junebug. The abstract melody "Wherever Junebugs Go" captures the play's tenuous underlying mood, the composition airs Junebug's confusion, and properly, the piece never resolves or concludes. After 1965 there aren't many Shepp compositions that approach this piece. Moreover, even his 1970s collaborations with Cal Massey turn out to be diffuse, a disappointment after Massey's valuable collaborations with Coltrane and Lee Morgan a decade earlier.

Over the years Shepp has created many diffuse recordings, but strong emotion rises to the challenge of unique repertoire in the Shepp-Horace Parlan *Goin' Home* (1977). This duet album is a program of classic spirituals; Shepp treats the noble melodies with respect, so that even his embroidery of "Steal Away to Jesus" and his split tones and fortes in "Amazing Grace" and "Go Down Moses" advance the atmosphere of reverence. He seems to be guided by the sensitivity of Parlan's piano accompaniment; the stylized simplicity of Paul Robeson's interpretations is just below the surface of *Goin' Home.* Throughout the 1970s and '80s Archie Shepp's main activity has been not performing but teaching, first at the University of Buffalo and then, with Max Roach, at the University of Massachusetts, where Shepp has been a tenured music professor since 1978. He says, "I don't think of keeping a group together the way I used to. I think in a sense we're guerrillas: we hide in trees, with camouflage, and we must be there until we and our music are respected. So I'm not anxious to play in clubs. . . . Performance, at least in the traditional sense of the word, of being on the bandstand, is not the primary thing. . . . I'm very involved with classical music. And to me classical music means *Black* classical music."[2]

Ornette Coleman's groups and John Coltrane were the most obvious influences on the disparate New York scene of the sixties. There were good, active rhythm section players, including bassists Gary Peacock, Lewis Worrell, Ronnie Boykins, and the wonderful Henry Grimes, and drummers

J. C. Moses, Barry Altschul, the adroit and adaptable Beaver Harris, and the innovators Sunny Murray and Milford Graves. Rhythm sections tended to be pianoless because Free horn players wanted to avoid the piano's traditional harmonic weight in accompaniments. The Freest pianists, then, like Paul Bley and early Don Pullen, either played solo or led groups.

Few of the pre-Free experimentalists accepted the challenges of the new jazz. Jimmy Giuffre was one who did, offering uniquely spaced and suspended woodwind studies with a bolder expressivity than previously. Trumpeter Ted Curson had been part of the fire of Mingus's 1960 groups. Curson's sophisticated sense of form sets his bright lyricism somewhat apart from the more discursive others in Shepp's *Fire Music* sextet; he is as forceful as anyone in solos like "Los Olvidados" and "Hambone," and more poised. Paul Bley's piano music, when he abandoned chord changes in the sixties, retained the characteristics of bop phrasing modified by Monk's sense of phrase spacing. The result is a romantic, unstructured, fragmentary, personal music that is sometimes flowing and ingenious, as in his 1972 self-duets on piano, electric piano, and synthesizer in "King Korn." No Free pianist could sound more different than Bley from the grand, expansive, high-energy music of Cecil Taylor, the dominant influence then and now.

The high-energy surface of tenormen such as Coltrane, Shepp, and Pharoah Sanders was transmitted to the alto sax by Marion Brown in *Fire Music* and Coltrane's *Ascension*. Over the years, then, Brown has shown equal mastery within successive Free styles, and in some seventies recordings, such as his *Duets*, his most personal qualities arise. They include a pastoral, sweet, bitter, faintly nostalgic sense, the effect of his line and his phrase spacing, a lingering aroma of the stories and poetry of Jean Toomer, with which Brown identifies.

Such improvising lacks the urban tensions of Brown's Free

contemporaries; altoist John Tchicai contains those tensions, but obliquely. For instance, he plays the phrases of John Coltrane without any suggestion of Coltrane's content; instead, Tchicai's limpid sound and slower but insistent pace are an instinctively Cool approach to Freedom. It is this insistence on his own dry, lyrical flow of movement that makes him sound so distinctive amid the aggressive contexts of various Shepp, Ayler, and Coltrane (*Ascension*) groups. Perhaps it's because he is a Dane, an African-European rather than an African-American, that his music seems to come from a parallel world.

The bop era trombonists played with clean-toned poise and precision; Free trombonist Roswell Rudd plays with the dirty smears, rips, and slides of the swing and Dixieland masters. In solos like "Skippy" he shows a Monk-like ingenuity for cubist reconstruction of distorted, displaced theme fragments. In general, though, his playing is loosely organized; his slashing, extroverted manner is dramatic, often sardonic. Rudd, Tchicai, Lewis Worrell, and Milford Graves were the New York Art Quartet, which, next to Albert Ayler's groups, was the most adventurous of the city's underground combos. In the terrain of the quartet's solo and collective improvisations, rhythms moved at will and in fact were seldom stated directly. There's a magical passage in "Number 6" in which the players improvise together, yet each is in a different, unhurried, unrelated tempo; here is a quartet embodying the complete freedom of Graves, who joined Sunny Murray in liberating the drums from the timekeeping function.

It's the responses and organization of Graves that lend continuity to the dry romances of the Art Quartet. The recordings have many brief, ingenious, intense solo drum passages. For example, after the final theme of "Rosmosis" Graves plays a bridge passage that softens to the faintest *ppp* before he taps a dance on a snare drum on which the springs are loosened; after this LeRoi Jones reads a poem. Great technique on a drum kit larger than Murray's leads Graves to a denser, more melodic style; despite his independence, he can embed punctuations and paraphrases of soloists' lines into his own motions (with Ayler in "Universal Indians"; behind Rudd at the beginning of "Rosmosis"). He's constantly in motion throughout Ayler's *Love Cry*, he seems to become by turns every drummer in a large equatorial African drum ensemble, and his polyrhythms move with a wonderful looseness; it was about Graves that LeRoi Jones told us, "The tap you hear is your own pulse, fellow being."

Bill Dixon's dark, earnest trumpet lyricism encompasses a wide range of rhythms and textures, something like the variety of Don Cherry's more spontaneous playing. Dixon's solos are carefully organized, sometimes with dramatic results ("Trio," with satire lurking in his melodies). In "The 12th December" (1963) the flow of trumpet line and dynamics is free of the compulsions of bop, and the nervous strain in split tones and indefinite pitches is Dixon's own. Dixon composed dark scores in which brooding impressionism is anchored by bass clef instruments. "Metamorphosis 1962–66" is in five movements in which the heavy weight of dissonant strings-woodwind textures is lightened by the busyness and density of two percussionists and by Dixon's fat and fast trumpet phrases, lyrical and nagging. Dixon's concerns are expressed in colorist terms—sonic, harmonic, rhythmic colors—and in fact, he is a painter as well as a musician.

It was Bill Dixon who organized the October 1964 concerts at the Cellar Café in New York, billed as the October Revolution in Jazz, to introduce the Free second wave to a wider audience that he was convinced would support the music. About forty groups played, to overflow crowds; emboldened by this success, Dixon invited a handful of other musicians—Shepp, Rudd, Tchicai, Cecil Taylor, Mike Mantler, Burton Greene, Sun Ra, and Carla and Paul Bley—to cooperate in producing musical events. The result was the Jazz Composers Guild, which began by offering four nights of concerts with eight ensembles at Judson Hall and continued with weekly concerts in a loft above the Village Vanguard nightclub.

None of the guild members was performing regularly; one of the guild's objectives was to become a bargaining entity, but member musicians began accepting opportunities to perform without seeking the guild's approval; other breaks in the united front appeared, and by mid-1955 the organization had quietly disintegrated. The guild's big band continued off and on as the Jazz Composers Orchestra, led by Mantler and Carla Bley, and in June 1966 Mantler was instrumental in forming a nonprofit organization, like a symphony orchestra's association, to subsidize the band. Some concerts occurred; the Jazz Composers Orchestra Association issued its first record album, a two-disc box of Mantler's 1968 settings for soloists (including Taylor, Rudd, Don Cherry, and Pharaoh Sanders). Recurringly active over subsequent years, the orchestra (with changing personnel) held workshop-concerts and issued six more albums; the JCOA's most visible activity, however, an activity that has lasted for more than a decade by now, is its New Music (record) Distribution Service, which wholesales the product of small, independent jazz (and some rock and classical music) labels.

This is a valuable service because with the decline in jazz recording in the sixties, the second wave of Free musicians was beginning to record itself. In the mid-fifties Charles Mingus and Max Roach ran their Debut Records, and Sun Ra began his Saturn Records; these ventures offered precedents. Milford Graves and pianist Don Pullen formed SRP to sell, by mail, albums of their stimulating 1966 Yale University concert, and thereafter a trickle of musicians' self-produced recordings became what is by now a flood: In 1983 a musician could produce and release his or her own album as a do-it-yourself project for less than $3000. One valuable musician-owned label is Paul Bley's I.A.I., which began activity in the 1970s.

Sun Ra and his Arkestras perform in their Halloween spacesuits decorated with Christmas glitter, invite us to travel through space with them ("Next stop Jupiter! Next stop Jupiter!") or at least through time, to the birth of civilization in ancient Egypt and Ethiopia. "I have a gift to offer this planet," he says, "and music is one of the bridges to the treasure house of it."

> I've chosen intergalactic music, or it has chosen me. Intergalactic music concerns the music of the galaxies. It concerns intergalactic thought, intergalactic travel, so it is really outside the realm of the future on the turning points of the impossible, but it is still existent, as astronomy testifies. [3]
> ... I'm actually painting pictures of infinity with my music, and that's why a lot of people can't understand it. But if they'd listen to this and other types of music, they'd find that mine has something else in it, something from another world.[4] Space music is an introductory prelude to the sound of greater infinity. ... It is a different order of sounds synchronized to the different order of being. ... It is of, for and to the Attributes of Natural Being of the Universe.[5]

Be warned: Sun Ra is a prophet, and you mock or scoff at him at your peril.

He was born Herman Blount in Birmingham, Alabama, around the early to middle teens of the century. He began playing music in high school and was pianist in Alabama bands before he moved to Chicago at the end of the 1930s. He spent a long career arranging music for the floor shows at the Club DeLisa, one of Chicago's most popular night spots, where Fletcher Henderson led the band and encouraged Sun Ra's talents. Ra also began leading his own bands in the late forties, with players in exotic costumes playing unusual African instruments. Even then he had the idea of sustaining a band comprised of his acolytes. "Sun Ra always had his little lectures: he just wants you to live clean and think brotherly," remembers Von Freeman, who played tenor in one of his early ensembles. ". . . Now this is the honest-to-goodness truth: he'd used to call me up and say, 'Von! Are you awake?', used to be 4:00 in the morning. I'd say, 'Yeah, Sunny,' he'd say, 'I've got an idea, I'd like you to hear it,' and he'd start playing this music, man. If he could have got some of that music into one of those monster films, that'd be enough."[6] Ra himself has said, "Sometimes I have an idea at three in the morning, and I wake everybody up. They don't want to get up, but they do; and they stay there, for hours if they have to. Or I might just write eight measures and then say, 'You can go now.' I tell my Arkestra that all humanity is in some kind of restricted limitation, but they're in the Ra jail, and it's the best in the world. The Creator has everybody in jail, for a life sentence."[7]

By the time Ra and his Arkestra were recording, in the 1950s, the band was playing a series of short- and long-term gigs; they were for years weekly fixtures at spots like the Pershing Hotel and the Wander Inn. The prophet Ra's objectives have always been ambitious—"The real aim of this music is to coordinate the minds of people into an intelligent reach for a better world, and an intelligent approach to the living future"[8]—and the motivation for his message is clear: "I would hate to pass through a planet and not leave it a better place. It's ridiculous to spend all that time and energy and then leave it the way it was.[9] What I'm doing . . . is about the destiny of humanity, and what I could possibly do to help."[3] So Ra's subject matter could hardly be of greater importance. For example, "People always seem to reject the good things in the world. It's very hard to develop a man who speaks of love and non-violence, like Martin Luther King. Very hard. And then the world destroys him. . . . Something will have to take his place. And a time will come when the forces that give things will say, "They don't want anything groovy, so they shall have something bad.' "[5]

Sun Ra's composing in the Arkestra's earliest albums sounds very hard boppish—kin to the kinds of music the Art Blakey and Horace Silver groups were playing in the mid-fifties, but for a larger and more exotic ensemble. Yet Ra's pieces, even swinging riff numbers such as "Brainville" and "Fall off the Log," must have sounded odd, what with their modal structures and distant, percussive harmonies in accompaniment. A drummer and a tympanist play interjections in the theme of "A Street Named Hell"; the big, broad baritone sax sound of Pat Patrick supports the horn section's weight, and the ending is not a rousing theme reprise but a slow waltz. Ra loved the sound of the baritone sax so much that for several years he kept a second baritonist, Charles Davis, in the Arkestra. Many compositions are stream of consciousness: "Enlightenment" is a long string of unrelated, sentimental pop tunes, beginning with a world-weary "Black Orpheus"-like theme on baritones (several years before the film *Black Orpheus* appeared); the fine, twisted Parker-like introduction to "Saturn" has nothing to do with the riff theme.

The chunky rhythms of "Call for All Demons"—bass, electric bass, drums, tympani, and Ra's sharply struck piano chords—hump and bump most fetchingly behind the theme, not a blues despite its twelve-bar form. In "Ancient Aiethopia" the stately percussion throb as Ra and then the baritones parade in like noblemen in review; flutes chirp over scratching and throbbing percussion that becomes insistent and yields a tympani passage; the warm, rich, low trumpet tones of Hobart Dotson are heard in a modal solo which gives way to Ra's piano thunder; between percussion passages, singers improvise low melodies in unknown languages. All these strange textures and wondrous colors conclude, unfortunately, with a conventional Latin riff; otherwise "Ancient

Aiethopia" is an illuminated composition that gathers the often separate strands of Ra's sounds, rhythms, and exotica.

The expanded percussion section serves less rewarding purposes, too. Beginning with "Sun Song," Ra composed the occasional lush, exotic piece very much like the pseudo-South Pacific islands mood music of the day, colored as it was by the pianisms of the likes of Liberace. Thus "Sun Song" and "Paradise" burble with bourgeois secrets, and over the years Sun Ra's most impenetrable music, as composer and improviser, has been influenced by the most flabby kinds of popular musics. He is the only jazz musician who ever recorded a version of "Holiday for Strings."

At the end of the 1950s Sun Ra and the Arkestra appeared in a curious film, *The Cry of Jazz*, which argues that this African-American art music, having by then achieved its heights of expression, was doomed to extinction because of its basis in the debased harmonic structures that the white man had imported from Europe. Sun Ra's music was certainly not doomed, though. Even at the time he was in the midst of a long process of reorganizing his concepts, and the Arkestra's music was now mostly percussion-oriented. Specifically bop developments are largely absent from *The Nubians of Plutonia* (1959); instead, the music is heavily rhythmic. "Africa" is in Ra's series-of-events structure, and after the musicians have hummed in harmony over rain forest tympani rhythms, the piece becomes a tympani solo by Jim Herndon, concluding in a few separated tones from the other instruments. It is an almost free-form culmination of Ra's percussion developments and a forerunner of his outside thinking.

In 1961, the Arkestra left Chicago for a two-week engagement in Montreal. On the second night of the gig, according to bassist Ronnie Boykins, "The owner kept coming to the bandstand and asking, 'When are you going to get into your specialty?' So Sun Ra stretched out, and he said, 'No, when are you going to get into it?' At the end of the night the man fired the band; he said, 'You all are playing God's music.' We found out then that we had been booked up there as a rock and roll band."[10] The Arkestra then stayed in a building near McGill University, played a month in a Quebec mountain resort, then went to New York, where they were stranded without funds or a vehicle with which to return to Chicago.

The Arkestra members lived as a cooperative in New York, much as several of them had lived in Chicago. As individuals they worked in the studios on pop recordings; they also took jobs with other leaders and pooled their money to record Arkestra albums. For the most part Sun Ra and the Arkestra continued creatively mainly as a rehearsal band, which they had already been for much of their Chicago period. At this juncture Sun Ra had experienced year after year of indifference, mockery, and rejection in three of the largest cities in America, and while he could view his stituation with detachment—"I want to be the only thing I could be without anybody stopping me in America—that is to be a failure. So I feel pretty good about it, I'm a total failure"[11]—the poverty and endless struggle left deep bitterness:

> I never wanted to be a part of planet Earth, and I did everything not to be a part of it. I never wanted their money or their fame, and anything I do for this planet is because the Creator of the universe is making me do it.... Everything they did I'm going to put on the books, on the books of heaven itself, because there is no excuse for people being the way they are, and I am not going to forgive anybody.... When people try to destroy the kindness and love in a person, they deserve the cruellest dimensions that the Creator can cast upon them. I am not going to pray for them, because enough good men have prayed for them and died for them.... If I can get out of enlightening this planet, I'll do so with the greatest of pleasure, and let them stay in their darkness, cruelty, hatred, ignorance, and the other things they got in their houses of deceit.[12]

Sun Ra's musicians were linked by devotion that was more than strictly musical. Given the most unusual and demanding kinds of music to interpret and improvise upon, they rose to the challenge: The woodwind players each doubled several instruments; all the musicians played various kinds of percussion. Among the catchy percussion works in the early sixties, albums such as *Cosmic Tones for Mental Therapy* began to appear, with its two pieces, "And Otherness" and "Hither and Yon," that present no reference to any traditional harmonic and rhythmic structures. Flutes, bass clarinet, and Marshall Allen's oboe in the foreground create a serenity that sounds, paradoxically, willed; the electric organ tones of Ra's clavoline weave through their lines. There are apparently no composed elements in "Hither and Yon," only the asymmetric oboe melodies and the other players' responses, singly and together. It's amazing that such an ensemble creation even exists, considering that only a couple of years earlier these same musicians were completely involved with the idiomatic extensions of Charlie Parker—and when so many of their 1960s peers approached the new structures of jazz with a caution bordering on fear.

The Arkestra's music, in the mid- and later sixties, when it performed relatively frequently, was wholly improvised, the players in solo and various combinations cued by Ra at will. Mysterious low tones from unspecified sources thrum against the rattle of ghostly percussion; often there's no theme or line of discourse, simply a succession of phantom images. Sun Ra liked to offer pieces like "Of Heavenly Things," in which a single instrument or a pair of players (usually himself and/or the remarkable Boykins) create central lines and textures, with improvised commentary, interludes, and developments by other players cued by Ra. Within this world of Free motion and constantly changing sounds and textures, many elements sound unfinished, so that it's the rambling, discursive long performances that fulfill the Arkestra's destiny. Ronnie

Boykins's tragic bowed bass line is the center of "The Sun Myth"; there are comments in slaps and cries, the clavoline pursues, a mass of horns appears in a fast section, trumpet and alto sax solo; the collective subsides, and we are left with Boykins's sorrow, at last supported by the clavoline.

"The Magic City" is a parable of disillusionment. Sun Ra's pilgrimage begins in faint, yearning chords; the chirping of many flutes surrounds the reedy line of his clavoline; after a dialogue of bass clarinet and bass, Ra and Boykins join in a slowly meandering journey, now twining and fading sadly in space, now led by a piccolo's piping to agitated fragments of sound. Suddenly, more than halfway through the performance, come the honk and wail of many horns: The pilgrims have arrived at the Magic City. Danny Davis's alto, unaccompanied, sounds indeed magical, but there's also pain that gathers in his long multiphonics cries. In a driving fast tempo, Pat Patrick on baritone and two other altoists solo in brilliantly colored lines that lead to the wildness and exhilaration of a collective improvisation, with agitation and harshness among the components of the ecstasy. The exalted ensemble breaks; the brief, sorrowing cadences of the clavoline recall the yearning of the work's piano opening, but now Sun Ra is vanquished in a loud, dissonant wailing of horns; now there is no turning back from the Magic City. The performance certainly wanders, the main line of discourse is always abstract and usually a mixture of emotions, and the Arkestra's range of feelings and sound is expressed in a design that's simply unprecedented in jazz: "The Magic City" attempts to be, and almost is, monumental.

The soloists in the earlier Arkestras were mainstream period players, none more so than tenorist John Gilmore, with his blunt sound and hard bop rhythms; especially the deep expressive blues of Marshall Allen's alto in "Ankhnation" and "Blues at Midnight" and the post-Parker baritonists would have found places in many hard bop ensembles. What's amazing is the transformation of these improvisers when they abandoned the Parker heritage to create Free jazz which depends on their vital inner resources, with probably a few of Coltrane's and Ayler's techniques. Patrick's rhythmic variety blossoms in his solos in "The Magic City" and "Cosmic Chaos." Allen's outside playing, so sparkling and aggressive, became the source of the styles of the Arkestra's alto sax section—Danny Thompson, Harry Spencer, Danny Davis. And of course, there's Boykins, whose role in the Arkestras was the most demanding, apart from Ra's own role.

As for Sun Ra's own improvising on his keyboard instruments, there is his trivial, lush cocktail-organ improvising in "Moon Dance" and "Sun Song." His piano playing is boppish in one piece, heavily percussive in another piece, cleverly suggesting Ellington or even Herbie Nichols in "El Is a Sound of Joy." "Nebulae" begins as an outer-space cocktail-celeste solo and moves through fast lines into opposition of hands and of celeste and piano, a sort of impressionist Cecil Taylor. Electric instruments dominated Ra's thought in the sixties; his clavoline and roksichord sound like stops on an especially fancy electric organ. He plays the synthesizer as if the instrument were invented specifically for him. It sounds like a cold wind blowing around hollowed wood, less a sound than an undertone, in "My Brother the Wind"; the long "The Code of Interdependence" is a synthesizer display piece, with ever-changing textures. The synthesizer extravaganzas that were such a prominent feature of his seventies performances had their prototype in "Atlantis," which he played on a "Solar Sound Organ" and a "Solar Sound Instrument." "Atlantis" begins with a tone hypnotically repeated in space, turning almost imperceptibly into chords; this spell is broken by the ugliest of low clavoline tones. The ensuing, rambling solo is a formidable, intricately decorated wall of electronic sound, leading only eventually to dark horn textures, moaning saxes, and the Arkestra choir singing about outer space.

And Sun Ra has turned back to the unamplified piano often since the mid-sixties. Among his several solo piano albums is *Monorails and Satellites, Volume 1,* with its explorations of chiaroscuro, but some other solo piano sets include cocktail music, without tension. On piano, with the Arkestra, he has offered vivid, hard-struck lines and clusters in "Continuation to Jupiter Festival." Possibly the improviser temperamentally most like Sun Ra is the vibist Walt Dickerson, whom Ra accompanies in improvisations on the film score of *A Patch of Blue.* The Dickerson-Ra *Visions* is even more revealing; here the two play unaccompanied fantasies, now in hard, percussive lines, now in soft, many-noted dissonances. "Space Dance" is a real duet, the two players are of a single mind in their delicate dreams; "Constructive Neutrons" is a long, nostalgic piece, most wistful and touching in Ra's solo.

In such a solo, or in the disillusioning parable of "The Magic City," Sun Ra's music seems to wish for a state of innocence, not a naïve kind of innocence so much as an absence of guilt—the guilt that follows cruelty, violence, inhumanity, the guilt that Sun Ra does not wish to participate in himself. "I felt that I should always be doing what I was supposed to do on this planet, regardless of whether the planet responded or not, so that the world could never say that I didn't try to do my spiritual duty. So if there is any reason they have not heard this music, it is most certainly not because I am not available to be heard."[3] In the last decade Sun Ra and his Arkestra have in fact been heard with far more frequency. Not only have they added to the dozens of Saturn recordings, but they have also recorded for other labels, and some of their major earlier works have been reissued. The Arkestra adds dancers, flashing disco lights, and sometimes films of the Arkestra to make their performances into multimedia events; at best, these are three-ring circuses, while musicians stroll through the audience singing "Space is the place! Space is the place!" An ever-changing array of soloists improvises before Sun Ra, in his flowing robes, ceases his dancing and grand gestures to the audiences, sits at his bank of keyboard instruments, and improvises long, wandering, clashing, profuse solos. The Arkestra has added works by Ellington, Thelonious Monk, Fletcher Henderson to its repertoire; for some years now it has been based in Philadelphia, from which it travels throughout the world.

The second wave of Free players was not limited in location to New York. Altoist-flutist Prince Lasha (Lawsha) went to high school in Fort Worth, Texas, with Ornette Coleman and in the sixties began recording Free jazz in California. One of his regular partners was Coleman-inspired altoist Sonny Simmons, who played frequently with trumpeter Barbara Donald. Another Coleman mate from high school was tenorman Dewey Redman, based in the San Francisco Bay Area, while Coleman's ex-sideman Bobby Bradford (who grew up in Dallas, thirty miles from Coleman's boyhood home) met another high school friend of Coleman's, woodwind player John Carter, in 1965, when both were living in Los Angeles (it was Coleman who introduced them). Actually the California Free jazz scene was small and scattered; though the Carter-Bradford group rehearsed often, they seldom performed publicly, and it was not until 1969 that they recorded, as the New Art Jazz Ensemble.

Carter's alto and tenor playing and his songs were subdued versions of Coleman; some of his solos were wholly legato. By the late seventies he had abandoned his other instruments to play the clarinet exclusively, and as he has turned to more extended forms, he features the softer, less expressive sounds of clarinet, flute, and trumpet in his scores. That first Carter-Bradford album includes the trumpeter's solo in "Song for the Unsung," which unites blues phrasing, a wonderful variety of phrase shape, and lyric flow with such elegant poise as to announce a major voice in the new music. Subsequent Bradford performances have strengthened this first impression, and two features are most important to his art. First is his gift for organic form: Despite his expansiveness, his lines flow with grace and naturalness, and his solos are often thematically organized. Second is his rhythmic virtuosity, because he is one of the most rhythmically vital of all improvisers. He sounds somewhat detached from his ensembles' pulses, yet his personal tempo alters to enter theirs, speed, or delay, as he chooses, sometimes from moment to moment.

His playing in the exciting collective improvisation "His Majesty Louis [Armstrong]" (1971) is a vivid example of this rhythmic suppleness. In "Love's Dream" (1973) he sounds on the verge of bursting with lyric ideas. He sustains tension throughout this solo by way of short (but not brittle) phrases that are extended into lines that dart this way and that: His accenting is so free that he seems ecstatically liberated; the performance dazzles; there is glory in Bobby Bradford's music.

·7·

Albert Ayler

Everything about Albert Ayler's music was astonishing. With him, the new music broke its last lingering ties with not just bop but the entire jazz tradition. Every one of the noisy horrors the first Free wave was accused of, he gladly embraced. He screamed through his tenor saxophone in multiphonics and almost uncontrolled overtones, absolutely never in a straight saxophone sound or in any identifiable pitch. His ensembles really did improvise with utter abandon, and they related their music to each other's in the most primal, irregular ways—when they related at all. Among the great jazz musicians, Ayler's emotional range may be the most limited: In his most creative years, frenzied ecstasy in the fastest tempo that's humanly possible alternated with the most maudlin ballads imaginable, and these two forms of hysteria were the sole content of his soloing. He never swung, not even in the standard settings of his earliest recordings; instead, his fastest solos acquired momentum through the kinetic energy of his tornado speed lines. Indeed, he bypassed the entire history of jazz to go back to attitudes and ideas about music that predated the art's inception; he then built up his own art out of primitive discoveries.

"It's late now for the world. And if I can help raise people to new plateaus of peace and understanding, I'll feel my life has been worth living as a spiritual artist."[1] Albert Ayler said this in 1966, and shortly thereafter he began playing the crudest possible kind of pop music, complete with doggerel lyrics. It was not only his mysterious death at the age of thirty-four that prevented the fulfillment of his mission. His career in the new music lasted around nine years, and after his five years of innovation, his music disintegrated thoroughly and quickly. Charismatic, with an ego as vast as Armstrong's or Parker's, he could not conceive of his new idiom without his total destruction of the jazz heritage. Nonetheless, it was left to others to build with Ayler's new resources amid the rubble he left; poignantly, their finished structures began to appear while he was losing faith in his art.

Albert Ayler (born in 1936) spent his first twenty-one years in Cleveland. At an early age he began a rigorous course of musical study with his father, a semiprofessional violinist and alto saxophonist; as a second grader Ayler gave alto sax recitals in school. On Sundays father and son played saxophone duets in church; they attended jazz concerts together and at home listened to records by swing and then-new bebop musicians. For seven years, beginning at age ten, Ayler took lessons from an experienced, well-traveled jazzman at Cleveland's Academy of Music; by his mid-teens Ayler was playing in young jazz and rhythm and blues bands. Captain of his high school golf team—when Cleveland courses were still largely segregated—he was also on easy terms with the shadow world of local hustlers and pimps, and for the rest of his life he maintained a city slicker's extravagant, colorful wardrobe. In his teens he spent two summers on the grueling, ill-paid blues circuit with the band of Little Walter, whose career predicted Ayler's in some surprising ways—the nattily tailored Walter was a pioneer of sound (on harmonica), an innovator among the first electric bluesmen; he was murdered when he was only thirty-seven—and for the middle-class lad, "being out there amongst those really deep-rooted people" was an essential learning experience.[2] Ayler's mastery of bebop style and the standard repertoire earned him the nickname Little Bird on the small Cleveland jazz scene. He entered the army in 1958, switched to tenor saxophone, and traveled throughout Europe with a special services band.

It was during that army period that ideas of Free jazz overwhelmed Ayler and changed him for all time. He found time to practice, jam, and develop his new music; discharged in 1961, he went to play in California and, like Coleman, was rejected; he then confounded his old Cleveland friends with his big tone, sonic extremes, and refusal to play on chord changes. "The music was not quite formulated in my head. I played it, but it came slowly...."[3] He then drifted in Europe, with almost no opportunity to play his original music, even though a few established players as diverse as Sonny Rollins, Don Byas, and Errol Garner encouraged him. Occasionally he did get to open up musically, like the times he played with Don Cherry (trumpet) and Henry Grimes (bass) while the latter two toured with Rollins; sometimes Ayler appeared as the fourth, unpaid member of Cecil Taylor's group.

In October 1962 he made a private recording that is amazing and perverse. His huge tenor sound is full of resonance, split tones, overtones, r&b techniques come to madness; his pitch is so imprecise that the themes he plays ("I'll Remember April," Miles Davis's "Tune Up," Rollins's "No Moe") are recognizable only from their rhythmic configurations—definitely not from any melodic features. His discontinuous phrasing is short, blunt, and bop-shaped, but his next recording, only three months later, in January 1963, is in a far more advanced style: *My Name is Albert Ayler,* taped for a Danish radio show.

In this fascinating program, he offers his only recorded soprano saxophone solo, "Bye Bye Blackbird," and a twelve-bar Parker blues, "Billie's Bounce." The meandering "C.T." is a themeless Free piece without fixed rhythmic or harmonic structure. He is wrenched by opposite pulls in "Green Dolphin Street," as his solo seems to be two simultaneous solos. One solo is inside, in observance of the bland harmonic structure (he pays dogged attention to turnbacks, chorus outline, alarming turns of phrases from free motions to inside tonality), and the other solo is outside by way of his sound (alternately gigantic, braying, slurring, or else whiny and querulous) and his occasional phrasing (fast, arhythmic, spiraling upward like fireworks from which smaller explosions shoot off). There's no doubt that in these performances Ayler's music is in great crisis; "Summertime," the album's remaining track, accepts the crisis, balancing the standard setting against his ideas of sound and his drifting sense of tonality to result in a long, tragic masterpiece.

In "Summertime" the rhythms of life become the rise and fall of dynamic structure. It is a series of four-bar statements that begin with big, emphatic tones; his volume then subsides slowly through the rest of the phrase until the line tails off into distant, wandering tonalities, barely audible. His vibrato is wide and almost uncontrolled in the big tones that begin phrases; he bends and blurs the subsequent tones, to lead to the wounded phrase endings. In these ways, each direct statement—such as the melodic beginning of a phrase—is modified by an afterthought, which then has its own afterthought attached. As "Summertime" progresses, the most varied playing occurs in the subsiding ends of the four-bar cycles— the progressively more harmonically distant areas. Ayler's timing is always precise here, and bent and ambiguous sounds are perfectly played even as long tones extend into slurs or when vibrato is so extreme that pitch is indeterminate. The performance is too extravagant to permit a conventional climax, though the arches of sound that lead to the concluding cadenza are indeed conclusive; in place of resolution, there is only a final subsidence of sobbing.

The stylistic crisis in *My Name Is Albert Ayler* may be primarily a result of his having to accommodate his bop rhythm section. Originally he'd intended to use Cecil Taylor's group as his accompanists on the radio program; but Taylor became unavailable, and instead, Ayler used three Danish players. Whatever the reason, the conflicts in his art produced a masterpiece of layered emotional complexity in "Summertime" that he would never equal again.

It all came together with a vengeance after Ayler had returned to America in 1963, when the second wave of Free players had begun to emerge. Back home in Cleveland he met bassist Earle Henderson and a trumpeter, Norman Howard, whose studio was rehearsal space for the city's handful of avant-gardists. Ayler settled in New York, played occasionally with Cecil Taylor and others, and the characteristically astonishing Albert Ayler idiom first wreaked havoc on record in *Witches and Devils* (February 1964, a year and a month after *My Name Is Albert Ayler*). His sidemen are Howard, Henderson, drummer Sunny Murray, whom he'd met in Cecil Taylor's group, and, alternating with Henderson, the brilliant bassist Henry Grimes. Bawling horns, with held notes and vast vibrato, exemplify bathos in the "Witches and Devils" theme, the track with both bassists; this and "Saints" are slowly moving, rubato pieces. As eccentric as the emotion is the surface denial of ensemble relationships in these pieces: Each player is committed to his separate world, perhaps responding to the others at moments but certainly not supporting anyone else's lines. Howard's playing is Ayler-based: He adapts blurred, approximate lines and a slow, wide vibrato to the trumpet, and his textures are far from the lyric sounds of Don Cherry, Bill Dixon, or Bobby Bradford. Drummer Murray is most independent: Rarely do his snare taps and cymbal drone rise to coincide with Ayler's calls and answers; the basic lines are discontinuous.

There are two pieces taken at freakishly fast tempos, "Spirits" and "Holy Holy."* At this speed and without harmonic centers, Ayler abandons the last sense of playing notes on his saxophone. Instead, he blares a slurred line that breaks often into the extreme heights and depths of his range, in spasms of multiphonics and overtones. His phrase differentiation is more distinct here than on the records to come, so the logic of his soloing is clearer to the listener: There is a flow and contrast to phrase shape, even thematic improvisation, in his music that are not merely freakish sounds played at overwhelming speed. Albert Ayler really does think and move that fast.

Witches and Devils was the first album of the best-documented year of Ayler's career. In March he applied his strange, quavery tenor saxophone sound to a program of spirituals, which he plays, it seems, as straightforwardly as possible. The rest of his 1964 records—the trio sets in the summer, the collective jam session, and the two European tour discs— use drummer Murray and bassist Gary Peacock and continue with the two kinds of material set forth in *Witches and Devils:* bathetic dirges and maniacally fast songs. Ayler's themes are invariably diatonic, usually in triadic harmonies: "We play folk from all over the world.... Like very, very old tunes, you know, from before I was even born, just come into my mind."[4] Nineteenth-century European nursery songs seem to be the source of "Ghosts" and most of the other fast pieces.

These fast pieces all are played at the same tempo, the fastest possible tempo, and they constitute about seventy-five percent of his performances. They begin with medium-speed statements of the archaic themes, after which, like a child's rickety wagon going downhill, the improvisations emerge.

---

* Ayler was inclined to be careless about his songs' titles. So some of his songs were given alternative titles when he subsequently recorded them; some of his song titles are used for more than one song.

Very quickly Ayler is erupting with earthshaking sounds and energy, with Murray's line implicitly sustaining Ayler's tempo and Peacock's sound discontinuous, in pitch (unlike the tenorist), and perhaps in tempo, perhaps not. For the first time in jazz, chaos becomes the premise of an ensemble. After all, rhythm sections can't provide support for either the rubato dirges or Ayler's insanely fast tempos; what a bassist and drummer *can* do is create a general atmosphere and play responses to Ayler's lead. As the three play independently, ensemble sound in itself becomes the trio's primary interest. Intermediate between the gigantic rawness of the tenor sax and the butterfly lightness of Murray's drums is the bass line, freewheeling in rhythm, atonal, and irregularly related to the others' lines. Sometimes Peacock quarters, halves, or abandons tempo, for he is the most independent player of the three, but his line is coherent and lends density to the ensemble.

Sunny Murray requires special attention because in many ways his innovations are as important as Ayler's. Remember that hard bop drummers joined their lead instruments in the forefront of creating musical lines and that Edward Blackwell's deep interaction with Coleman was an advance on hard bop polyphony; Elvin Jones and Tony Williams then strained the drummer's role within the jazz ensemble to the limits. Sunny Murray (born in 1937 in Idabel, Oklahoma) had played in New York since 1956 with Dixieland and bop musicians, and in Cecil Taylor's tracks on *Into the Hot* (1961) maintaining tempo and meter are only secondary functions to him, carried only by his sock cymbal. With Taylor in Copenhagen the next year, Murray abandoned timekeeping altogether, in keeping with the pianist's headlong, unmetric lines. Now the whole of Murray's style was cymbal-snare interplay with the melody instruments; with this dissolution of function, Murray liberated jazz percussion. (Of course, Milford Graves and Rashied Ali would also free jazz drumming from timekeeping then.) Murray's work with Albert Ayler, beginning with *Witches and Devils,* advances in detail and complexity over his playing with Taylor.

How does this completely liberated drummer play? He interacts with soloists on the complex levels of Elvin Jones, without Jones's distracted timekeeping. Or he plays responses, to horns' lines, so dense and intimate that he moves far away from the horns' directions. Or he plays pure sound, thus creating an essential element of ensemble atmosphere without motivating the performance rhythmically. From passage to passage, his playing is any of these. Whether it is rhythmic, arhythmic, or polyrhythmic, his mastery is thorough and complex even when seemingly simple. The entire mass of his playing is committed to impulsive abstraction, to moving away from surface engagement despite his many junctions with the main lines of the performances. Thus he deliberately pursues a policy of mystification, in keeping with Ayler's mysticism.

As opposed to the typically loud drummers of the period, Murray developed his sense of dynamic contrast particularly in terms of volume gradations, often playing with brushes or even knitting needles ("I played with Cecil for six years, never played loud 'cause Cecil didn't really play loud at first . . .").[5] Moreover, Murray has always used a standard drum kit or even pared down his traps to a minimum of drums and cymbals; no exotic percussion or wide selection of cymbals and auxiliary percussion for him. He doesn't beat the drums; instead, his playing moves in impulses and waves that, even as sound density or polyrhythms accumulate, do not overwhelm. He has the most delicate touch of all drummers, and possibly for this reason he is only infrequently well recorded next to the vast Ayler tenor sound. Typically in Ayler works, Murray's line begins in arhythmic calm and grows in waves; then tides of sonic or polyrhythmic density appear, reflecting changes in the horn lines; his swells of abstraction are inclined to crest in fast, even snare rapping, which, however, does not mark tempo.

Sunny Murray and Albert Ayler did not merely break through bar lines; they abolished them altogether. This lack of meter is essential to the Ayler idiom. Implicit in this is the players' freedom of tempo, as they play simultaneously but without uniting in a single speed and as they multiply or divide tempos. Because Ayler's music lacks the natural tension of meter, his saxophone cries are ecstatic, and it's his tenor sax sound that most delighted or shocked his audiences. Never before or since has there been such naked aggression in jazz; never had anyone created an entire world out of raw fantastic saxophone wailing. Young musicians first becoming acquainted with their instruments make freak sounds through lack of instrumental control, and they're taught to discipline such sounds out of their playing. Ayler, though, chose to play in nothing but those "noises," from huge, deep honks through middle-register multiphonics to long, high overtone squeals. He used the hardest of plastic reeds in his saxophone; he continuously overblew, and he manipulated pitch with his embouchure, so that his extraordinary manipulation of facial muscles replaced the standard fingers-on-saxophone-keys techniques.

Ayler was inspired by the way Sidney Bechet dominated Dixieland ensembles with his big, vibrato-rich soprano sax and clarinet: "It helped me a lot to learn that a man could get that kind of tone. It was hypnotizing—the strength of it, the strength of the vibrato . . . he represented the true spirit, the full force of life. . . ." And, "You have to purify and crystallize your sound in order to hypnotize."[1] With his minimum of melodic and rhythmic referrents, sound itself now had become the whole of Ayler's communication. Donald Ayler, Albert's trumpeter brother, said, ". . . try to move your imagination toward the sound. It's a matter of following the sound . . . the pitches, the colors, you have to watch them move."[1]

Albert Ayler's tenor solos abandon subtlety and emotional shading altogether in his frenzied quest for ecstasy, a quest implicit at the very origins of music, before humankind discovered any but the simplest ways to organize sound. As 1964 progressed, he gravitated more and more to the high and low extremes of his horn. Many solos are wholly in overtone squeals broken, for contrast, by low honks; the briefest of breathing spaces are the only rests in his jagged lightning lines. This is the kind of playing that the mid-sixties energy music aesthetic was based upon; value derives from the passion of playing with such sound and speed. Indeed, it is exhilarating music, especially when several players join in the wild babble, and Ayler's own energy music holds intrinsic interest beyond its powerful immediacy. With his approximate, imprecise pitches he varies and caricatures his themes in the midst of his improvisations. And his improvising is in squalls differentiated not by melodic qualities but by duration, range, and sound character. Often in the trio recordings his solos observe a kind of structural golden mean: After irregular lines in middle and high registers, around sixty percent through a solo he blasts spaced low honks; these honks set off rising squeals, which subside again into irregular phrasing; about ninety percent through, the spaced honks reappear, followed by a climactic summary of his solo argument, including a final perversion of the theme.

Among the trio performances are some of his major works, including the ESP 3030 "Ghosts, Second Variation" (actually this is "Spirits") and the ESP 3030 "Wizard." The ESP 1002 "Ghosts: Second Variation" has Ayler's dark shattering of the theme and central passages in a welter of "unknown" pitches, booms, cruel rising phrases. The passion and the extreme internal disorder of this catharsis are among the most intense moments in the career of this most intense of artists. Even more than the maudlin slow pieces, the fast works show the terrifying melancholy that, despite Ayler's ego and gregariousness, is ever an undertone in his music. An agonized yearning is inherent in the rising long lines that, in song after song, are smashed by the growls, multiphonics honks, helpless eruptions. Here are the conflicts of a Hamlet, more fantastic because Ayler lived amid the incomprehensible chaos of an age more betrayed than the ancient prince's, asserting his lonely nobility despite the certainty of its denial.

"Al was really a sad person despite his charisma and everything," said his colleague altoist Charles Tyler. "That 'old-time religion' was what caused his sadness; it was in his music."[2] In fact, Ayler's playing has its sermonlike qualities, the way certain preachers' vocal straining and emerging song may enter into indefinite or atonal musical line. The slow Ayler pieces offer obvious links to evangelism, beginning with the church-inspired vibrato of his horn (his vocalized techniques are common procedure for gospel sax soloists). A dirge entitled "Spirits" (not the earlier "Spirits") is an imposing gothic structure, and the thematic conclusion offers, for Ayler, a surprising sense of uplift. "Prophecy" is a pyramid structure with volume contrasts on the grand scale of "Summertime." There are dynamic and rhythmic contrasts within phrases; they progress to contrasts of phrase against phrase; fast phrases enter and by degrees begin to dominate, projecting a fast tempo. After the bass solo Ayler's second solo gradually reduces the fast phrasing until he's back at the original tempo. Only on the surface does this suggest the interaction of evangelist and congregation: The tragedy that Ayler evolves in the extremes of "Prophecy" does not admit salvation or any other alternative.

In mid-1964—three and a half years after Coleman's *Free Jazz* and almost a year before Coltrane's *Ascension*—the Ayler trio was joined by Don Cherry (trumpet), John Tchicai (alto), and Roswell Rudd (trombone) in a Free jam session that was later used in a film sound track, *New York Eye and Ear Control*. Though less famous than these Coleman and Coltrane group improvisations, *Eye and Ear* was an advance on them because of its free motion—of tempo (often slow, usually fast); of ensemble density (players enter and depart at will); of linear movement. Ayler tends to be the catalyst because of his big sound and superior structural sense; Tchicai's stubbornly detached playing resists Ayler's dominance. The spontaneity shared here predicts the informal Free jazz gatherings of the years to come.

Cherry sat in with Ayler several times that year, and at the end of summer he joined Ayler's group to make a quartet for a European tour. On the Copenhagen LP Cherry appropri ates aspects of Ayler's style—never before or since has he played so many notes so fast—but he is no extension of Ayler. Rather, in the way he commented upon Sonny Rollins, he became a leavening agent in Ayler's music, too. His blasts of punctuation, his joining in ensemble improvisations, his broken phrase responses lend the music the intimacy of sympathetic, recognizable emotion, as opposed to Ayler's extravagance. The melodic beauty of his long, graceful tones in the Hilversum concert "Angels" convey emotion as profoundly as Ayler's overstatements of timbre and range. The slow "Mothers" demonstrates Ayler and Cherry creating a unity out of their divergence. The Victorian sentiment of the tenorist's quavery vibrato is heartfelt, a dusty lithograph of faithful Old Shep dying on a lace curtain. Much of Cherry's ensuing solo is a haunting, clear-toned statement emphasizing the theme's yearning lyricism without Ayler's grotesquerie; after Ayler has returned, there is a bridge in which Cherry's low tones rise to an interlude of bright, quick trumpet against the stately, obese sax. Self-pity is a most unlikely source for, of all things, a major jazz performance; even so, "Mothers" is one of Ayler's finest works.

Back in America, Cherry recorded with Ayler one more time, in Sunny Murray's album *Sunny's Time Now*. Trumpet and tenor improvise in opposition to the grim Murray tides and the two rumbling basses in "Virtue," and an intense LeRoi Jones poem ("We want poems that kill!"), is answered by the flutter of drums and the tempoless, free-form quintet. Ayler does not dominate this recording, for a change, and he opens up in the "Justice" collective improvisations, responding to Cherry's longer lines with snapping and snarling.

Even while the Ayler quartet was touring Europe in 1964, Albert was planning musical changes. At his behest, his younger brother Donald, an alto saxophonist, switched to trumpet and began practicing Albert's music with altoist Charles Tyler in Cleveland. These two plus Murray and one or two bassists were Albert Ayler's 1965 sidemen. And now theme material became important to Ayler, not as music to be developed in solos so much as an added aspect, often constituting half his performances, sometimes the whole, as in the Paris "Holy Family." The themes Ayler composes are more simple and archaic than ever. The first theme of his "Spirits Rejoice" is "La Marseilleise" with a "Maryland My Maryland" bridge; the other themes are a bugle call and, to separate the solos, a repeated phrase from Ayler's "Truth Is Marching In." And the first of the three "Truth Is Marching In" themes is a Stephen Foster takeoff; "Omega" is a Christmas carol travesty; "Dancing Flowers" is as precious as "To a Wild Rose," from which it lifts a lick; "Our Prayer" is a nineteenth-century American Thanksgiving hymn which the Aylers play like a Beethoven finale. And so on.

All these, and the rest of the Ayler brothers' original themes, are played absolutely straightforwardly; not only is there never a hint of satire, but the fervor of the band's playing is always compelling. "Echoes of New Orleans marching bands," "like a Salvation Army band on LSD," "the music of central European firemen's bands," wrote three accurate critics, and the rest also loved to find precedents for the Ayler brothers. Ayler said he liked to "have different simple melodies going in and out of a piece. From simple melody to complicated textures to simplicity again and then back to the more dense, the more complex sounds."[1] And the more dense and complex sounds include a rasping like the attack of a giant mosquito: it's Donald Ayler playing trumpet in a small range of a few imprecise notes, each buzz lasting as long as breath permits. Tyler's little solos sound wild, primitive, with short, internally varied phrasing. The fast solos are almost static elements in the performances, sometimes too brief and too poorly recorded to communicate much more than sonority and range in what sound like almost unbroken spasms. Yet solos such as Donald Ayler's in "D.C." definitely demonstrate the logic of these player's choices.

So a typical Ayler group performance is now a series of themes, including a slow, sentimental one played by Albert on tenor; then a brief round of solos; a brief what-the-hell collective wailing; and the faster themes reprised. This is the original *Bells*, the Lörrach, Germany, "Bells," "Spirits Rejoice," "Truth Is Marching In," and so on; the performances are unbroken medleys. There are, of course, briefer, one-theme performances, too, such as the ones in *Love Cry*. The music of the Ayler brothers' groups is alternately good-natured and exciting, as Albert Ayler's more painful aspects—especially in the dark melancholy that could spill over into tragedy—become distant. One of the briefer 1965 pieces is a new "Angels," which has Call Cobbs's frilly lace harpsichord accompanying an Ayler tenor solo aching of nostalgia for cranky grandmothers who bake apple pies and quietly fart a lot; the tenor vibrato and big theme tones, with their little trailing away decorations, are charming and elephantine.

Ayler's late 1966 concert recordings are especially rewarding. A demon violinist, Michel Sampson, has replaced Charles Tyler in the group, and fiddles double-stopped lines in collective improvisations, complementing Ayler's new world of sound with church harmonies and frantic, intricate textures. Ayler never sounded grander. The scale of his ambitions was superhuman anyway, so the extravagance and uniqueness of the Ayler idiom were absolutely necessary. He told the jazz audience, "For me, the only way I can thank God for his ever-present creation is to offer to him a new music impressed of a beauty which nobody had previously understood. . . . The music we play is one long prayer, a message coming from God. . . ."[7] What is this new beauty? ". . . Like Coltrane, I'm playing about the beauty that is to come after all the tensions and anxieties. This is about postwar cries; I mean the cries of love that are already in the young and that will emerge as people seeking freedom come to spiritual freedom."[8] Not all audiences were ready for these revelations, by any means. On the 1966 tour the Ayler group recorded a television show in the BBC studios, reportedly a thirty-minute improvisation on "Ghosts." Network producers, seized with revulsion, refused to broadcast the Ayler program and destroyed the videotape.

Some fine Free musicians passed through these bands. Ayler's remarkable drummers included Sunny Murray, Ronald Shannon Jackson, Milford Graves, and his old army friend Beaver Harris; among the bassists were Peacock, Henry Grimes, Lewis Worrell, and Alan Silva. It's true that some of the spirit began to leave his music after 1966. For one thing he chose to play not tenor but alto sax throughout his February 1967 Village Theater concert and in *Love Cry*. The result is that he, despite straining, projects less resonance and less sonic variety, along with his losing the tenor's bottom registers; he plays "For John Coltrane" in almost straight alto saxophone sounds, and his playing thereby loses much of its emotive force. "For John Coltrane" is an interesting piece that presents an improvising string quartet surrounding Ayler with a current of dissonances and acidic sounds. Alan Silva plays a high violin role on his bass, and Joel Freedman plays a grave cello solo; for a change, Albert Ayler is the least radical player in his group.

Ayler's move from tenor to alto is his first recorded evidence of dissatisfaction with his musical idiom. Up to this point his art had developed quickly and steadily, as you can hear in a consecutive listening to his first eight recordings (1964–66) of his most popular tune, "Ghosts." There is the harrowing passion with which he plays it on ESP 1002; then there's the exultant Lörrach version (mistitled "Spirits") with tenor, trumpet, and violin rising to affirm Ayler's new beauty. It's true that the Ayler idiom was isolated from the main currents of Free jazz developments by its extreme specialization and its dependence on one individual. Yet up to this point his art was indeed an exalted one, and in fact, the Village Theater septet, with its four string players, was a striking first step in the direction of expanding his music's linear, harmonic, and sonic vistas. But his next moves away from the Ayler idiom mock his magnificence.

The effects of years of poverty are destructive and cumulative. Despite the wide publicity surrounding his music, despite the enthusiasm of his audiences and the respect of his own musical generation, despite such occasional periods of activity as the 1966 European tour and his new contract with a major record company, his life after 1965 was not a great deal more secure than it had been in the years of wandering through Europe. During Ayler's most difficult times in New York, John Coltrane had lent him money, and Coltrane and a few others had found him spots on concert programs. "But at the time there wasn't much money to be made," Donald Ayler points out. At the beginning of his *New Grass* album (September 1968) Albert Ayler states, "The music I have played in the past, I know I have played in another place and at a different time." With this—after having demolished and reinvented the jazz tradition—he forsook his musical vision: His next three albums are rock and modal collections. As the *New Grass* liners emphasize, he now fits his phrases to the patterns and harmonic areas of his new accompanists.

There are exceptions to his general deterioration. He plays a dark, almost unaccompanied tenor solo in "New Grass" and a dervishlike bagpipe solo in "Masonic Inborn Part 1." He first sang in the Paris 1966 "Ghosts"; some of his vocals in the 1968–69 albums are startling, for he sings "in tongues," without regard for pitch, just as he plays saxophone. But in "Sun Watcher" he peeps an ocarina solo, and that instrument's poverty of sound symbolizes his decline. Most of his playing on these dates is extremely simplified, secondary to the vocals of Mary Maria (Parks) and others; she is also credited as composer for almost all pieces on the final three Impulse LPs, including tracks on which she's absent. "O, this land is a desert, and we dwell in this land," she sings. "A man is like a tree; a tree is like a man." "Music is the healing force of the universe/It brings about a state of wholeness and purifies/Let it into the very interior of your soul. . . . Sometimes our very soul is in need of spiritual meditation/We do not need the pill and its contents. . . ." And so on.

These recordings appeared not long after the height of the popularity of LSD and the other powerful stimulants, and frankly the banal lyrics seemed to be an attempt to cash in on a fad. ("Peace, love, and understanding," cries the drunkard, clubbing you on the head with his spirituality.) Albert Ayler could not have been more in earnest. He felt that the objective of his music was to purify, to lead people into spiritual communion: "The music which we play today will help people to better understand themselves, and to find interior peace more easily."[7] In 1969 he described his visions in an open letter addressed to Amiri Baraka (LeRoi Jones), published in *The Cricket:* "It was revealed to me that we [Albert and Donald Ayler] had the right seal of God almighty on our forehead." His visions were of a flying saucer, the Second Coming of Jesus, the New Jerusalem.

> Remember, he said, you know not the minute or the hour, so let's be obedient children to God's laws. We live in darkness now; God almighty is the light of lights. You see there are mighty angels from Heaven and they are very large. Bright as the sun. . . .
>
> I saw in a vision the new Earth built by God coming out of Heaven. Years ago they called it New Jerusalem. It was a solid foundation built by God himself. It is not like the foundation we have now where men seek to kill each other's spirit.[9]

So the music on these three final studio albums is not a mere attempt to be fashionable. Instead, Albert Ayler had a message so important to him that he abandoned his most original ideas in order to communicate it.

Yet he turned toward more musically rewarding directions in a concert in France four months before his death. The albums of this concert include only one rock piece and only one Mary Maria vocal, although the rhapsodic cadences of pianist Call Cobbs add a sickly undercurrent to the rest of the music. The performance includes Ayler's fine, free, sensitive tenor sax interpretations of "Truth Is Marching In," "Spirits Rejoices," and "Universal Message." "Spiritual Reunion" is a powerful work; in his passionate development, Ayler shatters the tearful cast with two screamed notes that reveal the crazed agony at the music's source. There's a renewed sense of purpose in this final concert, as he turns away from rock and modal dabbling; possibly some major changes in his art were on the verge of occurring. But early in November 1970 Albert Ayler disappeared; three weeks later his body was found in New York's East River. Descriptions of his frame of mind in his final year are contradictory—he was optimistic, or he was worried and depressed, depending on who's talking about him—and the circumstances of his drowning remain a mystery or perhaps a secret.

Albert Ayler was one of those rare visionary artists who appear at exactly the right time in history. Almost immediately after he had begun playing in New York, he became a major inspiration, like Coleman and Coltrane. In fact, it was after Coleman had jammed with Ayler and Tyler in 1963 (and thus become involved with their ideas of sound) that his violin improvising began to appear, and Coltrane felt he played like Ayler in *Ascension,* one of his own musical breakthroughs. There are two discoveries of Ayler's that were developed into characteristic features of Free jazz in general: first, his new ideas of jazz ensembles; secondly, his world of sound.

What with shared concepts of harmony and rhythm, the musicians of the pre-Coleman generations could create together with comparatively little difficulty; obvious examples are the many all-star combos down through the decades that have included Dixieland, swing, and bop musicians together. But apart from their own immediate circles, the outside players lacked common ground (for example, try to imagine Coleman and Coltrane playing in each other's groups). Each individual who played the new music had a personal interpretation of what Freedom meant; as the music moved away from fixed tempo and meter, ensembles became precarious groupings of specialists. Ayler's music was so completely original that he accepted diversity and contradictions readily, so the 1964 groups of independent players somehow reinforced each other through their very faith in Freedom. Liberated groups such as the New York Art Quartet followed. Of course, his groups with Donald Ayler were rehearsed and trained to play in his original ensemble style, but it nonetheless incorporated much disparity. The fluidity of the Ayler ensembles from 1965 to 1967 may depend on Ayler's dominance, but it also depends on his accepting considerable give-and-take among his players.

Before Albert Ayler, jazz artists accepted—as they accepted the need to breathe—that music was founded in rhythm and scales. No, said Ayler; music begins with sound itself, and from there you can create what relationships you wish without the baggage of theory. Ayler's discoveries have nothing to do with parallel developments in Western music—minimalism, aleatory music, Partch's many-noted scales, electronic composition. These practices tend to result from musical theories, whereas the source of Ayler's music was playing a saxophone with hands and breath and nerves and mind. The most obvious aspects of his ideas of sound were heard in the energy music saxophonists of the second wave; the rather deeper implications of his ideas were at the source of Roscoe Mitchell's 1966 *Sound,* the next major advance in jazz communication.

Though Albert Ayler's choice of theme materials sounded eccentric in the mid-sixties, it doesn't at all anymore—not after the subsequent choices of the AACM musicians of Chicago, the European Free composers and improvisers, the world music of Don Cherry and others. Mingus and Shepp are fine artists whose larger compositional aims included the incorporation of folk materials. By contrast, Ayler made himself into a folk musician: Marches, old pop songs, "simple, folklike themes" were his reality, and the major third interval that he cherished in his tunes is the source and symbol of Western harmony, human as well as musical.

After leaving Ayler, Sunny Murray has played in or led any number of post-Coleman groups, ranging from the relative conservatism of his 1978 Untouchable Factor to Drums Inter-Actuel, the percussion ensemble he formed in 1981. The center of Drums Inter-Actuel is four trap drummers, Murray, Edward Blackwell, Dennis Charles, and Steve

McCall—all four are sensitive masters of percussion sound, and their separate Free concepts of rhythm and dynamics are as diverse as can be—among whom Murray, the most subtle and refined, contributes wholly in terms of arhythmic sound textures, a kind of distant commentary on his vivid partners. Here again is the Free paradox: Out of great differences, the players achieve ensemble unity.

Charles Tyler, who first appeared on record with Ayler's 1965 groups, performed and taught music in California in the 1970s, then returned to New York in 1974 and, for three years, operated The Brook, a Manhattan jazz loft. Throughout several different styles he has integrated his sonic discoveries of his period with Ayler into essentially swinging, lyrical music which retains aspects of bop harmony, r&b rhythms, and Ornette Coleman melody. In the 1981 "Just for Two" he plays a fervently yet closely unified solo with vivid, highly expressive phrasing, and this fusion of lyric content with expressive character is the special strength of his best playing. In recent years he has chosen to solo, as often as not, on baritone sax, in a style somewhat reminiscent of Sonny Rollins's tenor structures.

Tyler's fertile alto saxophone is heard almost continuously throughout his 1976 *tour de force, Saga of the Outlaws*. The work is a quintet collective improvisation in a flux of styles and moods, and it provides the logical sequel to Ornette Coleman's "Ramblin'" of 1959. The *Saga*'s length and texture embody the panorama of "Ramblin'," but now the frontier myth is devastated by reality: The duo basses rumble and tumble in multiple tempos, and keening and dissipated cries describe demoralization. Tyler's *Saga* is also a folktale, but this one shows the dissolution of faith that motivates "Ramblin'"; the two works heard in order summarize America's frontier story.

·8·

Chicago, Sound in Space, and St. Louis

It was only for kicks cracks and flacks
plicks and placks and plickers
    Lackplacker Lackplicker
    loundwadtti Daago
Nickers flickers lackpicker
Kicks flicks plack and ack lackflacmac
ack ack macflacklack
    Concladoso Oselacon Seaco
    Decoula Seaco Coonclaso
    oolinoundnighhentti
    ooo——tti nigoundhheintti
    ouncladose lacontti
    ooo——oun——tay
        —Roscoe Mitchell

The major regional centers of Free jazz activity were in the Midwest, more than 1,000 miles from the New York mainstream. When Sun Ra and his Arkestra left Chicago in 1961, the city seemed a barren place for advanced ideas in jazz. There were rare individualists such as the tenorman Fred Anderson, who was ignored by Chicago's boppers. There was the Ornette Coleman-inspired

Joe Daley Trio, which played occasionally and even recorded an album shortly after its 1963 Newport Jazz Festival appearance. The Wilson Junior College students who studied and jammed together—including bassist Malachi Favors and saxmen Joseph Jarman, Roscoe Mitchell, Anthony Braxton, and Henry Threadgill—played hard bop. Bassist Rafael (Donald) Garrett and pianist-composer Muhal Richard Abrams were the center of a small avant-garde circle on the South Side. These small clusters of people at first had little to do with each other. But then, in 1962, Abrams began leading a rehearsal band that got together weekly in a South Side tavern.

All musicians were welcome to play with this band, and young, daring ones in particular answered Abrams's invitation. The band's music was experimental in nature, so it became informally known as the Experimental Band; polytonality, chromaticism, and serialism were among the band's adventures, and Jarman once described the repertoire as third stream music with a heavy jazz bias. Abrams wrote most of the scores, and the band's other composers included Troy Robinson, Jack DeJohnette, Phil Cohran, Maurice McIntyre, Jarman, and Mitchell. The Experimental Band didn't play in public. Instead, it rehearsed continually at the Abraham Lincoln Center, one of Chicago's oldest settlement houses; jazz was truly unwelcome in Chicago's nightclubs by the mid-sixties. It was in the midst of this high creative activity and unpromising circumstances that four of the most experienced modernists—Abrams, Cohran, drummer Steve McCall, pianist Jodie Christian—initiated a do-it-yourself cooperative to produce concerts and invited everyone who had played in the Experimental Band to join them.

The co-op was named the Association for the Advancement of Creative Musicians (AACM) and chartered as a nonprofit organization in May 1965. The six original AACM groups were Christian's tough hard bop quintet, Cohran's pop-jazz Artistic Heritage Ensemble (featuring Cohran's solos on an electrically amplified thumb piano), altoist Robinson's cheerful modalists, the Experimental Band, and the groups of Jarman and Mitchell. What happened was an explosion of musical activity, and moreover—this was what surprised everyone—audiences, sometimes quite large ones, appeared to hear the music; it seems the new jazz only had to be made available. So the AACM musicians played not in nightclubs and jazz joints but in small theaters, a lodge hall, coffeehouses, churches, taverns dotted throughout Chicago, and Jarman led jam sessions in a student lounge at the University of Chicago. In mid-1966 Delmark Records began documenting some of the exciting young musicians, beginning with Roscoe Mitchell's sextet.

Mitchell (born in Chicago in 1940) began playing saxophones and clarinet in his teens, played in an army band with Albert Ayler in Germany at the beginning of the sixties, and played bop when he returned home in 1961. He also listened to Ornette Coleman's recordings and to Coltrane's "Out of This World" and *Africa/Brass;* he and saxman Joseph Jarman practiced at length together as they discovered the new music and as they studied with Abrams. Mitchell's breakthrough to Freedom did not come easily. "After I began to really listen to this music, I would be playing and I would feel the urge within myself to play things that I would hear, and I fought it for a long time because I wasn't really sure that this was what was happening. Then after I stopped fighting, it just started pouring out."[2] In 1965 the simple, soothing pop singing of Nick the Greek Gravenites in "Whole Lotta Soul" is suddenly blasted away by an explosion: It's Mitchell's alto sax break, Free, wild, and hilarious. This was Mitchell's recording debut; most of his subsequent recordings would offer similarly dramatic events.

The first record of the new Chicago jazz, Mitchell's *Sound* (1966), had a monumental impact. The main line of avant-garde development at the time was the energy music of the second wave New Yorkers, as heard in Cecil Taylor's works, the Ayler groups, and Coltrane's *Ascension*. In fact, the Mitchell Sextet's virtuoso piece "Ornette" exemplifies energy music methods within a structured context, but "Little Suite" and "Sound" introduce a bold and crucial development to jazz. At no point in "Sound" are the instruments' customary sounds heard; instead, distortion is the medium of communication, as the players create in overtones, harmonics tones, imprecise pitch, high and low tones that extend the ranges of the instruments. Of course, these were standard procedures with the Aylers and the other New Yorkers, but for them, intensity of execution—"kinetic energy" was the standard, and accurate, description—was the sustaining force in improvising. What the Mitchell Sextet did in "Sound" was to return music to its very basis: the discovery and relation of sounds within the natural force of silence.

So the mysterious, changing textures of the "Sound" theme appear slowly over sentinel bass tones and a distant, ominous current of cymbals—and then there is silence. In this void are heard very faint moans; then there is a faint, whistling trill; the primeval sounds become childlike whimpers played by Lester Bowie on his trumpet, all soft, all separated by silence. Then comes Kalaparush(a) Maurice McIntyre's tenor sax, pinched into separated overtones and undertones; space and the separated sounds create immense tension that yields a line almost in spite of itself. The tension is so extraordinary that when bassist Malachi Favors enters briefly to pluck dispute, McIntyre responds without disrupting his finely balanced line of sound and space. Lester Lashley's trombone is a thin teakettle whistle that makes a hazardous but, for the first time in "Sound," unbroken line, in angles and tangles; Mitchell's alto sax solo, wholly in multiphonics and overtones, is angry and tortured; Malachi Favors plays demon waves of harsh-toned, bowed bass, before Alvin Fielder's mysterious cymbals return "Sound" to its primeval beginnings.

"The Little Suite" has further revelations. Bells, gourds, toys—found objects that had never been used for improvising jazz—now convey lines through space in a "suite of colors." The scratching, peeping, and tinkling of these "little instruments" comment on each other, organized into sections by a harmonica-gourd duet, a pinball soldiers march, and two percussion climaxes. The ruling principle is the same as that of "Sound": *Music is the tension of sounds in the free space of silence;* sounds and silence are potentially equal elements in the creation of musical line. Musical freedom results from the interacting of sound and space.

Music of such originality and sensitivity requires most unusual players. Mitchell drew his sextet from colleagues in the Experimental Band, among whom bassist Malachi Favors (Maghostut) was among the most experienced. The usual biographies state that he was born in 1937, but Favors himself has written:

> Into being in this universe some 43,000 years ago. Moved around and then was ordered to this Planet Earth by the higher forces, Allah De Lawd Thank You Jesus Good God a Mighty, through the precious channels of Brother Isaac and Sister Maggie Mayfield Favors; of ten.
>
> Landed in Chicago by way of Lexington, Miss., for the purpose of serving my duty as a Music Messenger.[3]

He studied all of the modern bassists, particularly Chicago-based masters such as Israel Crosby and Wilbur Ware; already in his teens, he was active in all kinds of jazz groups and styles.

As for Lester Bowie, he was born in Frederick, Maryland, in 1941 and grew up in St. Louis, where he was inspired to play trumpet by Louis Armstrong records: "I read the story of how Louis Armstrong got with King Oliver, so I used to practice with my horn aimed out the window, hoping that Louis Armstrong would ride by and hear me and hire me to play with him."[4] He spent years of touring with rhythm and blues bands; he played in a carnival; he played bop; he led the band that accompanied his then-wife, the fine soul singer Fontella Bass. He also became part of the young avant-garde circle in St. Louis that rehearsed the new music in private, away from the disapproval of clubowners and older musicians. When he moved to Chicago in 1966, he was discouraged at the lack of stimulating jazz activity that he saw and stayed at home practicing with his Music Minus One records. But then one night a friend took him to an Experimental Band rehearsal, where he met Abrams, Mitchell, and the AACM.

Bowie was the foreground figure as a series of combos billed as the Roscoe Mitchell Art Ensemble was refined into the 1967 quartet. This group presented the versatility and distinctive roles of a musical commedia dell'arte troupe. Bowie played his trumpet, flügelhorn, steer horn, and kelp horn in arabesques through the air, teetering on toes or staggering backward precariously. He was alternately clown and tragedian, and his lines in space were the most literal of the ensemble gestures. Often as not, his "lead" was in response to the others' sounds. Favors was the music's core, with intensity that sometimes veered into anguished satire on bass, and banjo, zither, and Fender bass, too. Drummer Phillip Wilson offered a crueler, sharper wit, and he lent the quartet a Dada atmosphere; a genius of shading, he extended his drum kit with chimes, washboard, gongs, tablas. Mitchell directed the flow of the group's improvisations, usually from the background, signaling changes with perhaps nothing more than dynamic inflections, sonoric shifts, softly repeated motives. He was the instigator of the "little instruments," which by now included a parade bass drum and huge gongs, and he composed most of the themes in the group's repertoire.

The Mitchell group's medium was so fluid, so open to incorporating spontaneous events that theatrical elements became passing parts of the concerts. Poets sometimes read, or a player in a Lyndon Johnson mask would appear, bowing and gesturing grandiosely—Mitchell would demolish him with a custard pie. One concert opened with Favors playing banjo while drummer Abdullah Yakub (Leonard Smith) danced with a huge Raggedy Ann doll and Wilson stalked him with a shotgun; another began with the players marching onstage dressed as the Spirit of '76—fifers (Mitchell and Jarman), drummer, wounded flag bearer, and Favors in ragged costume strumming his banjo. The group's music was already dramatic, and the visuals were a logical extension of this.

The Mitchell Quartet of 1967 was one of the great jazz ensembles, though it was together for only six months. The players did not record together, though in 1975 an album was issued from a private tape of the group. It features "Old," an imaginary New Orleans with a bass pedal, snare press rolls, and trumpet blats and chatters, and "Quartet," an improvisation in free space in which Wilson becomes the catalyst for the others' movements, singly and together, an eloquent demonstration of his capacity to lead and respond. The cover of Bowie's LP *Numbers 1 & 2* is Mitchell's painting of Wilson, Bowie, and Favors playing together—it is a remarkably true-to-life painting—but Wilson is absent, and "Number 1" is a trio. This piece is Bowie's journey from broken and abstract areas to, finally, a dialogue of manifestos with Mitchell. "Number 2" adds themes and achieves more populated space with the addition of Jarman and his woodwinds and "little instruments."

The spontaneity at the source of this music is based on the premise of complex ensemble relations. By contrast, chance music operations restrict the players' range of choices; also by contrast, in the energy music of the day, the players' distinctive qualities were likely to vanish in collective orgies of speed and volume. But Mitchell, Bowie, Favors, and Wilson for a half year were free to draw upon all their knowledge and experiences as part of the ensemble movement. (Incidentally, their repertoire, while mainly original, included folk and bop tunes, Bach fugues, "Muskrat Ramble," and much more diverse stuff. Any player could introduce any theme into the group's improvisation as he chose.) In this new world of sound and space, there were from the beginning alternatives to the Mitchell groups' freedom of motion in Joseph Jarman's breakthroughs, including group improvisations that were planned in elaborate detail.

Jarman (born in 1937 in Pine Bluff, Arkansas) grew up in Chicago, studied drums in high school under the great teacher Walter Dyett, and began playing saxophone in the army in the fifties. While he and Mitchell were developing their original musics together and influencing each other, he had the crucial experience of hearing Coltrane and Dolphy play together in a club:

> ... if that was the way you had to play in order to be able to play, then I would absolutely never make it. . . . I don't mean that it wasn't possible for me to do this thing technically, but emotionally and whatever art is supposed to about-ly. We could sit down and learn a set of changes, and they do it in these schools all day every day. But that ain't music—but these guys were playing music. It made me angry because I knew that I would never, absolutely never deal if that was the standard. . . . Do you see what I'm trying to drive at? That I had discovered my mentors. . . . This was about goal and purpose and mental attitude. It's about, what do I want to paint, what colors do I want to use, it's about, will I have the nerve to step out there on a limb? It's about, will I be creative?

And what Jarman heard in their new music, most important of all, was *"the unmoving conviction that it was right."*[5]

He had written poetry since the fifties when he met Allen

Ginsberg, LeRoi Jones, and other well-known younger poets; later he studied dramatic techniques at the Second City Theater School and the Art Institute of Chicago School. He was especially interested in multimedia presentations, so his concerts were guaranteed to include a dancer or two, or a poet, or flashing lights, or "happenings," or usually a combination of these. His first LP (1966, four months after Mitchell's *Sound*) unites his poem "Non-Cognitive Aspects of the City" with his improvising quartet in complex balance. Disjunct and ambiguous sounds open to images of spiritual desolation, until "Exit the tenderness/for power" brings a drum roll and a blinding flash of Jarman's alto sax. Piano and bass move as the poem moves in the "quiet city" section, capturing "pain," rumbling at "doom." Then a piano interlude segues from this specificity to dark rhapsody; alto and rhythm conclude in a simple blues. Four distinctive personalities are revealed in this work's immensely fluid medium of free space: the vivid Jarman; the complex, brooding bassist Charles Clark; the romantic pianist Christopher Gaddy; the responsive drummer Thurman Barker.

In several other Jarman works, space is a medium of suspension. Density and sonic weight grow slowly out of suspended space in "Song For" and "Song for Christopher"; there are crescendos to highly active musical plateaus and decrescendos. In "As If It Were the Seasons" the stasis of floating space alternates with individuals playing or singing the precious theme; this is a work of minimal motion despite Jarman's jewellike contrasts of alto sax volume and sound. For him, space can be suspended, faintly mysterious, as an alternative to Mitchell or to the intensity of "Non-Cognitive." In two of the Anthony Braxton group's *Three Compositions* (1968) space is without tension; moreover, the music exists less in interplay than in separate, simultaneous movements.

A few saxophonists in previous eras (Coleman Hawkins,

Lee Konitz, Sonny Rollins) had created a cappella *tours de force*, but complete solo works on any instruments other than piano were virtually unknown before the Chicagoans. Mitchell carefully works out his unaccompanied "Solo" on bells, "little instruments," and woodwinds; this recording was a sketch for his and Favors's innovative 1967 concert of solos and duets. Side one of his *Congliptious* (1968) is three unaccompanied improvisations: a dense, intense Favors bass solo; a thematic, equally intense Mitchell solo; Bowie asking the alarmed question "Is jazz as we know it dead ... yet?," then freely associating lyricism and low humor in his trumpet solo, closing with "That all depends on what you know, heh, heh, heh." Indeed so! The next year the rest of jazzdom might have been stunned at Braxton's *For Alto*—two discs of well-sustained clever or charming or intense or brilliant alto saxophone solos—but Braxton's impressive development as an artist was no surprise in Chicago. These pioneering solo performances, and undocumented ones by Jarman and others, were the first of a flood of solos in the seventies.

There were common features among the members that helped hold the AACM together: They lived in the South Side black community, had at least some experience in blues and gospel music—these were particularly lively, innovative arts in Chicago—and, most important, had united under the leadership of Muhal Richard Abrams in the Experimental Band. In the fifties Abrams maintained a busy, successful career as a bop composer-pianist, yet he grew progressively unfulfilled by bop's confines. He began listening closely to Art Tatum's solo piano recordings: "I found out from Art Tatum that I needed to adhere to my rhythmic feelings more, and then I would have less trouble keeping up with what wanted to come out. ... The real genius of Tatum was his rhythmic concept. Expansion and contraction of rhythm: my system always seemed to need that. ... I never discarded it."[6]

Abrams has said: "I always had composing music to tell a story in mind"; the stories are, of course, collaborations between the composer and sympathetic improvisers. "I plot a story, and the music is just furthering the symbolism." By the later 1960s Abrams's direct control of his concerts was almost minimal: "You don't need much to get off the ground when your musicians are spontaneous enough—just rehearse and let things happen. Donald Garrett used to tell me that someday there wouldn't have to be written compositions—he saw it before I did. I had to write quite a bit until I had musicians who could *create* a part, and then I wrote less and less. Now I can take eight measures and play a concert."[6]

Except for its abbreviated length, Abrams's album *Levels and Degrees of Light* is characteristic of his sixties concerts. Metal shimmers around his high clarinet shrieks in "Levels and Degrees"; otherwise, fast tempos and freely outlined improvising dominate the music. "Bird Song" is a poem and then collective twittering that crescendos in orchestra instruments. Though individual characteristics are subsumed here, the mixture of greater and lesser sympathies in Abrams's players gives his groups their flavor, and "My Thoughts Are My Future" is a fine example. Most vivid is the contrast of Braxton's frustrated, squalling alto solo and the poise of Maurice McIntyre's tenor solo, with rhythmically self-assured lines that speed or slow impulsively over the driving rhythm, floating momentarily, then barreling forward with angry argument. Here and in the equally fine "Young at Heart," Abrams's piano solos are characteristic: fast ripples and tone clusters played with a light touch, with frequent acid sparkles of sound or oppositions of hands. His phrasing is turbulent, broken, constantly busy, yet his soloing sounds flowing, freely lyrical in contrast with the endless forms and contrasts of Cecil Taylor, the dominant Free piano stylist.

Of the dozens of musicians who appeared in AACM concerts in the sixties, almost all played in one or another of the groups that Abrams led. One of his favorite collaborators was Lester Lashley, whose trombone innovations in Mitchell's *Sound* were a major event in the instrument's history; he was almost equally proficient on bass and cello. It's a major loss to jazz that painter-teacher Lashley has remained musically almost totally silent in the last decade. A one-man hydroelectric generating plant named Alvin Fielder advanced jazz percussion by moving the polyrhythms of Elvin Jones into post-Coltrane ensembles, before departing Chicago in the early seventies. Charles Clark was the AACM's prodigy; the young bass virtuoso moved in dark abstraction or dissonant melodic areas and created extremely intense, dramatic catharses of densely packed lines, magnifying the prophecies of Charles Mingus. In the months before he died in 1969, he played in the Chicago Civic Orchestra, the Chicago Symphony's training orchestra.

Musically and socially the AACM was proving a success. The AACM school began in 1969; member musicians gave classes and tutored inner-city students, even found instruments for them to play; at times as many as fifty young musicians were enrolled. Musicians from the Black Artists Group (BAG) in St. Louis sometimes played at AACM events, and Chicagoans occasionally played in St. Louis and at the Artists Workshop community in Detroit. Other than these visits and obscure appearances by Jarman and the Mitchell and Braxton groups on the coasts, the AACM had been almost entirely a Chicago phenomenon. Since 1967 Steve McCall had lived in Europe, and records and magazine articles had introduced other AACM musicians to international jazz fans. In June 1969 the Art Ensemble (Jarman, Mitchell, Bowie, Favors) and the Anthony Braxton Trio (Leroy Jenkins, violin; Leo Smith, trumpet) pulled up stakes and left for an adventure in Europe; they had no promises of or prospects for performing opportunities.

The Art Ensemble (to whose name a sign painter added "of

Chicago") became famous almost immediately. Within two months of arriving in France, their first stop, they recorded six LPs, more than the total the four had led in the United States. The best performances on these albums, "Ericka," *People in Sorrow, Reese and the Smooth Ones,* are the Art Ensemble's freest-flowing recordings. The second section of *People in Sorrow* (about half of the second side) offers the lonely, blue trumpet against a violent bass, and after a passage dominated by cruel percussion, Jarman's ironic alto solo (sweet, classically pure sounds versus bent or growled tones) concludes the finely sustained, vividly varied tension of the Free ensemble improvisation; the third, final section is a furious collective improvisation.

The film sound track *Les Strances à Sophie* introduces drummer (Famoudou) Don Moye (born in 1946 in Rochester, New York) to the Art Ensemble. He had come to Europe with a group of outside Detroit musicians, had adventured through the Continent and northern Africa, and had played with Steve Lacy and others in Rome before meeting the Art Ensemble on the festival, concert, and television circuit. Moye's great array of percussion added to the group's hundreds of musical instruments, from gigantic gongs and bass saxophones to the tiniest of bells, to make an incomparable range of sound colors. A lot of his ideas were inspired by African drumming, and since his style depends on constant activity and polyrhythmic, polycolor density, he resists close interplay. Inevitably his complex excitement altered the group's direction. The aggressiveness of his playing became a unifying force, but it also largely vanquished space as a medium of ensemble improvisation. He joined Favors and Jarman in wearing African hats, costumes, and varidesign face makeup in the Art Ensemble's performances; visually as well as musically, they became a colorful spectacle.

As a quintet the Art Ensemble has made a number of fine records, among which *Urban Bushmen,* a two-LP concert, is the best document of the rich diversity and interaction it can achieve. Since resettling in the United States in 1971, the group has spent many dormant periods while the five players pursue separate activities. By now the group's name is an anachronism, since only Favors and Moye are based in Chicago, leading groups and performing with other AACM musicians; also since 1971, Moye has had homes and led groups in California and New York.

Lester Bowie is an ornery heir to the New Orleans trumpeters who came to his home city, St. Louis, on the riverboats of legend, for he reintroduced into the jazz mainstream their range of sensitive expression. You can glimpse the survival of the heroic age of jazz as he evokes comedy, tragedy, wit, crudity, joy, nastiness, at best in the most specific terms available to music's abstract language. For besides his melodic playing—brilliant zigzag slashes or haunting, breath-edged lyricism—he breathes misterioso through his horn, makes gothic horrible mouthpiece sounds, chatters subverbally, or moans, childlike. So his ballads include growls and insults; his bright, upbeat solos include choked, devastated whimpers; harsh, smutty tones convey pop songs such as "Hello, Dolly!" Bowie's highly original emotionality is subject to whim and fancy, and at the most unpredictable times light emotion gives way to depth of feeling. The Art Ensemble's medium of idiomatic flux is ideal for Bowie, so some of his own best recordings—"St. Louis Blues (Chicago Style)" or the grand "Great Pretender"—internalize this flux in his long solos.

Extravagance, flamboyance, adventure are basic to his personality. Twice during the seventies he left America to live in first Jamaica, then Nigeria. "Most of these places I go, I go broke. Like when I got to Jamaica, paid, tipped the cats, and everything, I had five bucks. I stayed two years."[7] In those two years he lived in a rural area, taught trumpet to young students, informally, and played only two gigs on the island (one was his own TV special). Broke again on his second day in Nigeria, he introduced himself to Fela Anikilapo Kuti, the controversial and enormously popular singer; he joined Fela's huge Afro-beat troupe, which included musicians, singers, and Fela's twenty-seven wives. He has toured with his gospel group From the Root to the Source, led his New York Hot Trumpet Quintet, and in 1979 organized his fifty-nine-piece Sho Nuff Orchestra for a New York concert, a dream come true. (The Sho Nuff Orchestra didn't record, but perhaps its musical character can be deduced from Bowie's 1969 twenty-one-piece band of European and American musicians in *Gettin' to Know Y'All*, with its wild mixtures of improvisers.) ". . . I've been doing the same thing my whole life: the dreams I have, I've had for years. I'm very proud of the time I spent in the carnival—that was great knowledge. The stuff I did with Joe Tex, the Art Ensemble, all the situations that I play in, to me, are equal. The spirit of the AACM permeates just about everything I stand for. Just the whole idea that cats can get together and do something in a town [Chicago] that has nothing to do with culture. . . ."[7]

The Free jazz scene that Lester Bowie left behind in St. Louis in 1966 was very secret. It was comprised of musicians who made their livings in bop and, primarily, rhythm and blues and who developed their original art in their leisure time in the park or at Oliver Lake's house. St. Louis drummers Abdullah Yakub and Phillip Wilson played briefly in Chicago, and alto saxophonist Lake spent part of 1967 in Chicago meeting AACM players, attending their concerts, and rehearsing (sometimes on the Lake Michigan beaches at 6:00 A.M.) with Jarman and Mitchell.

> Roscoe and Joseph and Muhal, when I went there, that was mind-blowing. Julius [Hemphill] and I and other players in St. Louis enjoyed playing in free form, free fashion, but we would always play it for ourselves and never thought seriously about performing it in front of an audience. We knew that it was impossible to get hired at a club doing that. . . . The norm is,

you played bebop if you wanted to play in public. And when you're younger, you always think about being discovered or something; you never think that you have to play the role of promoter, the ticket printer, the ticket seller, the guy who sweeps up after people leave. That's what the cats were doing in Chicago, and that blew me away and really inspired me. So it was from that trip that I came back and started my group and said, "Oh! What am I waiting for? *Do* it—*that's* the key! Just go out and find a place, present yourself." It was such a simple thing to do. I don't know, you just get, like a veil's lifted.[8]

The Black Artists Group (BAG) began in 1968; Lake, Yakub, altoist Hemphill, trumpeter Floyd LeFlore, and drummer Charles Bobo Shaw were among the founders; very quickly actors, dancers, poets, and visual artists were included, too. BAG began in a building in Gashouse Square, the nightclub district of St. Louis, and soon moved to a building large enough to include performance space, living quarters, a teaching area (AACM-like, BAG began tutoring young musicians). BAG was well funded, far better than the AACM, with aid from the National Endowment for the Arts and the Missouri Arts Council. After the funding had vanished in 1972, BAG dissolved.

Initially, Oliver Lake was a Jackie McLean enthusiast who studied the bop repertoire and bop licks, but he also heard too many other saxophonists playing the same way. "I just thought, 'Damn, there's got to be something else. If I learn this vocabulary, then I'm going to be able to recite all of the sentences that this guy can recite.' . . . Lester was influential in my playing from the standpoint of, what's the use of sounding like everyone else? Try to develop another thing that would maybe create my identity, rather than being Jackie McLean, Jr."[8] His eclectic Free style reinterprets first and second wave Free concepts—Shepp, Coleman, especially Eric Dolphy—in light of post-Ayler techniques of expression. He's naturally attracted to angular intervals and considerable dynamic variety, and these, along with his tendency to play phrases that don't flow together, result in a chiaroscuro art in solos such as the sonically dappled "Zaki." Basically his sound conveys a natural saxophone hardness, though he often plays with a softer, more "pure" tone; sound contrasts and intensity merge in his best hard-driving, sometimes wrenchingly harsh lines, such as in "Owshet" or the pieces for alto and three violins in *Heavy Spirits*. There are sometimes Lake improvisations on other instruments that equal the expressive vitality of his alto work (his soprano in "Hymn for the Old Year"), and a closely developed and sustained alto solo such as "Improv 1" contradicts the main course of his work. He has turned to Eric Dolphy for inspiration in the eighties, but unlike Dolphy, Lake doesn't whelm you skyward. Rather, his phrases are more broken, his sound coloring is un-Dolphy-like agitation; knobby, gnarled threats introduce "Clevont Fitzhubert," and he gives a new kind of complexity to the Dolphy songs he plays in *The Prophet*.

Julius Hemphill's alto sound is cleaner than Lake's, his technique and sense of sonic contrast far less active, but his attraction to fantasy and his romantic free association of phrase make him temperamentally the closest to Lake of all saxophonists. You can hear their likenesses and contrasts in *Buster Bee*, their album of duets, and the benign glow of this music persists in Hemphill's own recordings, especially his long flute solo "The Painter." Despite the angular, broken quality of his phrasing the innate sweetness of his musical temperament is evident, even when he plays cries and harsh sounds ("In Space"). Hemphill's major works to date are his two-disc albums *Roi Boyé and the Gotham Minstrels* and *Blue Boyé*, in which his flute and multiple saxophones are multiple-tracked, with no other musicians. *Roi Boyé* becomes steadily more agitated as it progresses, a babble of sounds in side 3, and then in side 4 nervous, harried alto over growling flute menaces that are only half-mocking. *Blue Boyé* includes the low flute groans, buzzes, and growls of "Antecedent," lumbering monsters struggling to rise out of primordial ooze. "Kansas City Line" is close to the heart of Julius Hemphill. It is an only slightly updated form of a Charlie Parker blues, a long solo full of Parker's phrasing and lyricism without Parker's anguish. These one-man multiple-tracked albums plus compositions such as "Lyric" show a deep love of wood-wind sound, blending in his orchestrations and bubbling in "ensemble" improvisations, that became the basis for the World Saxophone Quartet in the 1980s. In any case, in Hemphill's soloing, as his melodies curve and fly freely, the lyric instinct can overcome emotional development, resulting in solos such as "Pensive" that do not sustain interest (but then, pensiveness is not a sustained emotion either).

By 1975 most of the leading BAG musicians were settled in New York. The Lester Bowie-inspired trumpeter Bakaida Carroll, trombonist Joseph Bowie, big-toned baritone saxo-phonist Hamiet Bluiett, drummer Charles Bobo Shaw, and drummer Phillip Wilson are among the other important St. Louis avant-gardists who've contributed vitally to the jazz of the past decade. Wilson spent several years touring with rock bands after he had left Roscoe Mitchell's 1967 group, but he returned to jazz in the seventies. Especially in performances with Lester Bowie such as "TBM" and "3 in 1," he shows the great free sense of shading and empathy that marked his 1966–67 works.

Three generations of AACM players have arrived at crea-tive maturity by now, and remarkably, since most of the younger generations studied at the AACM school, they are not at all like their seniors. The strong, big-toned tenorist Fred Anderson was one of Chicago's first outside musicians, as far back as the 1950s. His long, blunt, formless lines rip raw flesh from bone, and he writes songs like "Saxoon" and

"Little Fox Run" that capture the rough blues cry of his improvising. Some of Chicago's finest musicians, from Jarman to
George Lewis, spent valuable years in Anderson's combos,
but no other saxophonist has played like him. Leroy Jenkins
plays Free violin without amplification even in the most aggressive of contexts, with traditional—that is, un-Coleman-
like—technique; though he has championed the cause of the
violin since the mid-sixties, no subsequent Chicagoan has
played the instrument. The intimate piano, organ, and vocal
music of Amina Claudine Myers presents a structural simplicity and directness that are warm, sometimes wistful, un-
cluttered even when most elaborate. Among outside
musicians she's unique for being far less a linear improviser
than an improvising arranger whose medium is reharmony,
reorchestration, redecoration. The harmonies and rhythms of
many generations of African-American sacred music run in
her bloodstream; it's no accident that she's the ideal interpreter of Marion Brown, possibly better than Brown himself,
since the pastoral grace of her own art has been consistent
through the years. Her most original music follows no schools
or trends, is quite detached from the mainstream of contemporary jazz tensions, so she is far less well known than she
ought to be and not influential at all.

When Myers and drummer Ajaramu (Jerol Donovan) led
their all-stars, the most active of sixties AACM groups, their
tenor saxophonist was usually Kalaparush(a) Maurice McIntyre,
who had created those immensely poised solos with Abrams
and Mitchell. Kalaparush has also raised the standard B-flat
clarinet to an instrument of high Free expression on occasion,
and on this instrument, too, his playing reveals a consistent
intensity. His great rhythmic poise does not obscure the iras-
cibility of his sensibility, and his stormy improvising has followed a difficult route over the years; his first album,
Humility (1969), and his *Ram's Run* (1981) are his best docu-

ments. In the latter LP his elaborate tenor lines suddenly
turn agonized and embroiled, fueling uncharacteristic double-time violence in altoist Julius Hemphill. The former has
an attractively varied program, and in "Humility in the Light
of the Creator" a near-classic elegance becomes Kalaparush's
main line of discourse. His anger is turned inside out here; his
yearning for transcendence, peaking in the closing cadenza,
is a moving self-revelation.

One senior Chicago avant-gardist, tenor saxman Von Freeman, never was part of the AACM. In fact, he began his
career before most AACM musicians were born, and he spent
years in bop, blues, and show bands before leading his own
quartets in the 1970s. Freeman's art is wonderfully swinging
and dramatic, and his most personal element is his large, rich
sound. Though he deals in a standard repertoire, he has as little regard as Ornette Coleman for conventions of pitch and
tuning, lending acute contrast to his most harmonically extreme ideas. The sense of form in this music is as classically
refined as Hawkins or Young, though Freeman's forms are
constantly, endlessly renewing themselves. There's a bluesy
intimacy about his music, even when his laid-back accenting
is coiled serpent power waiting to strike ("Time after Time,"
"Swinging the Blues") or when rubato warmth gives way to
fast, strangely diminished and augmented lines, with raw,
low choruses and bent, heady high tones ("I'll Close My
Eyes," "Mr. Lucky"). The wrenching of his outside passages
in "Have No Fear, Soul Is Here" is quite as compelling as
Coltrane; the difference is that Freeman's liberation is victo-
rious, unlike the new obstacles Coltrane discovered with
every advance. Incidentally, in both of Freeman's 1975
albums he and the sensitive drummer Wilbur Campbell
achieve remarkable unity.

The AACM school turned out to be a self-fulfilling prophecy. Chico Freeman, Mwata Bowden, Douglas Ewart (wood-

winds), Iqua (vocals) and Adegoke Steve (piano, composer) Colson, George Lewis (trombone), Pete Cosey (guitar) are probably the most visible new Chicago musicians of the seventies, and most studied at the AACM school. Freeman is the gifted tenor saxophonist son of Von Freeman, and at least in the United States he may be the most popular AACM musician. Very much unlike his father, Chico Freeman offers a highly stylized, post-Coltrane modal music, and some of his best work has occurred in the company of Muhal Richard Abrams. Ewart studied alto sax under Jarman and Mitchell, and as he progressed to the rest of the woodwind family, he also began making carefully crafted and handsomely decorated bamboo flutes of all sizes. His own improvising is a less intense synthesis of his AACM teachers, and his dramatic alto solo in "Homage to Charles Parker" is an excellent demonstration of the Chicago love of inflection and controlled sound manipulation. His clarinet quartet *Red Hills* is an energetic, unpretentious exploration of reedy sounds from gritty and growling tones to big swells and swoops, with individuals bobbing or leaping out of the mobile textures.

The widely admired composer-arranger George Lewis wrote the Parker homage, one of his several pieces for standard and electronic instruments together. As one of Free jazz's leading trombonists, Lewis plays like a tailgate revivalist at Armageddon in "Another Place" and "BFG-12" and then sensitively developed solos like "Olobo" and "Music for Trombone and B Flat Soprano" that suggest kinship with Lester Lashley's fusion of abstraction and lyricism. The multiple-tracked "Piece for Three Trombones Simultaneously," full of little phrase curls, fiercely contested chases, and grand solos, is the most enthusiastic work of this most enthusiastic player. His longtime Chicago trombone friend Ray Anderson has proved his match in terms of extroversion and exuberance. Never a part of the AACM, Anderson offers a ready, broad wit, a rough sound, and an expressive style that's an updated, more flowing Roswell Rudd.

One of the most violent jazz performances of the 1970s is Wallace McMillan's tenor saxophone holocaust in "Triumph of the Outcasts Coming." Multiwoodwind expert McMillan was the only St. Louisan who came to Chicago and stayed, for a decade; he was one of the last holdouts as one by one the earlier Chicago generations abandoned the AACM's home city. New York, especially, was where these musicians settled, for New York audiences had been highly responsive to the new Chicago jazz ever since the Braxton Trio and McCall returned to America and gave concerts, adding Abrams and bassist Richard Davis, in May 1970. These highly colored performances were not, of course, at all like the energy music that New York was used to. The excellent concerts were enthusiastically received and issued on two *Creative Construction Company* albums; Braxton and Leroy Jenkins then settled in New York, initiating the AACM's eastward trickle.

Henry Threadgill had played saxophones in the Experimental Band, but instead of participating in the subsequent Chicago ferment, he toured the United States, playing alto in church revival services, then played in a rock band in the army. In 1969 he became active in the AACM's new worlds of sound. One day he was driving on Chicago's Dan Ryan Expressway, when

> there was a guy on Maxwell Street, that you could see from the expressway, that had all of these hubcaps in his junkyard: the sun was hitting them, and they were *shining*, it was just lighting up the whole expressway—it was blinding. So I came off the expressway to see what it was. And when I started looking at them, they were so incredible—looking at the coat of arms on these hubcaps, you know—when I was going through them, I would drop some trying to get to others, and I

got involved in the sound when I was dropping them. I took some of them home and cleaned them up and began to beat on them and test them for sound; I designed a frame and everything and put it together.[9]

Threadgill plays his hubkaphone, along with his flutes and saxes, in the trio Air, which he formed when asked to perform Scott Joplin's music in a play. The other Airmen were drummer Steve McCall and bassist Fred Hopkins, who played in the Civic Orchestra, having received the Chicago Symphony's Charles Clark Memorial Scholarship. The Joplin rags, with multiple themes which Air played in two and four beat, were the means of developing ensemble unity. Soon Threadgill had taken a distinctive approach to composing for the trio:

> I began thinking about the personalities in the group and how they played. I kind of got into writing for people rather than just writing music. So often, you hear this one instrument out front, and these other two instruments are some kind of accompaniment. Well, I'm really trying to get away from that. So I'm writing music from the concept as if I were a drummer. Sometimes I go from the bass, but right now I'm involved in writing from the drums. . . .
>
> It changes the whole frame of reference in terms of what accompaniment is all about, you know. It kind of kills accompaniment and puts everything on an equal footing, and that's what I'm after.[9]

His "No. 2" is built up from the drums; the brief theme is quick, staccato tones, distant and spaced. McCall's drum solo is first, beginning as soft sound in intensely charged space; his motions rise and fall in volume and density without ever becoming loud. Over the almost arhythmic drumming, Hopkins and then Threadgill's alto add to the remoteness. The waltz "Dance of the Beast" is built up from a complex Hopkins solo, organized around heavily accented downbeats and minor third modulations. What there is of composition in these works is not a great quantity; settings and overall organization are sufficient for the three remarkable improvisers. By complete contrast, "Subtraction," an experiment in sound/space tension, is almost entirely composed.

"Abra" is a funky, weary theme in a slow three; Threadgill plays quarrelsome tenor passages, but the work ends in a fatigued droop. The fast "Air Raid" is built around a series of seven scales; Threadgill's alto solo is broken at first, then continues in long lines of unbroken, violent sound. The studio recording of "Keep Right on Playing Through the Mirror over the Water" closely evolves intensity from the opening drum solo, an anxious creation broken by a stark tenor theme that bursts into an angry solo. Hopkins's composition "R.B." offers elaborate textures: bowed bass with hubcaps and low drums; a theme by bass flute; powerful passages of tenor, bass, and drums, as sorrow erupts into anger. Air's most successful recordings are its first three studio albums, *Air Song* (recorded in Chicago, 1975), *Air Raid* (recorded in New York, 1976, after the group had become based there), and *Air Time* (Chicago, 1977); these feature Threadgill's best improvising. Initially it seemed he created different styles for each of his woodwinds: the melodic flute ("Air Song"), the brittle alto ("No. 2," "Dance of the Beast"), the huge, brawling baritone ("The Great Body of the Riddle"), the authoritative tenor ("Untitled Tango," "Midnight Sun," the studio "Keep Right On Playing"). "Untitled" is a marvelously exciting piece, with Threadgill's solo constructed in the best 1956 Sonny Rollins fashion, organized around pivotal long tones, with dramatic contrasts of phrase shape and character. Since 1977 his playing has often been in the enigmatic style of his "No. 2" solo.

Fred Hopkins is heir to the ensemble empathy of Chicago bassists Ware and Favors, and sometimes, as in "Dance of the Beast," his lines are so closely wedded to Threadgill's—

"coattailing"—that one person seems to be playing both instruments. His natural inclination is to complexity; his lines are many-noted; the result is not ornamentation at all, but power and drive. Steve McCall, Air's drummer until 1982, is one of the wonders of the world. He creates a special climate of sound and rhythms for each piece—delicate, or aggressively leading, or highly contrasting, or humorous, hard boppish, thundering, infectious—that is a refinement of the already refined hard bop masters such as Max Roach and Wilbur Campbell. In McCall, this sensitivity becomes a fervent emotionalism, a passion that's a new development in jazz drumming. McCall's emotional range, then, equals that of a melodic instrumentalist, and his playing, like Lester Young's, can even break your heart.

> Quite a few musicians who play highly commercial music didn't start out that way. You won't find one musician who's been out here 10 or 15 years who hasn't seriously thought about just going all commercial. Those who did I guess felt they deserved it after so much struggling.... There are hordes of very fine musicians across the country who play like the AACM who never get promoted. The AACM inspires musicians to band together to do what they do, because otherwise it wouldn't be done.... From what they've told us, we've commanded the respect of musicians all over the world, especially in the states. And it's not so much because of the music itself, but the idea. Because if the AACM is anything, it's a very excellent idea. It's not so much what is or isn't done, it's the idea and what it could mean to different groups, depending on their energy. The idea: to pool our energies to a common cause.[10]

Muhal Richard Abrams made these remarks in 1975, just before the AACM's tenth anniversary. "We're local musicians when we're at home," he added, "but there's no mistake that our intentions always were for a world audience."

By then the AACM and BAG musicians were an accepted part of the New York and international jazz scenes, and any number of music-producing cooperatives had appeared, some to thrive, others to disappear, from California to Connecticut and also in Europe. In the seventies Abrams had a sextet (including saxmen Threadgill, Kalaparush, and McMillan) that played nightclubs, concerts, and tours; he also led the AACM big band in weekly concerts, and he played solo piano concerts and traveled and recorded with the Art Ensemble, Braxton, Mitchell, and Chico Freeman. Finally, he, too, moved to New York, in 1977, and an era in the AACM's history came to a symbolic end.

Abrams has made two categories of recordings after 1975. First are his piano albums, solo and duet improvisations in which his art tends to be romantic, enigmatic. Abrams has never lost his early wonder at the vast possibilities of Free music; his experimentalism is irrepressible, a faith, even, that can sometimes lead to querulous results or to pleasantries such as boogie and ragtime duets with Amina and Braxton. The other category of Abrams recordings is his combo and band works. At least some are from his early adventures in Freedom—"Blues Forever" is a twenty-year-old Experimental Band standard—and most apparently date from the seventies and eighties. When they were composed is unimportant; the fact that they are being documented is definitely important because they are major steps along the frontiers of today's jazz.

What precipitates these recordings is Abrams's experimentalism based on his knowledge of his players' capacities and inclinations; here are players, as he says, "creating their parts." This very atmosphere of experiment leads to some inspired improvising, such as the alto saxophone exchanges (Ewart and Jarman) in "Bud P," the raw insults of Wallace McMillan's alto in "Balu," and, in the big band LPs, Bakaida Carroll's trumpet, George Lewis's trombone, Vincent Chancey's French horn, and the bent, bruised, floating lyricism of alto saxophonist Jimmie Vass. The best of these improvisers is Abrams himself, in solo and in ensemble; it is his forceful, astringent, lyrical piano lines that lead the duets of "Charlie in the Parker," "Arhythm Songy," and "Ritob." Abrams's aim is to encompass an always-moving range of sound and color combinations; the intensely played "Ja Do Thu" compresses an entire Abrams set of regrouped instruments into eight minutes; "Spihumonesty" ventures into synthesizer mysteries, with monstrous harmonies of human and electronic sounds.

Abrams's 1980s big bands bring an increasing importance of closely organized orchestration. Again, sound textures are constantly mobile, ever regrouping, with improvisations now leading, now subjugated; Abrams explores directions that George Russell and Johnny Carisi long ago abandoned. Snatches of church-style and fast themes develop alternately in "Mama and Daddy"; here are opposing instincts that then develop in solos. Similarly, in "Cluster for Many Worlds," separate motives by four instruments each grow into shifting clusters of orchestra sound; then, as talkers recite a motto, free improvisation in space grows from a few players to many. "Quartet to Quartet" opens with Free sax quartet counterpoint; then soloists and the full band play in a fast tempo; the third section is a Free brass quartet. The succession of events in "Malic" and "Chambea" is kaleidoscopic; the romantic "Duet for One World" begins as a variation of "Chambea" and continues in a three-part counterpoint of improvising French horn, trumpet, and band.

Thorough, never-ending change is the one constancy in these Abrams recordings. He says, "I can say 'God,' 'Allah,' 'Jehovah,' but all people don't relate to that. Everybody relates to change, and I think change is synonymous with any conception of the deity. It's something basic to mankind, it's in the physical make-up, the deterioration and rebuilding of cells, and there's no thing man-made that gets beyond change."[10] Abrams's and AACM's response to change as a spiritual principle has been not just willing acceptance, but actively seeking and embracing it. This, of course, is the way a new world is brought into being.

·9·

——— **• • •** ———

Cecil Taylor

One of the running threads in the story of today's jazz is that so many of the music's advances first appeared in Cecil Taylor's music. Like Herbie Nichols, pianist Taylor was ahead of his time in the 1950s; fortunately, unlike Nichols, he lived to come into his time. His very first record placed him unmistakably among the jazz avant-garde, back when John Coltrane was beginning his career with Miles Davis and still discovering himself in bop; when Eric Dolphy was playing bop in Los Angeles and Ornette Coleman's cataclysmic first LP was more than two years in the offing. Subsequently Cecil Taylor performed in obscurity and supported his art by washing dishes, delivering sandwiches, working in a record store. When he did get opportunities to create music, he knocked on the forbidden doors of atonality, composed thorny post-song form scores, and conducted the Free debuts of some of today's leading outside musicians (including Steve Lacy, Archie Shepp, Sunny Murray) during the years while hard bop grew to fulfillment and declined and the era of Free jazz began. The intense energy and superhuman virtuosity of his sixties music led to the energy music obsessions of the avant-garde mainstream, but actually it was not until the seventies that his basic investigations of jazz structure became the shared concerns of an avant-garde generation. He remains among the most challenging of improvisers simply because there is no comfortable way to listen to him, no way of accepting or even understanding him within the terms of any aesthetics but his own. His lonely example has given heart to many others, and now, in the post-Coltrane, post-Ayler era, he is obscure no longer.

To a large extent the jazz piano tradition is a parallel to as well as a part of the jazz ensemble tradition. Among the greatest jazz pianists, some accommodated their creativity to the musicians they played with, without any diminution of their powers. Some others, like Earl Hines, Art Tatum, and Thelonious Monk, challenged their horn soloists with the orchestral powers of their instruments; as the years passed, Hines and Tatum created their major works alone, and thereby uninhibited. Herbie Nichols composed for piano and recorded without horns; the greatest of all pianists, Jimmy Yancey, always played alone, except when his wife sang. Cecil Taylor performs either solo or else in groups in which he is the ongoing center of attention, and this places him in the tradition of great pianists—contrary to the criticisms that he's too active or too distinctive.

Isolating specific influences on Cecil Taylor's piano playing makes an interesting game. "Oh, I've always been a sponge for the people I felt were great," he says, and his inspirations include most of the masters named above, as well as Fats Waller, Lennie Tristano, early Dave Brubeck, and early Errol Garner; among other jazz improvisers, Miles Davis and Milt Jackson; among composers, Stravinsky, Ellington, Basie, and Bartók ("Bartók showed me what you can do with folk material"). Interestingly, Tatum, with his dazzling artifice, his endless destruction of flow, his continual rhythmic resetting, did not seem so crucial as the others to Taylor's self-discovery, and it was not Bud Powell so much as Powell's younger apostle, Horace Silver, whose intensity liberated Taylor's conception. In the 1950s Silver was often a rummage sale of ideas—rhythm and blues, pop, and folk licks, swing and bop riffs—played as nervously as if he were balanced on a tightwire, over an ongoing, almost distracted mutter of brittle, staccato bass chording. Certain Silver solos (for example, the funky call-response development in his second "Sister Sadie" chorus) are like nothing else in fifties jazz *except* certain choruses of Cecil Taylor.

Taylor was born (1933) and reared on Long Island, New York, and grew up listening to classical music and the big swing bands. He began studying piano at age five, and later percussion, with one of Toscanini's musicians. He attended the New York College of Music, then, for three years, the New England Conservatory of Music, and his intensive involvement with the twentieth-century classical masters was paralleled by his introduction to the wonders of improvising jazz. During the early fifties he played gigs with swing players such as Hot Lips Page, Johnny Hodges, and a trumpeter named McCoy or Coy: "That may have been more informative than any other jobs. . . . Ah, he would never hire a bass player and he would play at such god awful tempos, I mean he would play at the fastest tempos, and he would. . . . The realm of his playing demanded that the piano left hand would speak and so as he was pausing he would lean over and say, 'Boy, where is your left hand?' "[1] By the mid-fifties Cecil Taylor was playing, though infrequently in public, with his own groups in New York City.

He led his first album in December 1955, when he was twenty-two. This is a high-spirited date in which his harmony, though not his rhythm, is already in a world far advanced beyond bop. His soloing consists of one contrast after another: simple dissonances versus tone clusters, wide versus narrow octave ranges, calls versus responses (call-response is his most common means of phrasing). The beautiful flow of chords in Ellington's "Azure" is broken up by Taylor's brittle decorations; theme developments lead to stabbing bass pains, riffs and double-time lines violate the melancholy mood, his two hands contradict each other; Taylor's assertion of individuality is consciously perverse. Really, it's the perversity of a young musician who is discovering the variety of all the things he can do; these are long solos, with a general air of enthusiasm and even good humor, buoyed by the generous swing of Dennis Charles's drums. In his early albums, in the company of bop musicians, Taylor deserves his reputation for playing far out; his chords and his willingness to let his lines lead him often make his tonality ambiguous; Gunther Schuller has noted that sometimes bassist Buell Neidlinger is also moved to wander away from the chord changes.

Again and again Taylor makes a point of the distances between his more mainstream associates and his own fusion of jazz and classical idioms. What Taylor does is attempt ensemble unity by closing the distances; thus in "Charge 'Em Blues" his accompaniment imitates Steve Lacy's soprano sax phrases, and then he and Dennis Charles take turns echoing and mocking each other. Vibist Earl Griffith strolls with bass and drums through much of "Excursion on a Wobbly Rail," and when Taylor eventually adds accompaniments, they are a real impetus to the soloist's lines. These quartet pieces often seem to be a melodic instrument soloing over the orchestra in Taylor's piano, so Lacy gets a riffing jump band accompaniment in "Johnny Come Lately"; the same eighty-eight-key orchestra develops theme material behind Griffith in "Luyah! The Glorious Step," and vibes and piano together generate heat in this one.

Above all, you get a sense of zealous audacity from this early Taylor music, not so far removed from the audacity of Earl Hines, for Taylor shares his cruel streak; this is almost literal in Taylor's comic-insulting opening to "Get out of Town." The only failure among Taylor's pre-1961 recordings is the most promising session, the one with Coltrane; each of the others represents a step forward. In 1959 he mocked "Love for Sale" and "I Love Paris" by extracting riffs from the themes and rocking with them. His piano solos become more flowing, while actually gaining conflicts and internal contrasts; his solos in "Little Lees" are as closely argued as Thelonious Monk of the period. In Ted Curson (one of Curson's first appearances on records) Taylor now has a soloist of kindred temperament: rich-sounding, bold, ironic note choices, spontaneously dramatic, a Lee Morgan without Morgan's depth of vulgarity (and just to that extent Morgan is the greater artist).

The blues on his early LPs seem to be wholly improvised; but Taylor also had compositional aims, and "Tune 2" (1957) is a breakthrough for him. It's an eighty-eight-bar theme, with twelve strains (four to eight bars long) developing three principal themes and, to generate tension, a pedal point strain. Obviously the standard twelve-, sixteen-, or thirty-two-bar pop song heritage isn't fulfilling enough if the young Taylor has to write such a long, complicated piece to provide lines and structures varied enough to enjoy playing. Of course, eighty-eight bars in a medium tempo are plumb unwieldy, so in 1958 he offered "Toll," which predicts a line of development he'd follow in compositions to come. Here are three tempos and a quartet in shifting balance for the theme: vibes alone with walking bass; piano unaccompanied, but with bass and/or drum comments; and the four players together. It's something of an abstract expressionist approach to jazz composition.

At the end of the decade the hit of the Off-Broadway theaters was a play, *The Connection*, which included the Freddie Redd Quartet in its cast. For a while in 1960 the hard bop Redd group was replaced by Cecil Taylor's quartet—the faithful Buell Neidlinger and Dennis Charles and tenor saxophonist Archie Shepp. "Air" resolves a particularly high point of tension in the play: Taylor offers abstract juxtapositions of lyric phrase and painfully struck dissonances before Shepp begins his fast solo. The high drama that would give such vitality to Shepp's own early albums is not so evident in his solos with Taylor, but the grainy-edged richness of his sound adds a welcome weight to "Cell Walk for Celeste" (January 1961). This piece is yet a farther step forward into abstraction, beyond "Toll" and beyond the atomization of Monk's original "Evidence," in fact, almost into Taylor's mid-sixties unit structures. "Cell Walk" begins in an exchange of spattered notes; there's a tenor-piano dialogue, moving to soft, low chords; bass and drums interject comments before the fast solos begin, and the concluding theme is also disjunct and fragmentary. It's a highly detailed composition—clearly the solutions of bop had no more relevance to Taylor because now this idiom is thoroughly personal—and the complexities of this composition parallel the emerging complexities in Taylor's piano improvising.

"Air" is in *The World of Cecil Taylor,* which demonstrates that the multiple facets of his initially problematic piano style were in balance by 1960. It was the most accessible of his recordings up to then, with five varilength performances (three originals, two pop standards), each with its distinctive character. There's a relaxed swing in his medium-tempo standards, which are not abstract statements at all. In "This Nearly Was Mine" his ebb and flow of consonance and dissonance, of lyricism and dramatic statement are a natural emotional organization; just as naturally, he becomes a pastoral impressionist in "Lazy Afternoon," improvising not on the theme or chord changes but on the (unheard) lyrics. These are about cows sleeping, beetle bugs zooming, speckled trout leaping, "a place that's quiet 'cept for daisies runnin' riot," and after a floating, wandering piano introduction, he ripples behind the meandering Shepp. Then comes a precisely structured piano solo as Taylor isolates a ripple, develops it into eddies of notes, a momentary cloud of low tones, and so on until he fades into droplets of triplet chords; it's the most charming of evocations. There's no greater contrast than the conflict that begins his solo in "Air"—soft chords answered by hard, shocking, rising treble tones. The central section of this solo and most of his long "E.B." solo are long, irregular lines of fast triplets in a high, small treble area, punctuated by sparse, vague bass chords, at a very fast pace. The soft treble lines seem rather withdrawn in the context of Taylor's otherwise forthright music, but this softer mood would develop in significance in his recordings to come.

The important "Cell Walk for Celeste" was done for a recording of which Buell Neidlinger was the ostensible leader, so it was actually a year, including most of 1961, between *The World* and the next session that documents Taylor's own musical choices, Gil Evans's *Into the Hot*.

> 1961 was a very important year. That was the year my father died. That was the final honing of the musical character because what most people perceive as either independence or insanity or whatever was supported lovingly by a father who was concerned about his son—whether he would be any of those things people said he was—but it was *his* son, his *continuance,* and he supported all my musical endeavors and my intemperateness. But he was no longer there. This man that loved was not there and economically that rock wasn't there. And one had to decide finally, what it is really all about.
>
> So, from the possible apex of becoming a figure of similar economic magnitude of, say, an Oscar Peterson, I found myself washing dishes. It was an extreme piece of irony that around that time there was an article that came out on the music that we were doing, in *Down Beat,* and I found myself, soon after it appeared, washing dishes, but by that time I knew *why* I was washing dishes.

What Cecil Taylor chose to do was to turn away from standard material and the temptation to alter or at least modify his style in order to "reach an audience." Thirteen years later he said:

In retrospect, in view of the development of the Unit's cultural base, I don't regret the decision that I made (to retain the artistic prerogative of ultimate choice). The thing I can say, for those people who *did* accept the call of becoming a commercial entity, people who have decided to make music the business by which they become financially secure—although it may be obscured by obviously deceitful talk about communication—is that *the artist's first responsibility is to communicate with himself* [italics added to last phrase only.][2]

Gil Evans did not compose or conduct any of the music on his album *Into the Hot;* instead, it's a showcase for his friends Taylor and Johnny Carisi. By now Shepp's sax sound is amplified by Jimmy Lyons's alto, in unison, octaves, and dissonant harmonies, a duo-sax sound that Taylor cherished, for he uses it in vamps that accompany his own improvisations in "Bulbs" and "Mixed." The three Taylor multipart compositions are in multitempos as well; "Pots" has striking phrases that begin on piano, then are carried by saxes; the sadness of "Mixed" is voiced by lonely trumpet and trombone, rubato, and then in anger by the crying saxes' ostinato and thudding, frustrated piano. What must have seemed an insoluble problem in "Tune 2" has been resolved by characteristic Taylor courage over the years and his good fortune in attracting soloists who can handle tonally ambiguous harmonic structures. *Into the Hot* is the bridge between Taylor's first career, in which almost every performance is an advance in scope and technique, and his second, his present career.

Johnny Carisi is a rare individual in jazz, in more than one sense. He studied under the dynamic, and neglected, classical composer Stefan Wolpe, then maintained a long career as trumpeter in big bands. In 1949 he composed the major works "Israel" (for Miles Davis's *Birth of the Cool*) and "Lestorian Mode" (for Brew Moore's septet); both are three-minute works originally issued in 78 rpm discs. These are virtuoso displays of shifting lines and sound colors; then in

1961 came his three longer works for *Into the Hot*. Carisi called these 1961 pieces "tonal and serial"; they are almost entirely composed, and they bring the world of uncertain tonality of "Israel" to a big band. Thus "Moon Taj" is the Taj Mahal by moonlight: Bits of melodies gleam here and there; alto sax thirds, vivid against suspended textures, flutter up and disappear; a piano calls in the void, and various groups of instruments make vibrant response; coruscating phrases are in constant motion among the musicians; and "Moon Taj" fades on a vamp. There is no theme or conventional structure here; the eternal motion of pure, brilliant sound is its own reward, the unity of the structure is the will of Nature herself. Despite the Asian subject matter, there are no Orientalisms in either this or "Angkor Wat"; on the contrary, the latter includes tuba and alto solos with gospel church band responses. Rhythmically these pieces are late swing, bop at the most advanced; Carisi's rhythmic world would not admit interpretation by Curson or Dennis Charles, let alone Archie Shepp or Jimmy Lyons. To my knowledge, the only subsequent Carisi jazz work is a diminution in vitality, a collection of jazz-rock scores for a studio trumpeter, Marvin Stamm. But Carisi's 1961 pieces are an unforgettable advance in the jazz sensibility.

Jimmy Lyons's alto sax and Sunny Murray's drums are in Taylor's *Into the Hot* pieces, and the next year these three players constituted the Cecil Taylor Unit. Their November 1962 Copenhagen performances offer a new kind of unity for the new jazz. This music has two basic moods: ballad-rubato and whirlwind fast, seemingly as fast as the human physique can stand to play or the human ear can distinguish between notes. Here is the arrival of energy music; such tempo extremes vitiate the possibility (and the issue) of swing, so in the cyclone tempos, continuity is sustained by kinetic force. In fact, Cecil Taylor is introducing an entirely new concept of rhythm to jazz, in which rubato and terrifically fast speeds are not opposites but alternative aspects of a single tempo. For example, two versions of "Nefertiti, the Beautiful One Has Come" begin in apparent free time, but when notes in smaller values accumulate, the density and gathering of accents begin to imply tempo. During all this, drummer Murray plays comments, but his line thickens, too, becoming a counterpoint; imperceptibly a fast tempo emerges out of the increasing density of texture, and by the time Lyons enters the superhuman tempo is explicit. There are other good illustrations of this approach to rhythm in the album; a good one is the way Taylor uses layers of intensity to multiply and divide tempo in the first take of "Nefertiti." Of course, Taylor's idea that all tempos are one tempo is a step beyond bop, but it's not the same as the free flow of tempo, meter, and space/sound that the Chicagoans would discover four years later.

What kind of music is the 1962 Cecil Taylor Unit playing? The repertoire includes one standard song that's a solo feature for Lyons, to point out the Charlie Parker qualities that linger in his playing. The other pieces include "Call," a ballad with a grand climax of piano chording, and the grandest side of the album is the long "D Trad That's What," which at least seems to be wholly improvised. This one has the fast treble rippling of "E.B." at great length, but now the ambiguous left-hand chords acquire a life of their own, an undercurrent of muttering that rhythmically expands and contracts against the main line. The second Lyons solo in "D Trad" becomes a collective improvisation with a difference: The alto plays the top line, the drums a bottom line (*not* an accompaniment), and the incredibly active piano plays all the other parts of a large ensemble blowout. There is no doubt at all that Taylor has abandoned his early mature style; there would be no more ironic distortions and concentrated investigations of standards, no more straightforward emotional structures such as "Mixed." These must have seemed more superficial areas of emotionality to him, in the face of the exploding density and complexity he was discovering. Taylor's often-quoted statement that "To feel is the most terrifying thing in this society" now becomes a crucial point of departure. For his discoveries of the early sixties were demanding deeper investigation of feeling, a certain restructuring of sensibility, in order to search inward—and the alternative to this inward search is psychic death.

The Taylor Unit made more discoveries in 1962. It was in this period that Sunny Murray abandoned timekeeping and began playing his *total* countermelody style; it was on the European jaunt that produced the Copenhagen LPs that Albert Ayler played with the group. Actually the European trip is one of the few times that the Unit performed publicly in the early sixties, and Taylor did not record again for more than two years. "I've had to simulate the working jazzman's progress," he said, "I've had to create situations of growth. . . ."[3] For a time welfare provided his income; in any case he rehearsed weekly with his group. And then in 1966 came three remarkable albums, two Blue Note recordings and a two-LP Paris performance preserved by French radio.

Andrew Cyrille is now Taylor's drummer. Like Sunny Murray, Cyrille does not mark time; unlike Murray, he directly accents the other players. This adds variable densities and vigor to the forward ensemble movement, and now Taylor adds the string bass to his Unit. The Blue Notes include not just one bassist but two of them, as very different orchestral elements, which is certainly not the way Coltrane sometimes used duo bassists as adjuncts to ensemble strength. Henry Grimes, with his big tone and drive, was one of the most powerful and forceful jazzmen of the sixties, with deep instincts for enforcing ensemble motions, as various Sonny Rollins and Albert Ayler groups, as well as Taylor's Unit, discovered. The other bassist is Alan Silva, whose role in the ensemble suggests a bass-playing Sunny Murray. Silva is thoroughly impulsive. He does not play tempo or any other similarly integral part; rather, he bows lines, most often in high, whistling ranges, that respond to the other players and add an irregular bitterness of color and fancy to the ensemble sound. Bill Dixon plays trumpet in *Conquistador,* which features possibly the best group Cecil Taylor ever led; of course, economics prevented this sextet's existing outside the recording studio, and in any case Dixon and Grimes had other interests that would have forbidden their remaining with Taylor for very long.

The Blue Note albums include some of Taylor's most colorful music, and his most abstract. The major element is the additional complexity of his forms. The album title *Unit Structures* is an accurate term for his way of organizing these ensemble performances. In his book *Free Jazz* Ekkehard Jost has a valuable analysis of how Taylor organizes primary and secondary theme material, along with introductory, ornamental, and contrasting units in a long piece titled "Unit Structure/As of a Now/Section." Briefly, there are fifteen units in the first five minutes, introducing the seven players in changing combinations, in constant and generally polyphonic motion. Theme elements appear; the primary theme is a series of short, separated motives; tempos and meters appear and quickly evaporate; there are small developments of various motives; the units are brief, usually no longer than a few seconds, so there's no possibility of a straight line of development. This is a long series of ambiguities and disruptions, composed and improvised. In the solos that ensue, the tempos and the relationships of the players stabilize, become continuous.

Essentially the other ensemble works on the Blue Notes proceed in similar fashion, though the solos in "Enter, Evening" are in free time and "Conquistador" is a relatively less complex work. The obvious ancestor of these unit structures is "Cell Walk for Celeste"; less obviously, the range of Taylor's piano style provides a model for these intricacies, as "Tales (8 Whisps)" suggests. There are any number of immediately attractive events on these recordings. My own favorites include the sound of low oboe and long, bent bass tones in "Enter, Evening"; the melodies Jimmy Lyons creates in "Enter, Evening"; the lonely opening theme of "With (Exit)"; all of Bill Dixon's playing. His trumpet solo in "With (Exit)" is almost classically contoured, in contrast with Taylor's kind of complexity, over a driving tempo. The long tones that begin and end this Dixon solo enforce his distance from the rhythm section's intensity, but most of the solo is fugitive rips and spits of sound, in which motives appear and dissolve, joining and accentuating the accompanist's great aggression. His specific lyricism in "Conquistador" is contrary to the flux of sounds and motives in the rest of Taylor's music. Dixon is unique; Cecil Taylor seldom again had the advantage of an ensemble member who resisted him this well.

The Unit in Paris in November was Taylor, Lyons, Silva, and Cyrille. "Amplitude" is suspended in a mystery of soft sounds: bass moans, strange scratching and strumming (including piano strings), sax cries; there's also a piano solo that Taylor makes indistinct by placing metal sheets over the strings. The fine "Student Studies" is full of foreboding. A stark, repeated alto tone and low, grim piano tones are central, as the players encounter space; danger continues to lurk in rubato and in fast tempo, in a dense piano-drums duet and in stuttering alto with stormy bass. "Niggle Feuigle" begins a trend of emotionality that, on the evidence of records, almost exclusively dominates Taylor's communications for several years. From the beginning it is violent, a whirling fire storm played as fast as the musicians possibly can. Obviously this had been a tendency in Taylor since 1962, but now the speed and density are without relief—except that most obvious kind, when the exhausted altoist drops out of the ensemble and Taylor's duet line becomes a solo by default.

And as Taylor found more opportunities to play in the late sixties, he also acquired a reputation for this kind of playing at great length—as if energy music were by definition a sort of race, and Taylor's stamina had made him the champion. The finest work in the 1968 Jazz Composers Orchestra collection is Mike Mantler's massive orchestration—Wagnerian? Stan Kenton-ish, at least—of Taylor; in it, Taylor plays a long solo in his kinetic energy vein. *The Great Concert of Cecil Taylor* is nearly two hours of almost unrelieved speed, with solos and collective improvisations. The music is single-minded, without lyricism or respite (except in a sax duet that interrupts), almost without emotion despite the violence of the playing and the extreme straining of the saxophones to outside sounds. What survives of emotion is excitement divorced from stimulus other than its own kinetic force. This is almost a trance, or perhaps intoxicated state, like the athlete whose continuous, concentrated exertion causes the release of a stimulant (manufactured by the human body) into the bloodstream. Taylor's concert attire is a sweat suit, and it should be no surprise that he was a high school athlete:

> ... when I was a basketball player I was probably the most aggressive basketball player ... I was fast.
> Interviewer: Play dirty?
> Taylor: Ah ... I was not foolish, since everybody was a lot larger than I was. ... I took advantage of my size, so certain people humored me ... but I made my share of baskets.[1]

So the demanding qualities of Cecil Taylor's music begin with the physical demands he makes on himself; his ensembles are, of course, built up from the piano. He has stated that his Unit creates music in constant whole-body motion

        as sound within
the *whole* body; which must be brought
to level of total depersonalized
realization[4]

The players' energies become, together, a "fissional construct." Taylor cautions, "The physical force that goes into
the making of Black music—if that is misunderstood, it leads
to screaming. . . ."[5] Nonetheless, there are many passages
in performances such as *The Great Concert* that sound
like only more complex, technically sophisticated kinds of
screaming.

In 1970 Cecil Taylor began teaching courses in black
music history and black aesthetics at the main campus of the
University of Wisconsin, in Madison. He also formed a student big band and composed music for it: "I gathered a
group of musicians in the rehearsal room on the first day and
told them, 'Now we'll play a blues.' They played, and I sat
back and listened, and it wasn't, quite. It's best that I had no
preconceived ideas—I let them inform me, so we could exchange ideas and create something together."[5] The student
musicians, some of whom had never played jazz before, interpreted and improvised on some of Taylor's most remarkable music. Here was the sound of the Unit expanded to
fifteen, twenty, or more musicians; here were the full-blown,
dense Taylor harmonies and continuous orchestral motion
being played by a real orchestra, with the advantage of daily
rehearsals together for months on end. Two years later he
moved from Wisconsin to Antioch College in Yellow Springs,
Ohio, where Lyons and Cyrille—the rest of his Unit—joined
him on the faculty. Again there was a student band; again the
band did not record. Taylor's big band compositions were
among the major products of his career—it's a revelation to
hear them—and it's most regrettable that they have not been
documented.

At last, in 1973–1974, came Cecil Taylor's first solo piano albums—and his most concentrated, highly organized performances. The four wonderful Tokyo solos range from the grand, flashy intensity of "Choral of Voice (Elesion)" to the tight thematic developments of "Lono." One Tokyo track titled "Indent" includes, near the beginning, fast, resounding lines that landslide down the keyboard, and these become climactic events in the full *Indent* performance, recorded at Antioch. *Indent* is built in three "layers" (Taylor's term). The first is basically in a rubato medium despite fast passages that culminate in the landslides. The second layer consists of every kind of musical conflict imaginable, beginning with oppositions of treble-bass, loud-soft, call-response; the third layer is in his most intense fashion, the great landslides reappearing twice. This is monumental as can be, and *Indent* is the best of Taylor's grand manner works.

The seven tracks in *Silent Tongues* are, for Taylor, not long ones, so the structure of the music becomes more apparent to the listener than usual; beyond the multitudinous upheavals in his improvising, the distinctive qualities of each movement are discernible. The theme of "Abyss" is an undercurrent at the beginning and develops to a conclusion of magnificent opposites crashing and toppling. "Petals and Filaments" begins with a rhythmic shape; he rebuilds it into a melodic phrase, then disassembles it, meanwhile alternating the repetitions with all sorts of flying hands, scrambling fingers, and low bass stabs. The "Abyss" theme is the distant source for extensive developments in "Crossing," alternating with an opposition of low, fixed phrases against treble leaps, then swoops, then fireworks explosions. Lyricism as well as immense complexity is the content of the final movement "After All"—and by then Taylor is so infused with the enthusiasm of the music that he offers two encores.

More than ever before, the piano is a wonderful orchestra to Taylor:

Just in the keyboard element I can, if I want to, have four or five bodies of sound existing in a duality of dimension. In other words, I might decide to have three or four different voices or choirs existing and moving with different weight propelling their ongoing motion . . . so that one can have—say that two or three octaves below middle C is the area of the abyss, and the middle range is the surface of the earth, the astral being the upper range—you have three constituted bodies also outlined by a specific range, a specific function of how the innards of these groups relate to themselves and then to each other. You have, therefore, what starts out as a linear voice becoming within itself like horizontal because of the plurality of exchange between the voices.[2]

How much of *Indent* (three layers) and *Silent Tongues* (five movements) is composed? His next solo piano album, *Air Above Mountains (Buildings Within)* (1976), is less obviously composed; in fact, it has the feeling of a completely improvised piece. The three-note phrase that begins is subjected to much sequencing as he develops it; after a few minutes another figure becomes the thematic cell, and there's another cell figure a few minutes later, and so on. Actually this is an advanced verison of his 1962 "Nefertiti" form, far more polished, far more technically skillful; it is also the form of the piano solo half of *Spring of 2 Blue-Js* (1973), which is Taylor's solo masterpiece. Ballad phrasing finds low, angry responses that pass in chords, then rise through the keyboard. Friction of phrasing brings phrase fragmentation; lyricism turns into clusters that form arcs attached, like kites, to the cruel bass chords. A barrage of clusters and fragments pummels the piano, as he plays all possible permutations of low bass chords and meteorite arcs in opposition. The performance is less magnificent (apart from its value) than the other solos, as he allows the more impressionist moods to develop and intensity to disperse. The oppositions here remain to the solo's end, never fusing as they do in, for example, "Crossing."

The very idea of the Cecil Taylor-Mary Lou Williams *Embraced* concert (1977) is madness. Williams was a swing and boogie pianist from thirties Kansas City who modified her style to accommodate bop in the forties; she was the only pianist to record Herbie Nichols's songs, apart from Nichols himself, and in the seventies she was also playing romantic modal pieces. In *Embraced,* she improvises on a series of blues, each in a different style. Rejecting her song forms, Taylor seizes on phrases she plays to mount a grand fantasia in extremely long, complex lines, as turbulent as ever and at his fastest speed; the two improvise in their separate worlds without remotely approaching communication, except for passages in the two longest tracks. Here is the most concrete example of the romantic foundation of Taylor's native constructionism; his completely separate world is rich, self-sufficient, all-embracing, all-transforming, and the demolition of Williams passes unnoticed.

In the early 1960s, during the years of poverty, Cecil Taylor predicted that eventually he would acquire an income from his own music to equal the income of a good chamber musician. According to Jimmy Lyons, it was from the time of Taylor's residency at Wisconsin that the Unit (still Taylor, Lyons, Cyrille) at last began working enough to support the players. Their 1973 first tour to Japan yielded, besides a solo piano album, the terrifically exuberant *Akisakila* concert album, two LPs of unrelieved intensity at the characteristic fantastic speed. Late in 1973 came *Spring of 2 Blue-Js,* with bassist Sirone (Norris Jones) making the Unit a quartet; since the quartet side presents advances in Jimmy Lyons's music, this is a good place to discuss his art.

Back in 1962 Lyons's alto style had seemed largely an adaptation of Parker, but in time he became progressively more indebted to Taylor's piano intensity, though Lyons's version necessarily seems fragmented simply because the alto saxophone is not a grand piano. Once, in "Chorus of Seed" (1976), Lyons even plays an alto approximation of a swooping, crashing Taylor climax (followed by Taylor's own grand swoop). In fact, he is so influenced by Taylor that even in his own albums he gravitates naturally to the speed and intensity that usually characterize the Unit. The other side of the coin is his beautiful blue tone in passages like the opening of "Student Studies"; in any case, Lyons's technique is highly refined and flexible. In *Blue-Js* he begins with a sweet ballad, unruffled in the face of the other players' disparate activity. Suddenly he joins Taylor's extremely fast tempo, and the piece becomes hot, exuberant, intense. At times, then, Taylor plays as if accompanying him; at other times he plays fragments as if accompanying Taylor; his fragmentary lines grow longer and more angular, then shatter into honks and overtone squeals. Taylor attempts to conclude this group improvisation with a circle and swoop into a gigantic low crash—but Lyons wails on, and the intense passages do not end until *he* signals a ritard with a repeated phrase.

In the years since Cyrille left the Unit in 1975, Taylor and Lyons have been joined by a changing cast of musicians. There was a sextet in the first half of 1978 that was important in broadening Taylor's scope; besides Taylor, Lyons, and Sirone, the players were Raphe Malik, a bright-sounding trumpeter who'd been a Taylor student at Antioch, and violinist Ramsey Ameen and drummer Ronald Shannon Jackson. Like Ayler's fiddlers, Ameen is an accompanist as well as a soloist. He's as harmonically free as you'd expect, but by no means as angular as Taylor; the textures of piano and multiple-stopped violin are dense, sometimes intense; sometimes Ameen asserts lyric emotions in the midst of the other players' extreme, fascinating activity, as in "Serdab." Halfway through the final side of *One Too Many Salty Swift and Not Goodbye* he plays a solo in a vein of melancholy that Taylor ordinarily suppresses, but this time the piano accompaniment is quiet and simple, and though harsh passages enter, they're allowed to expire in crying slurs; the two players share the exacerbated sadness to the concert's conclusion.

"Idut" begins as a polyphonic dance built up from the violin; piano interludes not only separate the many varicolored events (dancing or riffing or intense) but also prevent "Idut" from hurtling into the narrower dimension of tornado tempos and unrelieved intensity. "Serdab" begins with warm, impressionist blues melodies; this piece has no passages of sustained violent intensity until near the end of the piano solo. There's no mistaking that Taylor's music has become freer, that lightning speeds and violent enthusiasms are not inevitable, that Taylor's range of emotion has broadened. Moreover, this sextet is an *ensemble;* the players may be disparate individuals, but they share a newfound freedom to assert statements, comment on and reinforce each other, regroup and alter the music's flow. The most eccentric player here is drummer Ronald Shannon Jackson. Often as not he amplifies and underlines the free motions of the other players as well as any drummer who played with Taylor; he also likes to impose patterns on the group, cleverly extracting phrases (especially from the piano) to repeat and vary in fixed tempos as bugle-drum corps rhythms. This is, of course, a conservative commentary on the group's radicalism—the Taylor-Mary Lou Williams relationship turned upside down.

All the trends to a new, all-embracing Freedom in Taylor's music are in *3 Phasis.* Throughout the first side Taylor plays solo interludes that one or more of the others join; musical sections, including some very intense ones, evolve at varying lengths (some are relatively quite long) before subsiding again to the pastoral piano. Six players exchange lead, accompaniment, and ensemble roles, each freely commenting on the others and developing the others' ideas in his own lines. Side 2 opens with a piano accompanied by irrelevant marching band drums; then this swinging drum pattern becomes the heart of the rhythm section's comic shuffle back-drop for Lyons's solo, which is fast, broken, sweltering in his extreme ranges. Drums play a different march for the re-maining piano solo and ensemble improvisation; altogether, the free play of ideas, the *readiness* of these musicians are what makes 3 *Phasis* so valuable. And the accompaniment to Lyons's solo is as broad humor as the Art Ensemble of Chi-cago offers.

Taylor's long piano solo in *It Is in the Brewing Luminous* (1980) is singular for its lack of grand dramatic gestures; inci-dentally, at the end Taylor sings, sounding like a meditative Screamin' Jay Hawkins, if you can imagine it. Nearly all of the piano solo LP *Fly! Fly! Fly! Fly! Fly! Fly!* (1980) is gen-erated by a single rhythmic pattern. This cell appears nearly intact in most of the pieces, in the low (abyss), high (astral), and mostly the middle (earth) ranges. This suite is not monu-mental or dazzling. Instead, it exists in a rhythmically open and free condition, of an inner pulse, beyond tempo and meter, that is deeper than relentless drive; here are the rhythms of life, not of will or of power. Not that Cecil Tay-lor's music in the 1980s can't achieve the same grandness as ever, but now he also chooses to play in other realms that prove to be as rewarding. Superficially Taylor's passion has resembled Coltrane's eternal quest, his endless unrest, but the natural progress of Taylor's recordings after the sixties has been toward acceptance of the variety of his emotional range. What results is not complacency but further discov-ery, in a career in which discovery, above all, is an essential.

By now Cecil Taylor is as loaded with honors and opportu-nities as an artist can be—teaching, working with dramatists and dancers, receiving foundation support, playing at Presi-dent Carter's 1979 White House Jazz Day. It's hard to keep up with him. For all that, his music has remained uncompro-mised; there has been no softening of his radical abstractions, his preoccupation with structure, his dwelling in musical extremes. Back in 1974 he said:

> I think the larger responsibility is now to let as many people hear us as possible. There's a marvelous thing that happens. There's a kind of development that goes on that is beyond the power of words to describe: the pleasure at seeing the music grow. Whether there is one person or whether there are a thousand as there were in Japan, one can see one's development.
>
> There are a large number of conscientious, loving, thinking people who are very serious in their dedication to poetry, music, dance, theater, who go there because it feeds them. There are more of these people around than is generally thought, and we've been meeting them.[2]

These meetings were not at all inevitable, of course—so for Cecil Taylor's persistence, let us be grateful.

·10·

Pop-Jazz, Fusion, and Romanticism

Jazz was a popular music for about half of its existence—during the swing era, jazz was among the *most* popular of American musics—even if jazz giants such as King Oliver and Fletcher Henderson never approached the commercial success of the Original Memphis Five or Tommy Dorsey. But eventually there were far fewer jazz performers among show business stars, simply because bop and its aftermaths were pretty far-out stuff to middle American audiences who'd grown accustomed to Patti Page and Pat Boone. By the standards of the television era, most famous jazz people, such as Dave Brubeck or the "soul" jazz groups, were only modest successes. Mainly "soul" jazz featured electric organs, which would approximate the volume and styles of riffing swing bands; a number of fine bop musicians thrived on organ-based combos, while the rest of jazzdom played for a specifically jazz-oriented—and declining—audience in the sixties. This kind of pop-jazz was distinguished by its forthrightness: The music was thoroughly blues-drenched; it emphasized the beat; people danced to it. The next kind of pop-jazz, the fusion music that grew out of the decadence of modes, subdued and eventually eliminated these features.

As Miles Davis's music declined in the late 1960s, the sales of his records declined, too, and this was during the period when the new management of Columbia Records was raising sales quotas. Davis's bosses ordered him to make a hit record or else; *Bitches Brew* was his response, in August 1969. The most overt rock element in the album is the Fender bassist, who, in each song, repeats one rhythm pattern over and over from beginning to end. The group includes three trap drummers and a hand drummer, none of whom plays loudly; there also are an electric guitar and two or three electric pianos in the accompaniment; a standard double bass adds decoration, and when the two horns solo, a bass clarinetist decorates with countermelodies. All this is the background for soloists Davis and Wayne Shorter; they are suspended over the modal harmonic structures in which the background bubbles, blurts, and mutters and the percussion rises and falls; each piece includes long, static sections which may or may not have been intended as guitar or piano solos accompanied by pianos or guitar; in any case, these sections are discontinuous.

Shorter plays soprano sax on the album, angling in and out of the "Bitches Brew" beat, floating in rhythms that expand and contract over the insistent currents of "Miles Runs the Voodoo Down." His tone is light, but it is not scrawny or inflexible; the soprano's customary post-Coltrane nasality is absent, and the instrument sounds lovely as Shorter creates fairy dances in his complex "Spanish Key" solo. Davis inflects every note of his "Voodoo" solo; this and "Spanish Key" feature his brightest playing in several years. By now his style is a balance of melodic and purely rhythmic phrases; but then in climactic passages, space closes, note values become smaller, and he blasts in high registers, then plays angry fluttering trills that expire down the scale. Apart from the wealth of inflection, Davis's style is more elemental: His sentences are simple, short, often monosyllabic, less lyrical, more tied to the beat. *Bitches Brew* became the most popular album Miles Davis ever made; it was quite the biggest of all jazz hits up to that time. Henceforth he played on the pop music concert circuit and abandoned nightclubs.

Stylistically there was no turning back. All of Davis's subsequent groups have been modeled on the modal, Fender bass-dominated *Bitches Brew* band; ensemble balances have been arranged—some groups have included sitars; hand percussionists have dominated the backgrounds of others—without affecting the new idiom's essential subduing of emotion. None of Davis's subsequent saxophonists were of Wayne Shorter quality, and Davis himself became a more austere trumpeter, as if he'd analyzed his art for maximum visceral impact and refined away the rest of his pre-1969 style. There are exceptions, such as two fine solos among his several in *Jack Johnson* (1970), but on the whole his soloing tended to set pieces, his diminished emotional range somewhat disguised by electronic ingenuity—echo chamber, multiple tracking, electric trumpet attachments, splicing (*Jack Johnson* sounds almost randomly patched together), and so on. Thus the content of his music declined to a search for the new idea or effect, and innovation became valueless. It is ironic that having chosen to play trumpet through a guitar amplifier, with a consequent narrowing of sound, in pieces such as "Ife" he further alters his sound with a wah-wah-pedal—this device had been invented to enable guitars to imitate plunger-muted trumpets! In 1975, after the vamping backgrounds of percussion and electric instruments were dominating his music completely, he retired from performing.

He did not return to an active career until the 1980s. While much of his current playing is as fragmented as in the seventies, he has returned to longer solos. His idiom is still dominated by rock patterns on Fender bass and drums; in place of the large ensembles of bubblers, blurters, and thumpers, his current group is an aggressive young quintet.

Miles Davis's trumpet tone is now coarse, and his pitch some-times imprecise, lending force to his flashy, flaring climactic phrases in solos such as "Fast Track." But there is the repeti-tive rhythm section to reassure us that Davis is not really conveying anger, and in any case, "Fast Track" consists of nothing but these climaxes. Lyrical phrasing returns in pas-sages of "Kix" (the "Swing Spring" mode) and "My Man's Gone Now," which is set to rock patterns. Overall, this new Miles Davis music is somewhat less meandering than his 1970s fusions of rock and jazz, but his trumpet playing has not yet escaped from limbo.

Within two weeks of *Bitches Brew* Wayne Shorter played soprano sax throughout an album of his own, *Super Nova,* eating up the beat in the fast, angry, rising phrases of "Super Nova," creating lyric melody in "Swee-Pea" and "Capri-corn." *Super Nova* is a jungle of exotic sounds, nowhere more so than the Brazilian carnival of "Dindi," and the vividness of the music depends on the other players' gathering around Shorter's lead. For Shorter is the drop of water that suspends these particles in a peculiar tension; without him there is no cohesion. This is most obviously true in the rubato "Capri-corn," but the entire album is distinguished by Shorter's poise and, even on the high, small saxophone, his authority. His solo in "More Than Human" seems abstract. It emerges in uncharacteristic, disconnected sections as though he were embodying, by turns, each of his accompanists' unrelated, si-multaneous, even random activity; he is sweet in some pas-sages, and others include his very hottest playing in the album.

Super Nova and its successor, *Moto Grosso Feio,* are ample evidence of Shorter's love of exotic atmosphere (the later *Na-tive Dancer* is more conventional). It was this love that led him to join Joe Zawinul in forming Weather Report after he had left Miles Davis in 1970. Zawinul also had played with

Davis, in 1969; previously he had played funk piano to order and written hit songs for Cannonball Adderley. With Weather Report he began playing several different electric pianos, synthesizers, and organs to vary the music's textures; the group also had an electric bassist, a jazz-rock drummer, and a second percussionist with a collection of hand drums and "little instruments," to add further color. As the band's leader and main composer Zawinul dealt in atmosphere; such pieces as "Waterfall" and "Morning Lake" evoke exactly what the titles say. He had a fine variety of materials to work with in this group, and though he lacked melodic gifts, he was quite sensitive to rhythm and sound fabric. And after all, there is Shorter to provide melodic life in his fast "Directions" solo, his free-ranging rhythmic detachment in "Seventh Arrow," his swinging, sustained long line in "Eurydice" that advances the sophisticated rhythmic world of his 1965 "Toy Tune." Zawinul rarely attempted other pieces as ambitious as his "Unknown Soldier," the subject of which is war and its aftermath; there are grim sections and a harsh tenor solo, but despite the threat of fast drums throughout the music, the closing elegiac section proposes the persistence of complacency.

Whereas Miles Davis's fusion of rock and jazz was an unending simmer of rhythmic and sonic ingredients, Weather Report sought more distinctive flavors in each piece. So Zawinul and Shorter deliberately underplay in "Tears" and "Waterfall," directing attention to the accompanying rhythms; or the line of "Orange Lady" is in long tones, in the odd sound of soprano and a bassoonlike bowed bass. Very early in Weather Report's career its focus on atmosphere shows signs of preciosity; "Second Sunday in August" is in long tones over fast rhythm and sustained organ chords; it includes no improvisation, and it is superior to Miles Davis's similar pieces mainly in its comparative brevity.

And as time passed and the personnel of Weather Report,

except for Zawinul and Shorter, changed several times, the increasing emphasis on simply impressionist surfaces and precious sonic values at the expense of inner vitality becomes unmistakable. There is no great difference between much of later Weather Report, such as the *Mr. Gone* LP, for instance, and the mood music of suburban radio stations. "Fusion music" became the name for the new idiom of Miles Davis, Weather Report, and the groups led by sometime Davis fusion music sidemen such as pianists Herbie Hancock, Keith Jarrett, Chick Corea, percussionist Airto Moreira, drummers Jack DeJohnette and Tony Williams (Williams's sidemen were Larry Young, organ, and John McLaughlin, guitar, both ex-Davis). In general, what fusion music fused was the atmospheric tendencies of modal jazz with the rhythm patterns of rock. The gravitational pull of the modern rock beat upon soloists' accenting discourages any but the simplest kinds of linear development; as a result, other features—atmosphere, color, small variation of subsidiary detail—become primary among the values of a music in which decoration is raised to the essential. This is fusion music's major break from the jazz tradition; creating a coherent musical line even becomes dispensable, and within this highly refined value system the evolution of the bop genre reaches its conclusion. But playing only fusion music is apparently insufficiently satisfying to a fairly large number of its famous players, who now and then return to playing modes or hard bop; some, when returning to straightforward jazz, including the marvelous Williams, Shorter, and tenor saxophonist Stanley Turrentine, present no diminution of their earlier jazz vitality.

As we've seen in Ornette Coleman and James "Blood" Ulmer, there are jazz artists who have used the materials of rock without accepting the values of fusion music. George Russell has incorporated rock rhythms among the many elements of his vertical form composition. While living and composing in Scandinavia in the 1960s, Russell chose no longer to contain his music in straightforward tempo and meter, so his vertical forms ("a state above time") offer simultaneous events in separate rhythmic and sonic worlds. The electronic sounds he overdubbed atop his 1968 improvised organ sonata became the basis of his vertical form *Electronic Sonata for Souls Loved by Nature* (1969; revised and rerecorded in 1980). The sheer multiplicity of event in his big band work *Living Time* is staggering: A world weighted with turmoil is marked by fusion, rock, blues, and Latin rhythms, Free, bop, and neoclassical gestures, in waves of low brass, piano ripples, band riffs, broken trumpet lines, sax screams, crescendos and decrescendos, and always, always massive movement. All this amassed simultaneous activity can be ponderous, as in *Living Time* or *Vertical Form VI* (1976), though a shorter vertical form work, "Listen to the Silence" (1970; recorded 1978), gives a sense of endless stylized blues. Interestingly, the most important (and first) of Russell's vertical form works does not include any rock elements. From the tolling bell opening, *Othello Ballet Suite* (1967) is sinister, full of inner strife and duplicities. Imagine the moaning of an entire sax section of Iagos; lines (solo and orchestral) are carried into flux, and tempos, densities, and orchestration are always changing; at last a growly, bent tenor sax (Jan Garbarek) is savaged into spaced fragments, suspended over the band's continually regrouping accusations. The dramatic services of Russell's panoramic art have never been more evident; here, then, is a successor to Duke Ellington's Shakespeare portraits of *Such Sweet Thunder*.

Don Ellis and Carla Bley were Russell colleagues of the early sixties who later also used rock elements as subsidiary features of some of their works. Trumpeter Ellis actually did his most important work with Russell's sextet and even as far back as 1960, when he began recording experiments in tone rows, free forms, free time, and outside harmonies. His daring partners in these adventures included pianist-altoist Jaki Byard and the remarkable Al Francis, who was the most liberated of Free vibes players; in 1961 Francis anticipates Bobby Hutcherson's most daring ideas, but Francis is more rigorous; there is no suggestion of Hutcherson's eventual conservatism. The enormously popular big bands that Ellis began leading in the mid-sixties specialized in pieces with odd meters; straight three or four beat became unconventional, and mixed meters, fourteen- and seventeen-beat bars, and India-derived rhythmic structures became much more standard. Ellis's musical values began to suggest a kid in a toyshop; his arrangements used rock patterns for some of the odd meters, he soloed through electronic trumpet attachments, and his horn sections added electronic attachments. The great lyricism and sonic sensitivity that marked his early work became casualties; the odd meters and instrumental paraphernalia quickly became stock stuff for hack arranger-composers.

Carla Bley composed songs for George Russell's sextet and for her ex-husband, Paul Bley, before *A Genuine Tong Funeral* (1967–68) established her as an important composer in extended forms. *Funeral* is a sort of modern concerto grosso with Gary Burton's quartet set against a section of five horns and Bley's own keyboards. The music is minor key and sometimes grim, with only one fast-tempo track, yet the balance and range of textures she gets are remarkable, with continual contrasts of sounds, rhythms, and regrouping ensembles (and the ingenuity of vibesman Burton), so the subject matter of the album, death, becomes bright and vital. Balance again is the essential in Bley's score for Charlie Haden's 1969 *Liberation Music Orchestra.* In this project the suite of Spanish Civil War songs includes film sound track clips and, above the band, the freely floating trumpet lyricism of Don Cherry and the emotive tenor of Gato Barbieri that turns into a long scream. The arhythmic, sensitive drumming of Paul Motian grows in disruption through the side 2 suite, which climaxes in an onomatopoeic version of the chaotic 1968 Democratic Convention in Chicago. The conclusion is "We Shall Overcome," the one element of hope amid the album's portraits of the crushing of personal liberty.

Subsequently Bley's recordings are with her own ensembles; sometimes they rise to the creative power of these early works. Her overture to *Escalator over the Hill* is the first of her satires; a musty fragrance of Kurt Weill decadence informs this music, enhanced by the somber trombone of Roswell Rudd and the tenor screams of Barbieri. *Escalator* is a three-LP "chronotransduction" with a cast of dozens of musicians, singers, and reciters playing characters named yodeling ventriloquist, sand shepherd, mutant, and so on, with words by Paul Haines ("Bullfrogs are/having their throats/cut. You pick hysterically/at your memory./O Rawalpindi!" . . . "Oh how beautiful the goatsuckers whirl/Serving our uncertainty"). "Ida Lupino" (1976) parodies soap opera thwarted love; "Drinking Music" is faintly, perfectly discordant and slobbering; "Dining Alone" is a stylized subtorch song with nonsense lyrics sung by Bley herself. Bley's most effective satires come back to the near-vertical forms of *Liberation Music*. A child's sobs, a fruity trumpet, and trombone mumbles develop the slow, weepy theme of "Jesus Maria and Other Spanish Strains" (1978); radio static and Spanish march and waltz themes are included. "Star Spangled Minor and Other Patriotic Songs" is certainly that, a real mélange of anthems in minor keys, with hysterical tenor sax, wah-wah guitar, Bley's organ funk, ending in a welter of rhythms, discords, and "Stars and Stripes Forever." The simple rock patterns in so much of her music tend to be less acrobatic, more fluid than the usual rock bases of fusion music; on the contrary, her use of rock even permits swing and lends further variety to the balance of elements that's so important to her.

By far the most influential pianist of the 1960s was Bill Evans. Earlier he'd worked in Charles Mingus and Miles Davis groups and had contributed valuable improvisations to George Russell's important 1957 Jazz Workshop sextet and early large-scale works, including the "All About Rosie" piano solo. (Incidentally, Evans then commissioned Russell's *Living Time* in the early 1970s.) Some of the spirit left his music by the 1960s, as he adopted a most distinctive touch, delicate as butterfly wings. This unique delicacy was excellent camouflage for Evans's unremarkable melodic conception; his ingenious artifice extended to creating illusions of activity out of a limited rhythmic range. Thus many Bill Evans solos are in triplets, variously accented, sped, slowed, which he occasionally alternates with the jazzy syncopations of dotted eighths-sixteenths; sometimes his juggling of these patterns is broken by less regular phrases which he sequences up and down the keyboard; he was quite a skillful technician, and his speed of execution helped maintain the sense of activity. His undramatic music was focused in the piano's middle octaves, and the summary of all these qualities is an art of understatement and an emotionality that ranges from hip to pretty to wistful: modest good manners raised to a world view.

Evans-inspired understatement came to characterize the most popular modal pianists such as Chick Corea and the eclectic Herbie Hancock, with his vague kind of impressionism. Hancock then turned to fusion music and became a leading seventies money-maker. His hit "Chameleon" erects a rhythm machine over a drum pattern in layers of half, double, and triple time by electric instruments, and atop these is a simple line on one of his several synthesizers. Sometimes

Hancock sings, too, but into a voice-distorting device rather than a microphone, in order to keep emotion at a distance. Occasionally Hancock's returns to jazz take the form of drifting modal duo-piano concerts with Chick Corea; in these the vagueness of his impressionism is doubled.

On his own, Corea led Circle, a valuable Free quartet (Anthony Braxton, woodwinds; David Holland, bass; Barry Altschul, drums) in 1970. Subsequently Corea led several combos named Return to Forever, which moved from Latin-edged, West Coast-ish postbop to loud jazz-rock fusion and then back. The appeal of his music is its optimism; his very popular *Light as a Feather* is modest in every way, with the light sounds of flutist and smooth-voiced singer joining Corea's own electric piano in pop-jazz tunes and fast sambas. Emotionally his world is as narrow as that of Evans, his nearest piano influence. Thus in 1981 Corea re-created Thelonious Monk as a happy innocent, without reflection, irony, or nostalgia and with touches of clever humor that are nothing like Monk's cruel jokes. But Monk was not deluded by attitudes like optimism or pessimism; the hard strain of realism that runs through his forms, rhythms, and harmonies is itself the best criticism of Corea.

Yet another extension of the Bill Evans sensibility is Gary Burton, who plays not piano, but vibes. Again, Burton is a technically thoroughly skillful musician and, moreover, one capable of rhythmically and harmonically stringent playing; his improvising in *A Genuine Tong Funeral* is stylistically no great exception. On the contrary, his technique also permits him to play in a style that's approximately that of Evans, as in "Crystal Silence." This piece is one of his many duets with Corea; the tendency of these pieces is for the pianist to voice recurring cadences in modern harmonies, matched by Burton in major triads, and above all, Burton is characterized by triad voicings. In fact, the weight of pastoral chords in his lines, especially triad climaxes and resolutions, makes the rest of his improvising at least seem purely decorative. The result of his "Vox Humana" cadences is a nostalgic ache, the sentimentality of a nineteenth-century love-lost heroine's opera aria.

There have been fusion music vocalists such as Flora Purim and Urszula Dudziak and rock-based fusion violinists such as Michal Urbaniak and Jean-Luc Ponty. In India, musicians such as violinist L. Subramaniam began fusing features of jazz and their own country's modally oriented musical traditions. Fusion music also brought the return of the guitar to pop-jazz. The great inspiration of fusion guitarists was rock star Jimi Hendrix, who led at first to such popular players as Larry Coryell and John McLaughlin. Miles Davis's 1969 records are the first demonstration of McLaughlin's extraordinary ability to recall and reproduce others' licks in a discontinuous fashion; subsequently he became the fastest and loudest of freak-out players, dealing in long strings of scales and arpeggios. I suspect most subsequent fusion guitarists, such as John Abercrombie, Ralph Towner, and Pat Metheny, were also influenced by John Fahey's improvised eclectic fantasias on American folk music, given the overwhelming dominance of pastoral moods in their musics. The nostalgic ache of sighing cadences is the ruling element of this latter-day pop-jazz; volume levels are low and all colors are muted, tending to pastel, varied not by contrast but by shading; despite the occasional undercurrent of percussion, rhythmic and linear event is kept at a minimum. It's hard to imagine music more soothing than Metheny's *Offramp* LP; these tranquilized sounds are divorced from emotion, from tension, from art or any other kind of vital communication. With such performances, fusion music arrives at a lingering condition of pure escape.

And pianist Keith Jarrett, the most romantic of individualists, presents escape into sensation as an ideal when he writes:

Improvisation is more than the word expresses. It is a greater responsibility . . . in that the participation with the moment is, hopefully, complete. It is a "blazing forth" of a "Divine Will" (Divine if only because of its greater force). This means that you (the pianist) are not only a victim of a message (impulse) quite beyond your own human ideas and thoughts, but you must put out (into the world of sound) as large a portion of it as possible (first having put complete trust in the "impulse").[1]

The crucial words here are "impulse" and "the moment." They are the whole of his perception of a divine will that is completely devoid of moral effect, as he likes to demonstrate in Kahlil Gibran-like statements without regard for truth: The piano provides "a more complete, more subtle, more vital language than words"; he abhors the very idea of originality because "All of jazz is based on the pressure to be unique—it's egotistical"; "We should try to be more/Like a flower/Which every day experiences its birth and death."[2] Divine revelations or not, Jarrett's dedication to "impulse," "the moment," is virtually the definition of "sensualism." In Jarrett's music the most obvious manifestations of pure sensation are the length of his ostinatos and his autoerotic groans, sighs, grunts, and moans as he leaps from his chair to thrust his pelvis at the keyboard while he plays. All this is part of Jarrett's charisma; for several years he has been the most popular of fusion musicians, though at least in America the Jarrett fad seems to have abated in the eighties. His escape into sensation, whether his own will or the divine will, is a familiar choice in the midst of the Me Generation's escape into the Self.

Keith Jarrett spent years playing hard bop, modes, and fusion music, in the mid-seventies leading a strangely restrained quartet of otherwise-fine players (Dewey Redman, tenor; Charlie Haden, bass; Paul Motian, drums). Over the past decade his primary medium has been his solo concerts;

to all conservatory students who, in their practice rooms, improvise music in the styles of various composers, Jarrett's solo methods are familiar. He plays long, unbroken wanders through a mostly bygone Europe, full of rocking vamps derived from American gospel music that turn imperceptibly into polonaise or Hungarian dance ostinatos. Mendelssohn, Brahms, Tchaikovsky, Dvořák are recalled; chromaticism mingles with extreme diatonicism; the anthems of Franck meet the young Debussy's melodies; the twentieth century enters with some alea and atonalisms. His fancy takes him from one style to another; the ostinato sections yield to hymns, sweetly pathetic melodies, up-down keyboard chases, strife resolving in bombast, and a wide variety of other stuff. The abundance of pathos in his music is an inevitable by-product of his devotion to sensation. Except for insane or intoxicated people, life is not a series of inspired impulses; no moment is ever preceded or succeeded by any equally intense experience. So Jarrett's very creativity is pathetically fleeting. The listener is left with an art of alternate waiting and vanishing, while Jarrett plays vamps that lead to blazing impulses, and then his precious melodies disappear; attractive lines get developed in progressively narrowing ways or are repeated long after their vitality is spent. You cannot expect emotional content apart from the obvious sensuality in such music; the pathos is a passive emotion, in the listener, not the pianist, who is playing on in his voracious quest of ecstasy.

There is one major romantic pianist who has spent his career in modes without his being enticed by the aesthetics of fusion or otherwise succumbing to post-hard bop's general etiolation. McCoy Tyner began his career as a Philadelphia teenager in rhythm and blues groups and in jazz bands such as Cal Massey's, and as we've seen, he became friends with John Coltrane in 1955. He has spent his entire adult life in the public spotlight. In 1960 he toured with the popular Jazztet; then later that year, when he had just turned twenty-one, he joined John Coltrane's newly formed quartet.

Already Tyner was a skillful sideman in the accepted style of the day. This was the style of Red Garland in Miles Davis's 1955–58 groups, with all its sophistication of technique and harmonic substitutions, mechanical structure, and block chord climaxes. All this mastery was apparently not wholly satisfying to Tyner because by spring 1961 changes in his art were already appearing as a direct response to Coltrane's own evolution. A straight-ahead piano solo such as "Blues Minor" now becomes an exception; more typical is solo movement by not linear development but contrast—multiple timing, trills, call-response passages, block chording, and grand downbeat pedal chords. The best portion of "Aisha" is Tyner's solo, fluttering with so many notes. Night after night he played one-chord vamps to accompany the tenor solos, and his own soloing began to absorb Coltrane's structures; thus Coltrane's cyclic form in "Out of This World" is reflected in Tyner's solo, with its recurring call-response developments. It's important that Tyner's soloing changed radically in 1965 to meet the demands of the great changes in Coltrane's own music. By *Meditations,* his final recording with the Coltrane group, his harmonic distances had become as free as they ever would, in passages of pure impressionism.

But by then Tyner was beginning to feel separate from Coltrane's grand quest:

> With him it became almost an obsession: music can become an obsession just like anything else. There was a struggle to find new things and it had reached that point where I think that anything eventually reaches its peak, and then it begins to taper off and new things have to be considered. And on a personal level, I saw the type of sacrifices that one has to make to get that involved in anything. I prefer to balance my life

and keep other things as important or in some cases, more important than music.[3]

Subsequently Tyner's career has taken three different directions, often simultaneously: as a composer-arranger, as a bandleader, and as a piano soloist. He was writing many of his most remarkable pieces from 1967 to 1970, for Blue Note LPs with a changing, varicolored cast of players. One of his groups is a quartet with Bobby Hutcherson's vibes; one sextet has Alice Coltrane's harp, for color; one septet has a front line of alto, vocal, and guitar; one nine-piece group has a *Birth of the Cool* instrumentation, and another includes a string quartet; almost always, his woodwind players double oboe, clarinet, and flutes; the sharp, resourceful team of Herbie Lewis, bass, and Freddie Waits, drums, plays on most of Tyner's Blue Note albums.

Some of his piano techniques are illuminated by these scores. One that he loves is a downbeat pedal chord call and a treble phrase response, which he voices for low brass and sax section in "The High Priest." Or his piano call-responses become piano-horns settings, or his piano trills become the trilling of flutes, and so on. These themes tend to be simple hard bop-modal tunes, often no more than riffs, though some swing on the rhythms of samba or African high life, but then "The High Priest" is a clever, odd-length line. He often likes Oriental modes, as in the aptly titled "Song of Happiness," with its kotolike cello, and "Forbidden Land," with woodwinds and rhythm instruments each playing separate lines. Among these colorful albums, *Expansions* (1968) offers the brightest spectrum, including such Free incidents as a clarinet-wooden flute improvisation or, especially, the pageant of "Smitty's Place," with its introductory snatch of fast stride piano and, instead of solos, a series of duets among the seven players.

The Blue Notes were recorded at a low ebb in Tyner's

fortunes, for with the jazz economy in decline, he was only slowly becoming established as a combo leader (in fact, several of the Blue Notes were not released until years after they had been recorded). In the seventies, then, Tyner became as popular as any of the fusion performers on the concert/club/festival circuit, leading groups that ranged from trios to septets. These groups usually feature Coltrane-based saxophonists, a Brazilian percussionist to provide color, and a traps drummer who, rock fashion, plays with stiff wrists and never strays from the beat, however busy his accenting patterns. The strong beats are accented heavily, and Tyner himself leads the attacks on the downbeat; as with the Coltrane Quartet, he plays vamps to accompany the horn soloists. His solos are earthquakes; the main content is ongoing sequences of four-note motives (he tends to use the same motive in most solos) relieved by powerful chords or call-response patterns. This is a thoroughly percussive style; he loves piano turmoil and harmonic complexity. Surely the most immediately exciting experience in jazz is when Tyner's hard-hitting bands begin their up-tempo sets, and the heart of these bands is the leader's piano.

Many times in Tyner's solos the accompanying rhythm halts, and he plays long unaccompanied sections; often, too, he offers entirely unaccompanied solos. It's these times when he plays alone that his most personal ideas appear, and you can hear his most crucial post-Coltrane advances. He is by no means a melodic improviser; his gifts are specifically in terms of highly contrasting structures, and like Cecil Taylor, he conceives of the piano as a convenient, self-contained orchestra. There's an indestructible weight and muscularity about his solos that derive not only from the solidity of his touch but especially from the quartal harmonies that are the core of his art. In Tyner, the major fourth interval replaces the major third as the symbol of unity and concord. These solos are marked by a great variety of chord densities, varied by decorative lines that wander off in many-noted, harmonically distant treble areas. There's no element of fusion's preciosity about his playing; on the contrary, the ballad character of "A Silent Tear" is enhanced by the heartfelt strength in his playing. Sometimes, as in "In a Sentimental Mood," themes become lost in the lush, thick foliage of his introductions and decorative afterthoughts. In fact, *Echoes of a Friend* (1972) is an album of piano solo extravaganzas in and out of tempo. Here "Naima" is treated both as a ballad and as a merry dance; another ballad, "Folks," turns to forthright calls and responses; the best is a fantasia on "My Favorite Things" that is full of rococo event. The grandest of these pieces is "The Discovery," which is a series of themes and decorations or variations; here are his ever-changing textures for a full seventeen minutes.

It's true that the great creativity in his early seventies unaccompanied piano pieces is not sustained over the years. Indeed, his later performances offer relatively predictable developments, despite the stimulation of varied settings (including several all-star combos), and even a reunion with Elvin Jones sounds somewhat forced (*Trident,* 1975). It's interesting that in 1979 he said, "I've always thought I could play with Ornette, although I never did anything with him. But I always felt that I could do something with him or any other horn player. Even now I feel as though I could go in either direction, because I've always done things like that, it's not an alien area for me."[4] Given the many fine Free passages in his unaccompanied performances, this is no surprise: Freedom remains one of the directions toward which he can still possibly develop, and the report that he actually has performed with Coleman in the eighties is tantalizing. In any case, Tyner's best music, after he left the security of the Coltrane group, demonstrates that romanticism is not necessarily an escape but instead can be an adventure into deep currents of emotion.

·II·

Free Jazz in Europe: American, National, International

Even as jazz was first spreading across the United States, it was making its way to Europe. By 1916 Louis Mitchell's Jazz Kings were making a popular tour of the British Isles, and they may not have been the first African-American jazz players to find success across the Atlantic. In the early 1920s it was not only expatriate American jazz artists who were finding a home in Europe; the Continent had its own musicians who were assimilating and imitating the fresh, "primitive" music from what was no longer the New World. For the next four decades the situation of the native European jazz musicians remained the same: Excellent and weak players alike depended on American originators for their ideas. The amazing Gypsy guitarist Django Reinhardt was the great exception, of course. Today, thirty years after his death, his ideas reappear not only in young avant-garde European guitarists but also again and again in American music, popular as well as jazz.

Even World War II did not slow the Old World's enthusiasm for jazz; on the contrary, there, as here, the music became a symbol of freedom (the Gestapo jailed jazz fans but couldn't suppress the spread of jazz). So it should be no surprise that after the war, while the recordings of Parker and Gillespie were yet new and controversial, bebop combos rose out of the rubble of central Europe. By the 1960s, while jazz commerce was declining in the United States, transatlantic audiences were welcoming our Free players; remember the experiences of Dolphy, Ayler, Taylor, Coleman, the Chicagoans. This led to two crucial developments in the 1970s. First, the European circuit of clubs, festivals, recording sessions, and concert halls became an essential means of support for Free musicians, even mediocre ones. Secondly, Europe-based modernists appeared one by one, evolved personal voices, and became the first internationally important European jazz generations. These musicians seldom appear in the Western Hemisphere. The currents of their own cultures provide them with inspiration and background that are at least as vital to them as the jazz tradition. Admittedly I use the word "jazz" with wide latitude here; for some, only their methodology is like Free jazz ideas, but still less does their music suggest any other traditions.

Of the American Free jazz expatriates, Steve Lacy is the major artist. A native New Yorker (born in 1933), he was inspired by Sidney Bechet to play soprano saxophone, then soon abandoned Dixieland to become the only soprano modernist of the 1950s. He's something of a high and light swing player on the first two Cecil Taylor albums (1955, 1957), sounding simple against the pianist's busy complexities. The musical concerns of a lifetime—for solo tension, solo organization—were evident very early. Instinctively he recognized that Thelonious Monk had solved some of the problems that concerned him, so beginning with an LP of Monk songs in 1958, he spent several years playing and recording almost nothing but the great composer's repertoire; he even talked Monk into hiring him for a season in 1960. The thoroughness of Lacy's absorption is stunning; even his solo in "Air," by Taylor (1961), is comprised mostly of Monk's piano figures.

The tension of Lacy's music tightened along Monk-ish lines, enhancing the delicate lyricism he had already projected with Taylor, leading to the real beauty in his 1963 solos such as "Monk's Mood." Best of all, the essential Monk rhythmic radicalism emerges, for example, in the floating phrases and freely flashing moods of "Monk's Dream" and "Bolivar Blues." He lacks Monk's harshest features and Monk's nostalgia; instead, his lyricism is becoming more liberated, and his interplay with trombonist Roswell Rudd is, if not quite Free, surely spontaneous. He says he and Rudd played the Monk songs "because it was a way of going through something to get to something else. We knew there was something on the other side. . . ."[1]

He had already encountered major steps toward Freedom in the Cecil Taylor Quartet; when Ornette Coleman and Don Cherry first played in New York, "that was the blow." Cherry, who plays the bright, incisive trumpet solos in Lacy's *Evidence* LP (1960), was a catalyst in the sopranoist's liberation:

> He used to come over to my house in '59 and '60, around that time, and he used to tell me, "Well, let's play." So I said "O.K. What shall we play?" And there it was. The dilemma. The problem. It was a terrible moment. I didn't know what to do. And it took me about five years to work myself out of that. To break through that wall. . . .
>
> It was a process that was partly playing tunes and playing tunes and finally getting to the point where it didn't seem to be important and it didn't do anything for you, to play the tunes. So you just drop the tunes. And you just played. It happened in gradual stages. There would be a moment here, a fifteen minutes there, a half hour there, an afternoon, an evening, and then all the time. . . . But it all had a lot to do with musical environment. You have to get some kindred spirits. And at the time that was in the air. It was happening everywhere.[2]

Clearly Steve Lacy had reached the Freedom "on the other side" by "Recitativo E Aria" in 1966; his long solo is distinguished by the paradox of his floating behind the beat tenacity. He recorded this solo in Italy, during two years of travel and playing in Europe and South America; returning to America in 1968, he found opportunities to play as scarce as when he'd left and took a day gig to support his music. When he went back to Europe in 1969, he stayed; he has made his home in Paris and Rome and married a Swiss musician, singer-cellist-violinist Irene Aebi, who performs in his combos. On records he is the most prolific musician since Coltrane, but most of his records are for European labels; it's only been in recent years that anything like a reasonable body of his work has been available in this country.

In the Free era of extraordinary instrumental execution at the speed of light, the truly amazing musician is the one who deals in simple materials. Lacy plays only soprano sax, with its small treble range, and moreover, the rhythmic inner character of his phrases is essentially as pre-Charlie Parker as Monk's phrasing. So the fine tension that he developed in his early playing must combine with close phrase relationships to produce the firm forms that he requires for the liberation of his lyricism. Don't expect heated blowing in his solos; instead, he offers patient exposition, step by step, tending to short phrases that are repeated, varied in small ways until they yield a conjunction of ideas or else give way to new, simple phrases. This is a very intimate approach to motivic transformation principles, resulting in solos like the unaccompanied "Threads," in which the evolution of variations leads up the soprano's range to fragmentary overtones and finally a high, spiky line in the most extreme piping, whistling sounds. In fact, he's become a virtuoso of soprano sound discovery and differentiation: The *tour de force* "Josephine" offers the faintest of high mouthpiece sounds; in "Micro Worlds" the highest possible whistling is altered, extended, and then sustained; *Axieme I* presents an exhibition of pecking, chirping, growling, and quacking; only someone uncommonly sensitive to the weight of every note can create unified solos like these out of such implausible material. These are a cappella solos, a medium Lacy was inspired to try after hearing an Anthony Braxton solo concert, around 1970; in his own soloing, says Lacy, "I try to concentrate on the rhythm, which is the most important element in a solo concert. In other words, rhythm for me is when you do something and what you do afterwards and the distance between and the proportions. Rhythm is the most difficult thing in solo concerts—and also the sound, because it's based on sound and no sound; that's all you have in solo performances."[3] This is a very Chicago-like approach to sound and space.

Thus Steve Lacy's art begins with the simplest of materials and then mounts solos the way sand dunes are built—that is, patiently, perfectly naturally. It's surely appropriate that he's set texts from the *Tao Te Ching* to music. These are performed in *The Way* by his mostly expatriate quintet, and the combination of his simple, repetitive composing and Aebi's classical vocal style results in a sort of German expressionist *Tao.* It is very picturesque music; the rustle of snares, a slow violin line, and faraway saxophone echoes suggest the unchanging eternity in "Life on Its Way"; "The Way" recalls a thirteenth century fan painting of mists and mountains with widely spaced alto phrases (by Steve Potts) over the low, abstract bowed bass. In "The Breath" he comes as close to genuinely agitated playing as he's ever come, while "Name" has one of his very best solos, a close development beginning in beautiful lines broken by a growl and then distorted sounds.

Lacy's 1958 Monk album began his relationship with pianist Mal Waldron, and after both had become expatriates they reunited often, even touring the United States as a duet in 1982. This is a stimulating partnership. Long ago the ingenious Waldron began developing a more harmonically detailed thematic repetition/transformation style, one that's simpler than Lacy's formal ideas. For Waldron, harmony takes the place of Lacy's linearity; in their *Snake-Out* concert, the piano patterns provide a steady, earthbound backdrop for the soprano's breakaways that rise and fall and then fly freely. Waldron's hard-hitting *Hard Talk* quintet provides the setting for some of Lacy's most liberated improvising, floating, rhythmically detached, yet emotionally at one with the darkly clouded ensemble. The Lacy style may be unique, but its pliability makes him readily assimilable in dozens of other combos that he's played in or led. *Threads* includes searching, highly intense trio improvisations by Lacy, pianist Frederic Rzewski, and multi-instrumentalist Alvin Curran; their constantly moving dissonances gather in bird flocks ("Rabbit"), become a ghostly, insane rattle ("Shambles"), lead to starkness without hope ("Broils"). *Trickles,* no less intense, is just the opposite, a merry quartet with Kent Carter, Lacy's regular bassist, trombonist Roswell Rudd, almost bubbling over with lyric high spirits, and the sensitive Beaver Harris, whose sound/rhythm textures show he understands Lacy better than any other drummer; there are the freedom of Lacy's motions in "Trickles" and the trombone slides and slashes that are just the right commentary on Lacy's neonursery rhymes in "The Bite."

Not to forget Lacy's many ducks, for jesting and iconoclasm—including the wandering solo "New Duck" (1972), the high, whipsawing solo "Duck" (1977), the woodsy quintet "Duckles" (1977), the ensemble improvisation "Swiss Duck" (1979), all with the same growled responses in the theme, all full of Lacy's quacking. (The 1976 trio "Ducks" appears to be mistitled, for it is completely unducky.)

One of the very first of all working Free jazz combos—in 1960, when Ornette Coleman was making his first New York sensation—was based in London, England. This was the ex-

periment-minded quintet of angular altoist Joe Harriott. They played some pieces without pulse, others in
freely moving tonalities, and even at their most conservative
they used freely modal settings at the least. Harriott and his
players commented at impulse on each other's solo lines; collective improvisation came naturally to them, so they projected a prophetic ensemble unity. The group's high
spontaneity and the lyricism of trumpeter Shake Keane are
among this music's most rewarding features; the twining of
players in the free movements of "Shadows" (1961) shows that
closely shared perceptions of line and sound colors were not
the exclusive territory of Coleman's quartet in the early
stages of the Free era.

Steve Lacy's important soprano solo, Don Cherry's trumpet arabesques, and a long piano solo by Giorgio Gaslini are
the major events of Gaslini's 1966 "Recitativo E Aria." Accu-
rately or not, any highly active, technically proficient pianist
who dwells within dissonances in the Free era is labeled a
Cecil Taylor type; Gaslini, however, shows a rare dedication
to Taylor-like ideas of solo structure in this solo. Clearly he is
a valuable pianist; moreover, his skillful group includes, besides three Americans, three other Italians like him, a French
bassist, and Gato Barbieri, the Argentine tenorist who later
became a pop-jazz star in America. Europe's Free players
were beginning to discover each other. By the late sixties
prominent Continental figures included the Dutch members
of the Instant Composers Pool (including the fine pianist
Misha Mengelberg, drummer Han Bennink, and saxman Willem Breuker) and the players in Alexander von Schlippenbach's Globe Unity Orchestra; the Southwest German
Radio's annual Free Jazz conclaves were already several
years old by the time Lester Bowie conducted *Gittin' to
Know Y'All* at the 1969 affair. For Americans, one of the first
signs of the vitality of the new European jazz was Günter
Hampel's *The 8th of July 1969*, with three Europeans and

three Americans. "Crepescule" begins in human breath (Anthony Braxton and his contrabass clarinet; vocalist Jeanne Lee's lips, mouth, and throat); despite its low-volume level, it remains tense and varied for half its twenty-five minutes, until Breuker's tenor at last rises from the calm to introduce more visceral intensity. Unquestionably this is an avant-garde performance for 1969; the only precedents for Hampel's form and choice of sounds were the Chicagoans' then still-recent discoveries.

Ever since the middle 1950s the German trombonist Albert Mangelsdorff had, to Americans, stood for the best in European jazz. He progressed through bop, hard bop, and modes, in a variety of groups, and jammed with all the traveling Americans and Europe-based Americans he could meet. By the end of the sixties, accompanied by his long-standing group, he had crossed into Freedom. In solos like "Never Let It End" his mastery of expressive technique is so subtle and thorough that he equals the American post-Parker sophisticates like Lee Morgan and Hank Mobley, and this solo is in his personal early Free style, with evolving lines and punctuation in blats and long trills. Mangelsdorff is usually credited with introducing trombone multiphonics that he makes by humming while playing, which releases his instrument's inherent overtones; thus in "Creole Love Call" he becomes all the soloists and sections of a big band, including single line calls and split tone, harmonized responses. This is an a cappella solo, for like Lacy and several of the best Chicagoans and Europeans, he began playing unaccompanied concerts. In "Tromboneliness" the modest elegance of his smooth tone and flowing line is mere surface; beneath it, vitality exudes, with all kinds of inner contrasts of phrase shape, rhythms, dynamics, coarse and split tones, broad phrases that tail off into grace tags. This sophistication admits humor with just an edge of irony. In the freest European groups such as the Globe Unity Orchestra or Brotzmann/Von Hove/Bennink, he often abandons bop sophistication entirely, to play passages of totally distorted trombone sounds.

"For Adolphe Saxe" is an outrageous mistitle for a 1967 Peter Brötzmann Trio piece; "For Albert Ayler," it should have been, since no other jazz group has so closely captured Ayler's 1964 trio. Brötzmann's own tenor sound is always distorted into multiphonics and screaming overtones; sometimes he plays passages that suggest Shepp and Kalaparush, too; his medium is screaming energy music with a deliberately manic edge, as in the long tones in "Filet Americaine" that rise as they tail off. For years he was joined by percussion collector Han Bennink and pianist Fred Van Hove, who cherished dissonances, in volleys of sound that savaged European harmonic and rhythmic traditions. This is a music of deliberate extremism, equaling the better mid-sixties New York energy music players. In "Florence Nightingale" a very Free trombone solo by guest Mangelsdorff is joined by tenor blurts and Bennink blowing multiphonics on a dhung, a large Tibetan horn; this has some of their wildest playing.

In Europe's musical traditions there is no precedent for Peter Brötzmann. But Chris McGregor maintains that there was a baritone saxophonist of an older generation in South Africa who anticipated many of Albert Ayler's ideas. McGregor was the pianist in the Blue Notes, a band that fused jazz with kwela music, the Black South African folk music; a racially mixed band, they scuffled for years in their native land, frustrated by its apartheid laws, until they settled in Europe, mostly in England, in 1965. Since then McGregor has organized several big bands named Brotherhood of Breath, comprised of ex-Blue Notes and English musicians, playing a kwela-inspired repertoire.

In contrast with better-known South African expatriates, such as Hugh Masekala and Dollar Brand, the Brotherhood's music is complex and explosive. Multiple simultaneous riffing is the Brotherhood's standard medium, at its most appealing in "MRA," a circle of swapped riffs between trumpet, trombone, and sax sections, but what's most immediate about the Brotherhood is the complicated tensions that it accepts so readily. Since "Davashe's Dream" is a ballad, it is atypical, the closest this ensemble comes to convention. Simple swing band harmonies underline a Dudu Pukwana alto line that wobbles through many sounds, in and out of tune and the chord changes, suddenly erupting in split tone screams or whimpering atonally. Mongezi Feza's trumpet solo adamantly rejects the song's harmonic structure, chattering compulsively, slurping at wounds; Pukwana's concluding solo growls to reckless atonality, and for all the stock material in the arrangement, the music's truth is in the tortured solos. The band's Willisau, Switzerland, concert album mingles swinging ensembles and catchy rhythms with collective cacophony; soloists arise from the chaos, from the delirious Pukwana and the furiously belligerent tenor of Evan Parker to the skittery, detached Feza. Agony and ecstasy mingle indescribably; the music is a volatile release of tensions, into— what? There's no conclusion to the music, no resolution, no catharsis, not even exhaustion.

Bassist Johnny Dyani, another ex-Blue Note, insists, "I am a folk musician." But in "Wish You Sunshine," after the folk-like riffs of the theme, his quartet becomes an Ornette Coleman group; Dyani's "Heart with Minor's Face" is a fine hard bop blues that initiates a nasty Free alto sax duel by Pukwana and John Tchicai, both superbly irascible. Other Dyani pieces include Brazilian pop rhythms; then again, "Magwaza," a traditional song, is sung to infectious rhythms before being treated to jazz sax lines. These Dyani combos, without the Brotherhood of Breath's extremes of tension, are at their best playing straightforward Free jazz; in the *Song for Biko* album, Makaya Ntshoko brings fervor to his drumming, while the trumpet solos by the American Don Cherry offer a sustained lyricism that's otherwise foreign to these South African-modeled albums.

The British composer Mike Westbrook's massive *Marching Song* project (1969) is a less subtle joining of inside and outside elements. This is effective program music, "An Anti-War Jazz Symphony" illustrating the progress of a war from inception to aftermath; the improvisers project various stages of sophistication with the languages of Freedom, in ingeniously manipulated textures and densities, with solos, duets, trios, stylistic clashes. Trombonist Malcolm Griffiths's sense of musical order is almost classic, just right for his role. The other trombone soloist is Paul Rutherford, whose incredible exhibition of virtuosity and utter illogic in "Landscape (II)" can be nothing other than a prelude to the progressive insanity of the "war" piece, a long, loud, cacophonous collective improvisation. Westbrook includes straight atmospheric and perverse patriotic pieces, including a parody anthem with wailing saxes; of course, the Haden-Bley *Liberation Music* also used inside-outside contrasts to show the horrors of war in 1969. Just because Westbrook's long work succeeds as music, it fails as a convincing document; this tension and excitement are stimulating, whereas his *Love Songs* (1970) are pop ditties salvaged only in the solo moments by Griffiths and Rutherford. If Westbrook's music is right, war is so much more interesting than love.

The program of *Marching Song* could be a television documentary. The program of Willem Breuker's big band Kollektief, formed in Holland a few years later, is left-wing propaganda cartoons set to the rhythms of clockwork mechanisms. The subject matter of Breuker's musical theater is Europe's bourgeois culture. He presents pageants, one piece always segueing into the next, of juxtapositions, exaggerations, perversions, pastiches of styles; the music is compulsively busy at a uniform volume level, to the pounding of fast, preferably two-beat rhythms. Tawdry, neurotic Valkyries ride in Breuker's Europe; lunatic Gypsies dance a neoboogie; a Rachmaninoff concerto slides into stride piano; fearful peasants dance in the middle of a funeral march; an oberek is contorted into a medieval dance; a correctly titled "Tango Superior" has slide whistle breaks and a blaring, stuttering alto solo; "Ham & Egg Stango" is a pure slapstick routine. Of course, television and radio bring America's cultural effluent to Europe, so the Kollektief can parody the authentic fake excitement of Las Vegas, for example, or mock the elderly teenaged cynicism of "Our Day Will Come"—sung in Dutch, surrounded by Xavier Cugat thumping. This music is full of tangos, polkas, habaneras, marches, rumbas, barroom accordionists, opera snatches, cheap theater orchestras, and whatever else original or plagiarized that can be serviceable. What's usually missing among the composed stuff is jazz, though Breuker's trombonist Willem van Manen offers "Swing Along with Babe," a Free parody of hard bop, and Breuker himself plays two saxes at once in a fierce parody of Rahsaan Roland Kirk.

The satire is almost relentless; often the band seems to be conducted by Donald Duck in a Gestapo uniform. Without the leavening of jazz, it would be oppressive, but agitated hard bop solos and post-Ayler saxophone multiphonics extend and comment upon the compositions. So in the "La Plagiata" rip-offs and lampoons, a drummer apes Gene Krupa, a tenorist plays an ignorant funk style, arthritic Latin rhythms liberate the tonality of a piano solo. Jazz provides characterization and relief in the "De Vuyle Wasch" pieces: The overbearing minor-key tunes of the overture part for tenor and trombone solos; during the funeral march Breuker pauses to mourn on bass clarinet. As a composer he is at best a harsher successor to Kurt Weill, and his Kollektief is *The Threepenny Opera* pit band fifty years later (reportedly Breuker has composed music to go with other Bertolt Brecht dramas). It's a small miracle that these high-spirited musicians usually manage to avoid outright novelty. But it seems to be true that Breuker loves drama for its own sake, even more than he loves his satiric program. There's a 1982 Breuker album that includes a perfectly straightforward performance of Gershwin's *Rhapsody in Blue*, that dusty staple of high school assemblies, and a long original piece, "Spanish Wells," which, minus the jazz solos, might have come from the sound track of a spaghetti western film. Will Breuker relent, soften his wit and anger, like so many other satirists—including Weill—and join the culture of fraud and illusion that he so ruthlessly has criticized?

For Breuker, contemporary high and low European culture is the mainstream of life that his modern jazz minstrels illuminate. Some of the composers who contribute to the Globe Unity Orchestra are Breukers in reverse. Free improvisation is the main ingredient in Peter Kowald's "Local Fair," even if a Greek folk singer, a twenty-five-piece accordion band, a barrel organist, and a parade brass band wander in and out of his mélange. With Kowald, we return to basic Freedom, which he considers synonymous with Let It All Happen. So like "Local Fair," his "Jahrmarkt" is hardly more than a succession of groupings and soloists, with plenty of bop snatches (especially Parker and Monk) amid the fun. Alexander von Schlippenbach likes to quote and arrange Monk songs, too; more important, he himself is a pianist and composer. The only obvious continuity in his "Kunstmusik II" (1975) is the very fragmentation of the Globe Unity players' phrases and the disassociation of their music in the many regroupings. This is a kind of musical abstract expressionism that's a little farther down the path of Anthony Braxton's *Three Compositions* (1968), so it's appropriate that Braxton joins the improvisers of "Kunstmusik II."

The Globe Unity Orchestra began in 1966, when Schlippenbach recruited a band to play his piece "Globe Unity," commissioned for the Berlin Jazz Festival. Subsequently the band got together again annually, sometimes several times annually, to play concerts, though the member musicians spend most of their time in independent careers. Kowald and Schlippenbach are far from Globe Unity's only composers. Sometimes the member musicians contribute conventional big band charts to the library; on the other hand, there are successes such as "The Forge," a hard-hitting, fast-driving Schlippenbach piece, mystifying personal statements such as Steve Lacy's "Worms," and plain experimentalism, like the crescendos of improvised disparities in Günter Christmann's "Trom-Bone It." But the really outstanding feature of the Globe Unity Orchestra is the quality of its individual players; these tend to be the best European Free players on their respective instruments and the most remarkable assemblies of outside jazz talent since the AACM big bands that Muhal Richard Abrams used to lead in Chicago. For example, Lacy (expatriate American), Peter Brötzmann (German), and Evan Parker (British) are usually in the reed section; the popular Enrico Rava (Italian) is among the trumpeters; Paul Rutherford (British) and Albert Mangelsdorff and Günter Christmann (both German) are the trombonists; "Every Single One of Us Is a Pearl" proclaims an Evan Parker piece that is possibly Globe Unity's finest performance, a twenty-five minute string of marvelous solos and duets. And the band's leader, Alexander von Schlippenbach, is one of the leading Free pianists, one of the unsentimental successors to Cecil Taylor without Taylor's depth of structural complexity.

The Globe Unity Orchestra suggests that Western Europe's jazz musicians constitute a thriving community. There is Free jazz in Eastern Europe, too, though how much and of what quality are largely unanswered questions on this side of the iron curtain. When musicians from Communist countries appear in the West, they are chaperoned by bureaucrats from their own countries, and they are not allowed to spend their native currencies beyond their borders; since advance payments to jazz artists are unusual, it's not easy to arrange visits by Soviet bloc jazz performers. From Russia comes the meandering Free pianist Sergey Kuryokhin. His album *The Ways of Freedom* comes from tapes that are sped so that his dissonant swoops and crashes sound like disoriented, humorless, comparatively simple versions of the American composer Conlon Nancarrow's piano rolls. Quite the most nationalistic of jazz musicians are the Russian trio of Vyacheslav Ganelin (piano, guitar), Vladimir Tarasov (percussion), and Vladimir Chekasin (woodwinds). Their basic material is popular and folk music, which they alter via the techniques of Free jazz into an endlessly energetic good-timey music, far from the post-Ayler seriousness and emotional range of their Western counterparts. The most remarkable Free musician from Eastern Europe that I've heard is Conrad Bauer, of East Germany, who is a key figure in today's revival of the jazz trombone.

The great Free achievement of Albert Mangelsdorff was his fusion of trombone liberation with hard bop and his own highly expressive emotionality. Conrad Bauer is the next advance in technique and the flowing forms that evolve from melody. In "Maxi" he holds a tone for seven minutes, improvising a multiphonics top line over it; sometimes the pedal tone changes pitch to become a slow-moving counterpoint, and in a key passage the top line accompanies the lower, unbroken tones; what's moving in "Maxi" is less this virtuosity than Bauer's naturalness of reflective solo structure. Again he becomes a one-man, one-instrument rock band in "Lotte," and he likes to evolve improvised structures out of rhythmically active themes ("Otto" is a bumblebee flight); this is warm-humored music. In "Rudiger" he proves willing to engage in the wild sonic fancies of his European trombone seniors Paul Rutherford and Günter Christmann.

Christmann is a tireless experimenter; Rutherford, an eternally surreal expressionist; surely there is no further avant-garde extreme for wind instrumentalists. Christmann also composes: "Mandolympia" for mandolins and typewriter, "Sinjuku," a collage of taped clips of street sounds, and "Airmade," four people inhaling and exhaling together, developing to a climax of a compressed air bottle—climax aside, the harmony of "Airmade" could not possibly be more natural. Like the pioneering Lester Lashley, Christmann is also a masterful bassist, while his free-association trombone solos are juxtapositions of the most eccentric sounds the instrument can make. Mangelsdorff and Bauer present prodigious instrumental facility, but Christmann is superhuman: Long sections of completely different tones, one after another in dizzying succession, high, low, here, there, everywhere on the horn are typical; so are freely spaced, soft, "freak" sounds ("Trombath" is a fine example). Rutherford exists in the same unbelievable world of lightning-speed trombone chatters, mumbles, whistles, pops, smears, clicks, growls, glides, gargles, overtones, and harmonics; the difference is that on some occasions Christmann may exhibit some momentary qualities of logic (as in his duet responses to cellist Tristan Honsinger), whereas Rutherford is the very soul of unreason. His 1974 solo LP *The Gentle Harm of the Bourgeoisie* is an advance on John Cage's practices just because Rutherford's chance operations are so utterly spontaneous, but of course, Free players have consciously pursued ideals of spontaneity ever since Lennie Tristano's first steps in 1949.

Among Free jazz activity in other European countries, in Denmark there is John Tchicai, whose alto sax sounded so intimate amid the more extroverted quests of the New York Free pioneers he joined in the early sixties. There is no loss of intimacy in his music of recent years, as he offers fragile responses to a variety of playing situations. Guitarist Pierre Dørge's *New Jungle Orchestra* moves the Brotherhood of

Breath's exoticism to central western Africa, with, instead of the Brotherhood's essential tensions, rather more detailed riff arrangements, rather more varied material, and definitely a more controlled relationship of improvisation and composition. "Jungle Rituals" and "Fullmoon in Brikama" are fetching pieces by these Scandinavians.

In France, Vinko Globokar is one of the most honored figures in avant-garde music, a classical composer, interpreter, and head researcher of "natural sounds" at the Institute of Acoustics and Music Coordination and Research (IRCAM), directed by Pierre Boulez. Globokar is also a trombonist who, as improviser, deals specifically with extreme techniques and unspecific pitches, without any suggestion of conventional musical lines. This is, of course, the province of Rutherford and Christmann, too; then in the quartet New Phonic Art, Globokar joins adventures in mobile multiphonics textures that at best ("Improvisation No. 2") suggest the most abstract adventures of the early Art Ensemble of Chicago. One of his frequent colleagues is woodwind soloist Michel Portal, who in his own album *Arrivederci le Chouartse* (1980) begins by developing a close melodic structure on alto before his tension dissipates and he presents successive versions of Roscoe Mitchell, the American modal altoist Sonny Fortune, Anthony Braxton, and Benny Goodman, on his various instruments. In earlier years he played like Coleman, Coltrane, and Albert Ayler's demoralized ocarina ("Walking Through the Lane," 1969); the sometime sensitivity to the weight of sound that he's acquired since then appears a legacy of the Chicagoans. The most original feature of this aggressive player's music is his frequent taste for the short, sensational phrase to begin solo sections or to decorate irrelevantly. The Portal recordings that I've heard tend to be emotionally cold and technically adept. He is apparently one of Europe's most respected Free jazzmen, which in a way is ominous.

* * *

The contemporary improviser faces a bewildering array of musical choices. Because he or she is a citizen of the world, without cultural imperatives, choosing to play within one genre or idiom can be arbitrary, self-limiting; even some kinds of Freedom can be restrictive if the player's message is thereby narrowed. One alternative is in the direction of dilettantism or eclecticism; a more promising alternative might be "free improvisation," which is what guitarist Derek Bailey calls his kind of music. The precedents of free improvisation, says Bailey in his book *Improvisation*, are in all kinds of music, and no single kind. As shown by Bailey and his friends, such as Christmann, Rutherford, and saxman Evan Parker, free improvisation means no fixed tempo, meter, melody, form, or any other given elements; these four players happen to be spectacular virtuoso instrumentalists, but that, too, is not really necessary for free improvisation. What is important is their sense of musical freedom. Bailey maintains that free improvisation is not an idiom but a way of creating music, a set of attitudes and methods.

Derek Bailey's records are hard to come by in this country. Despite that, his guitar techniques have influenced some young American string instrumentalists, and in recent years he's been coming to this continent at least annually, for weeks at a time, initiating concerts. Born of a family of professional musicians in Sheffield, England, he grew up playing the guitar, and by the early fifties the teenaged Bailey was a working musician.

> I'm not a trained musician, as they call it. The practical demands of making a living are about all the training I've received. But I've been fortunate enough to meet and work with musicians who were the repositories of a lot of information, which I've managed to wiggle out of them in many cases—that kind of thing. Teaching, I know nothing about; learning, I know a little bit about.

> I was interested in playing jazz when I first started playing. My interest sort of expired in the late fifties. . . . I mean, I was left with the feeling that it wasn't quite my music anyway. So I turned to the business of making a living, and I pursued that for about ten years, playing virtually every kind of music you can play on my instrument. There was a certain amount of jazz activity in England, in regard to conventional jazz—no full-time jazz activity—so I worked in dance halls, nightclubs, I accompanied singers, which I used to like very much, I worked in the studios. . . . You can find improvisation everywhere. Without the ability to improvise, making a living in the sort of demimonde of entertainment music is impossible; it's a necessary tool for the working musician, outside of classical areas. . . . It was in the later half of my working in studios that I got interested in my current activities.[4]

In 1963 Bailey was a member of a guitar-bass-drums trio that at first played jazz in fixed tempos and chord changes. Progressively over three years it eliminated tempo and meter, played modal improvisations, and then:

> . . . most of the music was improvised and solos were unaccompanied. Such accompaniment as happened was a sort of occasional commentary from the other instruments.
>
> So the whole was somewhat atonal in character, played in a discontinuous, episodic manner, with two instruments—amplified guitar and percussion—matched to the volume of a very softly played double bass.[5]

The trio stayed together for three years, doing most of its playing at a weekly gig in a Sheffield jazz club. Then in 1966 Bailey moved to London.

> There was some sort of Free jazz-cum-free improvised music—that's another fine division—activity taking place in London, mainly at a place called the Little Theater, mainly organized by a drummer called John Stevens. I started playing

with those guys—Evan Parker, Paul Rutherford, John Stevens, Trevor Watts. The Little Theater was a thriving place, but the audience was perhaps less thriving. We could play three or four nights a week in this ideal playing situation right in the center of London. That group of people went on working there through '68 and included also people like Kenny Wheeler [trumpeter] and Dave Holland and one or two other guys. By that time we started getting a few gigs, as well— usually outside England. Compared to now, I have to say that there was a lot of activity in all kinds of music. People didn't take as much notice, certainly, of what we were doing, but that was one of its satisfactions: We didn't worry about whether anyone liked it or not or whether it was right or wrong.[4]

The various Spontaneous Music Ensembles that John Stevens has led since 1966 have ranged from duets to thirty musicians improvising collectively. Stevens's most frequent partner is Trevor Watts, an Ornette Coleman-inspired altoist; the quintet Spontaneous Music Emsemble that recorded with Bobby Bradford (1971) really does dwell within a kind of spontaneous interplay that obviously develops out of Coleman's early groups and the second wave of New York Free players. Meanwhile, the groups that Derek Bailey and Evan Parker played with at the Little Theater led to their much less literal art with the Music Improvisation Company, which from 1968 to 1971 offered completely distant, abstract sounds. These were four musicians who played electronics, percussion, guitar, and saxes; they were later joined by a vocalist who, like Jeanne Lee, made mouth, lip, and throat sounds rather than sing. These musicians created separate improvisations in which they moved at odds with each other, met, reinforced one or more of the others, and formed relationships that did or did not pass quickly. The improvisations in the Music Improvisation Company's ECM album nearly all move into dry, abstruse collective energy improvisations.

This is a new idiom, all right, another successor to Albert

Ayler's groups, the first Roscoe Mitchell and Lester Bowie albums, post-Cage classical music. Absolute individual originality and pure interplay of personality are the objectives, ones that Bailey and Parker have pursued right to the present day, as the scope of free improvisation has broadened. Bailey has written that the free improviser, by definition, "doesn't have a tradition with which he can identify. But what he does have is the possibility to develop and maintain a personal authenticity."[5] His description of his own free improvising experiences has an occasional undertone of efforts to negate fashion, traditions, and any sort of representational music altogether: ". . . the sort of electric guitar open string sound that I had been at pains to avoid for years;" "All these moves constituted an attack on the harmonic and rhythmic framework . . . "; ". . . it became necessary to reject all tonal, modal, and atonal organisation in order to leave the way free to organise only through the powers of improvisation."[5] After a 1981 concert of Derek Bailey-George Lewis (trombone) duets, I asked the guitarist how the two players organized their program of improvisations. He said, "Intuitively, largely. I mean, I know quite a lot about George, I think he knows quite a lot about me, and there are all sorts of essential ingredients like goodwill and mutual interests and interest in interests that are not mutual—endless ingredients. But how it's organized is largely intuitive. I played with George quite a few times over the last eighteen months, but I never rehearsed with him."[4] Free improvisers like Bailey and Evan Parker spend their time playing solo or with one musical unit after another, seldom making regular affiliations. Though they recurringly play with certain musicians, the contexts are different each time they meet again.

Ordinarily the tenor saxophone is the most communicative of all the traditionally used jazz instruments. Its construction makes it among the easiest of instruments to manipulate fluently; its octave and dynamic ranges and the resonance and weight of its sound offer its player unrivaled scope of emotion, line, and expression. These classic tenor qualities are what Evan Parker has abandoned. He plays the soprano probably even more frequently than the tenor; the same descriptions apply to his work on both. Every note he plays is distorted, none is in an identifiable pitch; his sound is ever coarse, either shrilling or scraping. His phrases are in coarse, tiny chips, almost pulverized into fragments. Circular breathing techniques are characteristic: unbroken harsh tones which he assaults with multiphonics or inhumanly long, inflected arpeggio trills. Amid the keening and twittering of his long a cappella soprano solos "Aerobatics," "Fingerprints," and *Monoceros,* the recurrence of certain techniques such as these offers structural touchpoints. Even though his solo forms don't follow fixed routes, they tend to be flowing, perfectly logical, as in his mighty tenor assault that opens "Every One of Us Is a Pearl." "Abracadaver" opens with a violent squabble of barely audible subtone tenor gurgles, though eventually this phantasmagoria reaches almost "real" phrases before the fluttering overtones and downward stabs.

Somehow Greg Goodman manages to accompany this on piano; better yet, in *Real Time* Alvin Curran, on piano and synthesizer, provides not just support and color but irritation for Parker. Even more impressive than the prodigious energy level of his music is his concentration of energies. The conjunctions of conflicts in "Aerobatics," especially as they converge in the final stages, result in a form that proposes a hellish Sonny Rollins. But Evan Parker's harrowing, exacerbated streams of sound are not perverse; the internal logic of his responses to others and especially to his own ideas reveals a clearheaded, angry vision that is all the more fearsome for its single-minded intensity.

Even when Derek Bailey plays electric guitar, he plays softly, in sprinkles of sound that do not immediately reveal continuity. In his 1974 duets with Anthony Braxton, the quiet pinging and blipping of the guitar provide a fantasy that's elaborate in its way, a strangely empathetic accompaniment that responds with surprising quickness. Then in "Sarinu," a sunny duet with clarinetist Tony Coe, Bailey's lines glitter over the high ranges of his guitar, dissonant and spiky; rather amazingly he gives the illusion of playing in the same range, tonal areas, and forward momentum as Coe while maintaining imprecision of pitch and rhythm. Under any circumstances, Bailey loves to offer high detail, yet the album with Coe is unhurried. But Han Bennink, who turns Ornette Coleman's violin aesthetic into tirelessly extravagant percussion, clarinet, fiddle, etc., lunacy, inspires Bailey to very distant sorts of flamenco, rock, ballad, and raga playing; when he is spare and spaced over the volcanic drums of "Umberto Who?," Bennink suddenly halts, as if astonished at the guitarist's imperturbable distance. Yet another aspect of Derek Bailey is stimulated to intense duets, thoughtfully evolving, by Steve Lacy; in "Abandoned 2" the guitarist abstracts phrases from the first soprano improvisation to initiate his own close, dramatic thematic improvisation. The most impressive feature of Bailey's duetting is his instinctive senses of empathy, contrast, yet at the same time, distance; without violating his own world of sound and motion, he provides an uncanny sensitivity to his changing circumstances.

His solo album *Aida* is no less extroverted, even though his playing remains at a low-volume level. There's a passage in "Niigata Snow" of agitated, dissonant arpeggios through which high, delicate tones are interspersed in a separate, gentle line of commentary: yin and yang at one. The kaleidoscopic "Paris" has, here and there, faint suggestions of all kinds of idioms and forms. There's an early climax of riff chording that quickly becomes hard-struck chords in a one-player call-response passage; late in "Paris" this is reflected in urgently struck, bell-like chords, but in fact, the solo's organization is wholly freewheeling; he is no less sensitive to himself than he has been to other players.

The recordings with Lacy and Bennink come from various Company weeks that Derek Bailey has presented annually in London since the mid-seventies (and in New York in 1982). These are several consecutive nights of totally improvised music by Bailey and musicians he's worked with in the preceding year:

> Usually there are eight to twelve musicians. Everybody will have played with at least one person, sometimes two, but most of the people there they will not have played with before, though they might be familiar with each other's work in different ways. I usually try to introduce one person that *I* haven't worked with either. What they have in common is that they all, at some time or other, work through free improvisation. We meet each evening before the performance and discuss what groupings we will make for that evening. With ten people, I find that most of the groups are threes and fours. So throughout the week we usually never play as a ten-piece group; in fact, it very rarely gets over six.
>
> There are many interests that week for me. One of them is the way that alliances and aversions shift and realign. Anyway, we do that every night for five nights. The only thing that's constant is the method of working through free improvisation.[4]

Larger groups make for obscured interplay, so the small Company gatherings are the most revealing. One of the best is the 1980 quartet of *Fables:* the shattering Evan Parker, the sober and sly George Lewis, bassist Dave Holland, a lyricist amid unlyrical circumstances, and Bailey, who seems to resist his compatriots yet somehow manages to project the general ensemble flow in his own distant terms.

He points out that there are one or two younger free improvisation generations since his own. American expatriate Tristan Honsinger, one of the rising masters, plays cello brilliantly, even madly. In his *Earmeals* duets with Günter Christmann he begins with bowed birdcalls and goes lyrically on to energetic lines that suggest love of twentieth-century classical music (Ernest Bloch is apparently one of his special favorites). Surely Honsinger is the most theatrical cellist since Pablo Casals; sometimes he scats with his playing, and in one "Earmeal" he plays the cello while stomping his feet, moaning, and groaning in a Keith Jarrett parody. Among the younger American musicians in free improvisation circles, the techniques of string instrumentalists like Eugene Chadbourne and Henry Kaiser are surely Derek Bailey-inspired to some extent, a case of, finally, our own avant-garde improvisers' discovering their voices with help from European influences.

·12·

Leo Smith, Anthony Braxton, Joseph Jarman, and Roscoe Mitchell

"Jazz is the art of the young" goes the old cliché; most of the major jazz artists achieved an early maturity and made their greatest discoveries before they were thirty. This hasn't necessarily been true since Ornette Coleman opened the door to the vast possibilities of the present jazz era, perhaps because of the high degree of sophistication required in order to cope with the demands of outside jazz. When the AACM was new, the young Leo Smith, Anthony Braxton, Joseph Jarman, and Roscoe Mitchell dealt in totally Free improvising and also the opposite approach to music making—totally composed scores. They were investigating all the possible mixtures of improvisation and composition as well. "Primarily you [the AACM artist] sought to create pieces of music that were multi-textured and multi-structured," says Smith.[1] It was specifically this search that led to these four Chicagoans' discoveries of the 1970s and '80s. By now they're among the old masters of Free jazz; it's their explorations that best illuminate the frontiers of today's jazz.

Leo Smith was born in 1941 in Leland, Mississippi, blues

country, the Mississippi delta. In the sixth grade he began playing trumpet in the school band and soon was playing for cakewalks held by local social clubs. His stepfather is Little Bill Wallace, a prominent blues guitarist and bandleader in the area and in recent years a regular performer at mid-South blues festivals. Leo himself formed a blues band in his early teens, playing classics from the repertoires of post-Mississippi masters like John Lee Hooker, Elmore James, Howling Wolf: "My stepfather's blues was more in the range of Albert King and B. B. King, but ours was much more of a rural type of experience." The teenage band rehearsed hard for its first gig, and:

> All during the week all of them had made the rehearsal. That afternoon I walked to my friends' houses that were playing in the band, and they had got discouraged by their mothers, so they didn't want to play. So that night all the riffs and lines we had worked out for three horns had to be, some way, performed by the trumpet. I learned then that the individual is alone, that you cannot depend on anyone else, and that lesson has carried through to today.
>
> Earlier in the week I had asked my stepfather if I could play with him; he said, "Impossible, no way." He was playing in the same town I was playing in—this was Hollandale, Mississippi—about two blocks from me. On his intermission he came around to hear us, and he was quite surprised at what was happening. From then on, when I wasn't working with anybody else, I was playing with him.[2]

After high school, Leo Smith joined the army: "Since I wanted to go to Japan, and they always keep their promise, they kept me in the southern United States." He spent five years in five army bands, in frequent trouble with his immediate superiors not only for protesting racial conditions—successfully, for two protests to the judge advocate general resulted in official policy changes—but for the jazz he was beginning to play: In an army band in France he had to talk a director out of disciplining him for the way he improvised. It was also in the army that a fellow bandsman led him to the music of Ornette Coleman and, more important to Smith, Don Cherry. After the army he moved to Chicago, in 1967, and discovered the AACM; then, after his experiences in Europe with Anthony Braxton's group, he settled in New Haven, Connecticut, in 1970. He chose to live in New England partly at the urging of altoist Marion Brown, with whom he had begun playing regularly; another reason was: "I grew up in a small town and I did a lot of research on Charles Ives, Carl Ruggles, and on Ralph Waldo Emerson, Henry David Thoreau, and Frederick Douglass. I felt a sense of spiritual birth in America coming from these people on this part of the East Coast. I figured that would be the type of society I wanted to live in."[2]

He began to reveal a remarkable poise in his early-seventies recordings. Singing over the cymbal tides of "Young at Heart," sharply contrasting with, and even mocking, his changing accompaniments in "No More White Gloves," he balanced the ensembles by offering contrasts—his calmness against their fire; his heat against their rubato. His duets with Marion Brown are impressive for the quickness and sensitivity with which he evolves counterpoint and also for his blasting, intense phrases drawing away from the deceptive, incipient melancholy of his long and bent tones. His detachment certainly embodies the philosophic self-awareness of the individual player amid changing external and internal circumstances, and the objective of this kind of sensitivity— to bring not just balance but the balance that provides meaning to the musical contexts—indicates a self-awareness that's as neoclassical as Rollins, and in its way, as profound. The materials of his style are firmly set by his 1970 recordings. He cites as his trumpet influences, besides Don Cherry, the silences and long tones of Miles Davis ("a sense of purity") and the lyric abstraction of Booker Little. His essential techniques of contrast and spaced sounds, and the activity of his lines makes an obvious, happy connection to his friend from Chicago Lester Bowie, even though it's their differences that are most revealing: Bowie is a dramatic, wholly emotive artist, whereas Smith is a wholehearted lyricist.

There is no greater test of an individual's powers of creation in organization than an unaccompanied solo performance. Leo Smith recorded two solo albums, in 1971 and 1979. He seems to conceive of his a cappella solos as total lines, in a far from classical form: "My pieces are multi-improvisations—my first note is the development and climax already. I don't go from point to point because the points are already inherent in the start."[2] Some of these solos seem almost perfect: "Ep–1," totally in abstract mouthpiece and lip sounds; the clear-toned call and distorted response of "Aura"; the growth of "Nine Stones on a Mountain" ("little instruments" further his line in this) and "Love Is a Rare Beauty" through isolated tones and phrases in the fluid medium of space. His playing seems thoroughly abstract, partly because of his extraordinary resistance to recapitulation; the flow of his line includes contrasts and juxtapositions instead. Instead of riffs, recollected phrases, fixed responses or calls, there is space, as fluid as the varied lengths of his phrases.

It is this very alive space that separates and joins his sounds into statements. He says:

> You know how Lester Young tried to deal with the saxophone tradition of Coleman Hawkins? He couldn't *find* that way. And I haven't, from the very beginning, been able to get away from the silences. I organized a system, the rhythm unit system, based off of silence. . . . For me, a whole sound or a whole rhythm is dual; it's divided up into the audible property and the inaudible property—that is, the sound you hear and the sound you don't hear. In this system, whatever value that's given to any of the units must be equivalent, in a relative

sense, to the degree of silence that will be played from that sound. . . . If I play a tone that's approximately three beats long, I would forward that sound with approximately three beats of silence.[2]

One of his two monographs, *Rhythm*, illustrates his rhythm unit systems with exercises: "Those nine elements of rhythm are the shaping of sound *and* silence."[2] It's important that the rhythm unit system is something he deduced after listening to tapes of his improvising. The method follows the man. His basic attitude is an organic one. The calm tension of sound and silence is a force of nature, like the drops of water that become a trickle, then a stream, and eventually alter the landscape. The result is a virtually exclusive devotion to creating beauty. It is a devotion implicit in the choices of jazz musicians ever since Lester Young, yet Smith's joining of stylistic elements has no obvious precedent in the jazz tradition, so for some listeners the lack of conventional emotional impulse may suggest a kind of asceticism. For the rest of us the music is thoroughly graceful and the results all pleasing.

Leo Smith's other monograph, *Notes (8 Pieces)*, includes his concept of ensemble playing. Each player is an autonomous entity. The "center of the improvisation is continuously changing, depending on the force created by individual centers at any instance. . . . The idea is that each improviser creates as an element of the whole, only responding to that which is creating within himself instead of responding to the total creative energy of the different units. This attitude frees the sound-rhythm elements in an improvisation from being realized through dependent re-action . . . there is no intent towards time as a period of development."[3] This is a unique concept all right. It's related to the practices of Anthony Braxton's first two combo LPs, in which Smith played, and of Derek Bailey's ideas. It is, of course, a perilous approach; in two of the motley groups Bailey introduces in *Company 6,* only the edgy clarity of Smith's trumpet provides coherence. But in general, for Leo Smith this attitude is anything but a denial of ensemble unity. For example, in the *Touch the Earth* trio, Smith's measured lines are a perfect counterpoint to the melodrama of bassist Peter Kowald. Some of his best trumpet playing is in his meetings with Oliver Lake's alto. His poise sounds insolent as Lake snaps at him with wounded cries in their priceless "Picric Wobble" duet. "Song of Humanity" begins with Wes Brown's somber, disturbing bass solo, to which the muted trumpet's cadences provide a long-toned, warming contrast; Lake enters with a primitive cry of welcome and wrenched, broken melodies before Smith, again muted, returns to play an elegy; the piece is perfectly shaded, and only the concluding rubato piano is in the least conventional.

Smith's instinct for ensemble balance and his responsiveness, for all the sense of independence that he projects, are the most sensitive kind of jazz ensemble playing—the kind of improvising Joe Smith offered with Bessie Smith, or Johnny Dodds and George Mitchell with various mid-twenties bands. Some recordings by his New Dalta Akhri groups expand his own sensitivity among several players. Bassist Brown and pianist Anthony Davis join Smith in the "Reflectativity" flow of harmonic and rhythmic textures; the intimacy is wonderful. Here and in "Illuminations: The Nguzo Saba" and the *Divine Love* pieces Smith brings what seems a telepathic sense of precisely defined degrees of changing intensity to his combos. The perfection in "Images" was perhaps not easily arrived at. Some passages are wholly improvised, some wholly scored, and for the most part any from one to four players improvise while the rest play from the score. The flow of forward movement—in the absence of pulse, or pulses; Smith says "velocities"—and the ensemble balance change from moment to moment; space narrows and separates; the five players (and nine instruments) move together and apart. Always there is respect for space, both ensemble space and the personal space of the individuals; the responding of the players, each to the others, is a small miracle.

The same is true of "The Burning of Stones," except that here the instrumentation is most rare—three harps and a muted trumpet—and for all the delicacy of texture, the activity is in multiple levels, with ever-changing individual velocities; only Smith sounds truly pastoral here. A big band plays "Return to My Native Land II," a journey through flowing textures and shapes: The full ensemble weight progressively narrows to lower ranges and sparser groupings, then a twisted, snarled Lake alto solo, then trumpet blasts, a forest of flutes, a bass clarinet solo, the ring and sparkle of vibes, and at last imposing big band chords over percussion that agitates to a passage of wild collective improvisation. In these compositions as much as in his improvised works, Smith's beauty is joyous. Some of his compositions have yet to be recorded; others, including some played by a big band that he and Roscoe Mitchell led in 1980, have been recorded but not yet released. They are eagerly awaited, for his serenity and beauty are as true to the possibilities of life as his many tortured musical opposites.

Leo Smith's three woodwind associates from Chicago—Braxton, Jarman, and Mitchell—had already met as students at Wilson Junior College, in the early 1960s. They are disparate individuals whose musical choices are often quite unlike each other's. Again and again down through the years they've inspired, irritated, joined with, rivaled, or otherwise stimulated each other to some of their most valuable discoveries. Anthony Braxton is the youngest of the three by several years; he was born in 1945 in Chicago, and as early as 1966, while he was stationed in an army band in Korea, he acquired a personal voice through his perceptive adaptation of later Coltrane to the alto saxophone. He returned to Chicago at the end of that year and discovered an AACM jazz scene where sonic and structural exploration, unaccompanied horn solos, and the abandonment of ensemble roles—rhythm sectionless ensembles, for instance—were commonplace. His progress was swift. He began playing other woodwinds besides the alto, moved from playing in tempos to an approximation of Roscoe Mitchell's ensemble methods, wrote totally composed scores, and played a solo alto composition by Henry Threadgill in a concert, all this in little more than a year. He consciously sought to shed his devotion to Coltrane; in 1968 he arrived at the Free improvisation idiom of *Three Compositions*, and he also began recording the solos of *For Alto*. For all these thrusts in promising directions, Braxton was not satisfied:

> When I was in Chicago, we were working with certain principles; it wasn't fashionable to function in certain areas of music. In the AACM, the basic emphasis was on improvisatory structure, and because of the intensity of certain discoveries, I focused on these aspects. The rate of new information was so dynamic, I was learning so much from Roscoe and Joseph, that I was trying to find my own space, lest I become completely gobbled up by the enormity of what they were developing. I didn't want to simply copy them, but rather, I wanted to develop a viewpoint which would hopefully be as meaningful.[4]

The first demonstration of his depth and range is *For Alto*. The continuity in his unaccompanied solos derives from his strictly controlling the syntax of each. Thus the dedication to John Cage is in furiously burning energy lines; "Murray De Pillars" is in trills and longer note values; "Ann and Peter Allen" is slow and played subtone; "Kenny McKenny" is in distorted, nonconsecutive tones. His kinship with Jarman, even without Jarman's technique, is evident in the dedications to Leroy Jenkins and De Pillars, and in the dramatic dynamic contrasts of the latter the characteristic Braxton vibrato first appears, with ripe, juicy notes that bend in the middle. His form is free association, and one of his main lines of growth is the increasing quality and variety of stuff that he came to associate freely over the years. His series of "104° Kelvin" solos is in a repetition/evolution style that certainly suggests composer Philip Glass—the first of them (1971) is dedicated to Glass—but Braxton's ideas are intrinsically so much more vigorous than Glass's. The long "JMK-80 CFN-7"* (1971), dedicated to Maurice McIntyre, is an important step because it's an extravaganza of Braxton's sound distortion and alteration methods, sustained by a high tension that admits free space and all kinds of quick velocity and dynamic shifts. By his wonderful 1979 solos he could even look back with some humor at his early art: "KSZMK" passes through multiple stages of anger, from outrage to sarcasm to fury, by way of subtones, growls, and squalls that mock his early subservience to Coltrane.

At least in the sixties, his adventures in small groups lagged behind his progress in solo organization and invention. There were two early free-improvisation efforts, *Three Compositions* and *Anthony Braxton,* both with Leo Smith and violinist Leroy Jenkins, who went to Europe with him in 1969. In Paris he met a rhythm section, Chick Corea, David Holland, and Barry Altschul, that followed him closely, stimulated him ingeniously, and loved rhythmic risks; the four of them became Circle, and they stayed together for a year. In fact, the lyrical yet driving bassist Holland stayed with Braxton for at least seven years, and Altschul, whose most vital drumming extends the nervous, explosive energy of Tony Williams, played with them for most of that time. It may have been

---

* This is only an approximation of this title. The vast majority of Braxton's pieces are titled with diagrams and, in later years, drawings to which letters and numbers are attached. Leo Smith tells us, ". . . any advanced student of mysticism or metaphysical science can readily read the code and symbolism embedded in his titles."[5] But they are nonverbal, in any case.

the security of playing with Holland that enabled Braxton to make great strides forward with his clarinet and alto. There'ᵉ a twenty-seven-minute Moers Festival version of "6 ——— 77AR–36K (NJD) T" that swings madly, Braxton's alto voraciously devouring the beat. Holland's propulsion is terrific; Braxton plays ahead of the beat, and thus ahead of the bass, and this combined with his shifting of accents makes him sound airy and liberated, for all his furious energy.

To some extent Braxton's headlong attack is a legacy of his immersion in Coltrane, but in the month before this 1974 recording he played a solo that shows a newly emerging kinship. That solo is in "Marshmallow," a bubbling abstraction in displaced accents by tenorist Warne Marsh, and Braxton's subtly disorienting lines suggest Marsh's own playing as reinterpreted by Eric Dolphy angularities. A Lennie Tristano disciple in the late forties, Marsh is the purest of romantics, always with an eager prebeat attack and wildly spontaneous accenting. The raised eyebrow of Marsh peeps over such Braxton alto solos as "4038 – – NBS 373 6" (1975), with long lines turning savage over the brutal stop time, and the internal disputes of "H – 46M B-BW4," with un-Marsh-like cycles of fiercely entangled, exasperated honking. The nasty passages of this and so many other Braxton solos are not just a post-Coltrane convention. His "Embraceable You" is a free-association fantasy that's a bitter, sarcastic commentary on the standard theme, arhythmic, strongly stated, often harshly intoned; here's evidence of a cruel streak that's more than artifice. One way he increased in power in the seventies was the degree to which he measured his episodes of squalling and sound distortion, frustration and anger.

Most of his major work is on alto sax, but almost from the beginning he joined the other Chicago saxmen in doubling on many woodwinds. More than Jarman, Mitchell, or Kalaparush, it is Braxton who reattracted popular attention to the expressive versatility of the clarinet; his solo in "BFG-12 46842 337-4" is a fine example, flashing wildly with sounds and contrasts. He plays soprano and sopranino saxes at least as often; the continuously mobile textures of "2M K F" are his four overdubbed sopraninos. The Charlie Parker themes he plays on contrabass clarinet sound like mastodons attempting to jitterbug; the instrument's range is so low that notes tend to emerge as monotones. His most engaging quality is his nervous vitality, which he brings to all his instruments. He's absorbed all kinds of modern musical ideas from everywhere imaginable, from bop and Free jazz to postwar classical composers to sixties rhythm and blues. All this results from a romantic attitude that keeps finding new worlds to explore as well as familiar forms to revisit and refreshen.

Surely Braxton has played with the most varied collection of musicians this side of Don Cherry. Among the other horns in his straight-ahead combos have been trumpeters Kenny Wheeler and the joyful Hugh Ragin and the exuberant trombones of George Lewis and flamboyant Ray Anderson. He's brought his outside art to bop era contexts with his *In the Tradition* LPs and with people like Dave Brubeck. His totally improvised duets with Max Roach are straight-ahead works, whereas in his chamber jazz works, no players assume a rhythm section function: trios with Richard Teitelbaum's synthesizers and either Anderson or Leo Smith; duets with Muhal Richard Abrams's piano, with Derek Bailey's sensitive guitar, investigative duets with Roscoe Mitchell, ponderous, overdubbed duets with Joseph Jarman, passionate duets on standards with David Holland. Some of this prodigious activity is extremely valuable and some is not. What's consistent is his quality of enthusiasm, with his combination of sophistication and innocence, and, at best, a swift, sardonically inclined wit.

There is his composing. He wrote rather Ornette Cole-

man-like themes for his Chicago combos, but his natural tendency to eschew simplicity led to this kind of material's being
elongated and complicated. Eventually it led to marvelous
multipart themes such as "6 ———— 77AR–36K (NJD) T," the
themes in his *Montreux/Berlin* album, the meandering, diminished, paranoid theme of "4038–NBS 373 6." He also
began presenting fully composed pieces, but only after some
real struggles: "I have 10, 11, or 12 early compositions that
were completed by the end of 1967. But in that time zone it
was very difficult to get performances of totally notated compositions. What I would do was save up money and pay musicians to rehearse some of my music, so I could hear it; I did
the same in Paris. My biggest problem as a composer was
that I never got to hear nine tenths of the music I was writing."[4] Two of his long compositions advance his improvising
combos' methods. In *For Trio* (1977) and *Composition 98*
(1981) he begins to discover the unity in independence that
was missing from his sixties free-improvisation recordings. No
features of these are sustained for very long; the players in
these abstract works are given alternative abstractions to
play if they wish, and occasionally improvisation appears as
what Braxton calls "creative-sound-bursts"; the players are
constantly moving from instrument to instrument. *Composition 98* sounds, on record, more texturally consistent than
its predecessor, I suspect mainly because the players are Braxton's touring quartet (Ragin, Anderson, pianist Marilyn Crispell), who, through extensive experience in the music, invest
it with spirit and continuity.

For Two Pianos is completely different. The pianists double on melodicas and percussion briefly, but otherwise there
is no instrument switching. This is not a succession of colors,
fragments, little forays; instead, the composition flows in long
lines. There's one passage of hard-struck, four-handed chords
that die away in space; otherwise the harmonic textures are
uniquely spare, and all the energy is linear. It is so effec-

tive because its lyricism is unalloyed; on the record, the pianists let Braxton's music sing for itself. Of his large orchestra pieces, only the largest, *For Four Orchestras,* has been recorded. Here are abstractly associated sounds, textures, lines bouncing back and forth among four symphonies (160 musicians in all) for two hours—not the content but the form (alternating movements in fragments and in long note values) determine the length.

The sprawl of *For Four Orchestras,* its post-Webern idiom, and the textures and densities of its symphony instrumentation make it formidable. And monumentality is what Braxton intended. *For Four Orchestras* is the only completed work thus far in a series that will include pieces for 6, 8, 10 orchestras each in a different city, linked by satellite, then 100 orchestras. Thereafter Braxton hopes that humanity's outer space travel will be advanced enough to accommodate his compositions' linking orchestras on several planets, several solar systems (by 1995!) and then several galaxies. And why not? If the human race survives the next millennium, Anthony Braxton would be a great choice to provide the music for the celebration.

Just imagine the celebrants on all the planets in all the galaxies cheering to an all-American parade march like Braxton's "22 H03 M," infiltrated by Free soloists: Leo Smith's smudges of trumpet sound, George Lewis's antic trombone, and then Braxton's agitated clarinet over band textures that grow progressively more separate and dissonant. These big jazz band pieces by Braxton are his major compositions to date, the best proof of his ingenuity with sound colors and forms. Some pieces recall Sun Ra—mid-fifties Ra in the post-hard bop, augmented lines of "Z-42 0-500 NWK"; later Ra in the slow, weighty, melancholy line before the bass sax duet of "Q 473 NB-12." This and "G-10 62 Z04 K" are without main lines of discourse or dramatic organization, in the medium of joined disparities of *For Trio. Creative Orchestra Music 1976* closes with the desolate prophecy of "CD-4 P FKB": Broken sounds lead to Roscoe Mitchell's splintered, sputtered alto tones; grim disconnected chords lead to Braxton's acerbic, ugly chattering on sopranino; the piece dissolves in eternal hopelessness. Braxton certainly knows the odds against intergalactic celebration; in "CD-4 P FKB" he provides the opposite, a terrible threnody for humanity's funeral.

There may be no better demonstration of the inadequacy of jazz documents than the recording career of Joseph Jarman after the 1960s. He's recorded less frequently than Smith, Braxton, and Roscoe Mitchell, and while his albums are good ones, they don't reveal the depth of his advances over the years. From the beginning he offered a nonpareil mastery of the alto saxophone, with not only a brilliant, golden sound but also a precise control of the "freak" ranges of overtones and multiphonics. He often plays in wide, wild leaps that touch high harmonics, middle and low registers in a flash, each tone exactly delineated; amazingly he often brings mastery of this quality to his other saxophones as well. Moreover, he's a master of several different, original styles, and as his work with the Art Ensemble of Chicago shows, he's a theatrical, even flamboyant musician. His emotionality is subtle yet, in its way, direct: lyric abstraction, reasoned love, gentlemanly or primitive anger, satiric humor; at best he makes the meanings of the adjectives clear, without mixed emotions. His finest large compositions for large ensembles are natural outgrowths of a unique instinct for line determining texture, color, and form; in this he is the superior of Braxton and Muhal Richard Abrams. But none of these Jarman compositions has been recorded.

In the 1980s Jarman has become a more consistently excellent player than ever before. He is rather less flamboyant now; he's inclined to create pure streams of structured melody that, for all their elegance, teem with life-giving movement. His is a kind of aristocratic elegance that derives from the contours of vital lines and forms. In duets, he likes to weave luxurious tapestries of variations to surround the other horn's music, often derived from the other player's ideas. Some of his best music lately has been in the company of the drummer Reggie Nicholson; again, none of this is on records. There are some recent recorded examples of Jarman in his most creative mood—a tense, swinging, eager tenor solo in "Happiness Is"; an elaborate clarinet solo in "Urban Magic"—but not many. I'm afraid that until he is more frequently documented on his own, away from the Art Ensemble, he will remain one of our unacknowledged legislators.

Fortunately, Roscoe Mitchell's development as a saxophonist has been reasonably well documented. There is a cruel edge to even the most lyrical of his early alto concepts, such as the "Old" solo in which blues phrases alternate with simple, drifting outside lines. In "Number One," he begins with slow, sweet, rubato melodies, a vision of utter romance that turns melancholy in descent; his tone begins to coarsen, and recriminations, then anger arise from a broken, speeding, nagging line; a volley of funky insults calms, after the trumpet intervenes, to satiric blurting on two saxes simultaneously. The unaccompanied solo "TKHKE" is organized along the same general lines, with far less specific emotional referents; his intensity is ecstatic in the wildly changing moods of his later passages. What distinguishes Mitchell's solo work of the sixties is its ever-changing, many-sided character.

As we've seen, he spent most of 1969–71 in Europe with the Art Ensemble of Chicago. Back in the United States, he was the first Art Ensemble member to establish his primary career away from the group; he removed himself geographically, too, settling in rural Michigan. The ironic edge and formal inclusiveness had begun to disappear from his art as early as his European stay, and by his mid-seventies record-ings he was very definitely an iconoclast. Gone were the swift successions of moods; in their place he now played careful investigations of surprising thematic material—distant inter-vals, space, sonic characteristics unique to his horns—in which all but the central musical elements were extin-guished. His lyricism almost vanishes or sinks down into a bass saxophone in "Eeltwo"; his alto dances through "Line Fine Lyon 7," but the piece lasts only a minute. Mitchell is more interested in the extreme overtone keening of "7 Be-hind 9 97 or 7" and in the faint horn exhalations and space that are the content of "Enlorfe" and "Tnoona." Space is the crucial utensil to him now, leading to the most radical kind of linear fragmentation. Solos like "Jibbana" and "Oobina (Lit-tle Big Horn)" offer a dire isolation of sounds, and then in the various pieces titled "Cards" other players create motes of sound with him.

In method he is not so very far removed from Leo Smith's music. But while Smith's work of the period is the statement of the most patient, equanimous individual in Free Jazz, Mit-chell is always conscious of the immensity of what he is doing. All his drastic fragmentation stems from his very first Free document: He is separating the linear and timbral dis-coveries of *Sound* and making each component the subject of a separate investigation. Not only his own post-*Sound* reali-zations but the entire Western musical tradition had become irrelevant to him. What he needed was a completely new syntax, a new logic, a reordering of fundamentals, to accom-modate and communicate visions that he was only beginning to see. Albert Ayler's insights weren't enough: Ayler had dis-covered only sound, whereas Mitchell had discovered space, the means with which sound's mysteries are revealed. Abso-lutely there is no relation between him and fashionable mini-malist composers like Glass and Steve Reich; the acuteness of his search is the opposite of their manipulation of effects. His position is a lonely one, analogous, suggests critic Larry Kart, to that of medieval composers of Guillaume Dufay's era, when polyphony and harmony were yet new ideas in Europe:

> Their musical world was one in which the component parts of Western music were still vigorously independent. And that independence was the quality their music was trying to elaborate and preserve.
>
> Because Roscoe Mitchell's music, too, is homing in on first principles, it is natural that his work should resemble compositions that were created when Western music was taking shape. And in the process, he is discovering anew that when music is truly broken down into its component parts, a new order can emerge.[6]

The emergence of a new order becomes slowly more evident as the seventies pass. "Tahquemenon" is a successor to "Cards," but the interplay of autonomous parts is closer, far more coherent. In "A1 TAL2 LA" Malachi Favors's stately bowed bass line is actually enhanced by the alto's distance and fragmentation. In light of Mitchell's early work, the exclusive concentration of so much of his music in this period might seem to be a form of self-denial. The intrinsic fascination of solos like "Enlorfe" and "Jibbana" results from great internal tension, and if this tension is not released, the player is flirting with insanity. The explosions come in 1976 with "Ericka" and in 1977 with "Improvisation I." Their surface intensity is extraordinary. If totally free improvisation, unaccompanied, results in the truest baring of the artist's heart, then the steadily growing brutality of "Improvisation I" is downright frightening: It begins in harshness and ends in a blur of fanatic motion. "Ericka" is more frightening because it begins with loving elaborations of a beautiful Jarman melody, so the ensuing savagery seems the more vicious. Surely these two long solos are the most violent saxophone utterances since Coltrane. Interestingly, the general outlines are, for Mitchell, almost classic ones: "Improvisation I" is "TKHKE" turned vicious, while Jarman's own (unrecorded) early "Erickas" provided a model for this Mitchell version.

Through the seventies in the evolution of the "Nonaah" pieces you can hear Mitchell's new vision of music acquiring shape and significance. All the "Nonaahs," says Mitchell, "come from the same world or atmosphere ... Nonaah is a fictional character that I've come up with.... I suppose it could apply to me in a given situation or someone else.... The thing about Nonaah is that once you put yourself in that atmosphere you can ride on forever. The world has the properties of very large skips and it has notes that have accidental properties that are kept."[7] He composed the first "Nonaah" for the Art Ensemble in 1973, the year he began playing "Nonaahs" as small, staccato encores in solo alto concerts; the agitations and perversities of the period are crystallized in these brief, fierce pieces, like the spasmodically jerking one at the Pori, Finland, festival. The 1976 Willisau, Switzerland, performance was a crucial event, when Mitchell was a last-minute replacement on the festival program. Here he creates interplay with an unruly audience by repeating a tangled "Nonaah" phrase sixty-six times, at first to increasing jeers; with the forty-third repeat he is smearing tones, to a sudden cheer of recognition; even so, not until nearly seven minutes into the performance does he finally release tension by playing another phrase. But this is just a third of this "Nonaah"; not only are there two subsequent movements, but one is even legato, in lengthened note values.

Clearly "Nonaah" has expanded drastically. It is this three-movement form that is the outline for the alto sax quartet version, the fullest recorded revelation of "Nonaah's" world. The first movement is an endless perpetual motion machine; the legato movement is saxes slowly bobbing up and down in sweet-sour polyphony; the third movement begins in repetition again, but this time the constituent mechanisms grow increasingly awry until the music is a whirling babble. "Nonaah" has now become a parable of disintegration—by the end only centrifugal force contains the primitive, dangerous turbulence—but despite the finality of the concluding chord, its story is not yet finished: In the same period Mitchell was busy composing further "Nonaahs" for a string quartet, an orchestra, and a saxophone family quartet.

And now come an extension and expansion of the small, primordial sound properties of "Enlorfe." *S II Examples* is breath blown thrown through a soprano saxophone; the breath touches tones, timbres but faintly, gains subtone incarnation; the long, quiet timbres move slowly, almost imperceptibly, entirely in microtones and harmonics, in a tiny saxophone range. Nuance becomes the whole of a music which exists in an exalted atmosphere of calm, quiet meditation. Here is a long form, unlike any other form, to concretize the capabilities of *these* sounds. *S II* is one player with one instrument; the next step is three players with sixteen horns, and in fact, Mitchell composed *L-R-G* for three specific sound explorers: himself, Leo Smith, and George Lewis.

The form of *L-R-G* is what Mitchell calls sound collages. They are brightly lit, in constant motion; long and short, bent, modified, or straight tones, independent runs, one-note blasts, and so on—all exist alone or simultaneously, meet, mingle, draw away. There are structural touchpoints in very long, usually low tones by one or more men, even though the flow of velocities and brass-woodwind sound characters is ever-changing. More than anything else, *L-R-G* resembles a slowly revolving kaleidoscope. It is wholly composed, however freely interpreted, and in all the conjunctions of players there is no sense of harmony, rhythm, or melody. Because it is a succession of events, its method may seem related to Braxton's *For Trio*, but *L-R-G* is a whole piece, a vision, next to the looser Braxton work. There are aggressions, frustrations, and also sustained combinations in *For Trio*. *L-R-G* is free from agitation. Moreover, Mitchell not only chooses nothing but simultaneous autonomies, he finds fulfillment in the separateness of the musical lives. *L-R-G* is an existentialist statement, a condition of life, a state of being; it is Mitchell's most intimate revelation.

While the twentieth century is the era of percussion compositions, from Varèse to Stockhausen and Wuorinen, they all seem naïve *tours de force* next to the immense skill and finesse of *The Maze*. Mitchell composed it as a celebration of the originality of eight Chicago percussion virtuosos playing hundreds of standard and self-invented instruments, from ordinary drum kits to Henry Threadgill's hubkaphone, Braxton's sloshing can machine, and all kinds of bells, marimbas, gongs, rattles, frying pans, and whatnots. It is a startling composition. Again the form is sound collages, with no sustained aggressive passages; just the opposite, *The Maze* is a rich chiaroscuro of clearly defined, mobile wood and metal textures, with a great elegance of detail. *L-R-G* is a world of shared separatenesses; its antithesis is *The Maze*, a world of joinings that's as near to lyricism as percussion music comes. It may be a no less intimate composition, for it predicts some aspects of Mitchell's eighties music.

Today Mitchell's explorations of sound characters continue; in Gerald Oshita's "Textures for Trio" he joins in throbbing, sustained, very low bass clef harmonies under the scat countertenor singing of Tom Buckner. In fact, sound investigations are the special province of the Mitchell-Buckner-Oshita trio, and they continue in works like the "Cutouts" series by Mitchell's Sound Ensemble. This group is a quintet with trumpeter Hugh Ragin and a rhythm section, guitar, bass, and drums, of three longtime Mitchell associates from Michigan (though Mitchell has lived on a Wisconsin farm since 1977). The Sound Ensemble is an all-purpose group for which the leader writes pieces with multiple themes and juxtaposed characters; for example, the themes of

"Sing/Song" are a pastoral waltz, a fast staccato line. and a swinging medium-up melody. Like the outside rock pieces the Art Ensemble used to play, a number of Mitchell's recent works use catchy rock rhythms; in 1981 he revived a fifteen-year-old song, "JoJar"—the dedication is obvious—and set it to a rock rhythm.

The new element in Mitchell's music is sometimes manifest as an almost Jarman-like elaborateness, even elegance. You notice this when his alto solo follows Jarman's clarinet in "Urban Magic," and it is also in Mitchell's soprano phrasing in "Fanfare for Talib." The lyricism of the early Mitchell was edgy, tinged with irony. Today lyricism returns as an unalloyed musical quality, and in place of structural concerns he may well choose to play pure melody, on tenor in "Round Two," on alto in "JoJar" and "Snurdy McGurdy and Her Dancin' Shoes." Mitchell, Ragin, and drummer Tani Tabbal present gay, charming performances in *More Cutouts;* here the joinings and the lyricism are spontaneous. After the difficult route he chose in the seventies, and the discoveries that led to his triumphs in extended works, Mitchell's eighties choices are even surprising; clearly, the sensibility of this enormously vital artist is undergoing yet another transformation.

The California-based Rova Saxophone Quartet provide a rewarding addendum to Roscoe Mitchell's revelations. Their recordings are full of references to his pieces, especially the alto quartet version of "Nonaah" (for example, "Daredevils," "Trobar Clus"). The Rovas play multithematic pieces, sometimes themes and improvisations strung together, sometimes loosely. They like to divide into high and low sax pairs, to contrast straight and distorted sax sounds, and, in fact, to take all sorts of chances with space and sounds, in solos and in all possible combinations of four players and at least fifteen woodwinds. Their long pieces like "Ride upon the Belly of the

Waters" are veritable anthologies of sonic combinations and devices. Their very eclecticism and sometimes incongruity provide their own special values; solos, too, are sober, highly active, eclectic, at times imaginative, such as Andrew Voigt's pure-toned alto line, over soft, slow trilling, that somehow is both melancholy and sardonic in "That's How Strong." They are post-Chicago masters whose extravagance can sometimes yield aesthetic mistakes, like much of "Mal Que Arroz," but that's the chance you take when you're this daring.

·13·

Free Jazz Today

The main idioms of early jazz were stride piano and the New Orleans ensemble style. The swing generation was dominated by the big bands and Louis Armstrong's discoveries. Charlie Parker, bop, and hard bop were the mainstream of the bop era. These pre-Free decades of jazz had common ground in harmonic and rhythmic structures; except for the very earliest stylists, who could not join in a jam session on "I Got Rhythm" or the blues? By 1964 there was no such common ground among Free musicians. Try to imagine Coltrane playing "Ghosts" with Albert Ayler back then or Cecil Taylor joining in Ornette Coleman's "Ramblin'." The reason you cannot is that already these musicians represent four divergent idioms. Ever since the mid-sixties, it's been impossible to deduce a Free mainstream from the proliferation of unique musics. It's easy to see that modal and fusion musics were dead ends, but today do the other consequences of the revolution Coleman began a quarter century ago result in a thriving or languishing art?

For some listeners the present proliferation of artists' choices is alarming. There were traditionalists who thought that Louis Armstrong was subverting jazz; later critics wrote about how the allegedly European features of Ellington's and especially Gillespie's and Parker's musics were antiswing, antijazz noise. Today's heirs to this attitude raise the battle cry "Tradition!" in opposition to composers who create in large forms (heirs to Ellington's suites) and multi-instrumentalists who play extensively in Free time and space (antiswing). Horrors! Free musicians are not obeying the rules! Back in 1938, Jelly Roll Morton demonstrated how all kinds of musics went into the origins of jazz, from pop songs and marches to opera arias and Latin rhythms to, among newer African-American arts, ragtime and blues. To Free players, nonjazz musics such as blues, soul and rock musics, postwar classical musics, musical traditions from North and central Africa, Asia—these musics have been widely available on LPs in the West—can be just as significant in a Free player's current art as the jazz traditions. It's not just that griots (minstrels, poets, satirists) from Africa and master musicians from India have come to teach in America. Leading Free musicians have lived in Africa and the East for extended periods, experiencing the available local musics, participating in them, absorbing them into their own arts.

Pianist Ran Blake plays (as he tells his students) "an improvised synthesis of ethnic, cabaret, or Afro-American music with what has been called for the last few years European avant garde." He calls this third stream music, which is not exactly the same as the third stream composing of his friend Gunther Schuller. The result is shrewd artifice, in solos that concentrate contrasts of dynamics, harmonies, rhythmic values into usually small spaces. A very plastic sense of phrase spacing is his special tactic; setting, decoration, and revision are main elements in his pieces. It's an approach that makes for superior program music, as in his social document *The Blue Potato and Other Outrages*. There's an inherent dreamlike quality about his flux of emotions, a surrealism that can be gentle, sly, or acidulous. "Realization of a Dream" is just that, with his secret smile behind a succession of portraits from fantasy to nightmare. *Film Noir* is his dark arrangements

of movie memories, with a "Touch of Evil" that truly captures the starkness and phobia of the Orson Welles film.
Among his music's constituent elements, Blake's most obvious heritage is the jazz piano tradition from Hines to Monk
and Bill Evans, and he can certainly make cunning music.

The squashed trumpet with a bent mouthpiece that Don
Cherry plays on the early Ornette Coleman records is a Paki-
stani pocket trumpet. After Cherry's innovations with Coleman, Rollins, the New York Contemporary Five, and Ayler,
he began his long travels through the five continents, ingest-
ing and playing music wherever he went; "Oh, Don Cherry,
he's the Pied Piper," says Coleman. The Cherry-Edward
Blackwell duets (Blackwell himself lived a year in Morocco)
are free improvisations on catchy, folklike themes, the drummer's throb and high step setting off, sometimes leading
Cherry's piano rhythms, singing, and trumpet and wooden
flutes; by 1969 he had become reasonably versatile on small
African and Indian flutes. As a rule this music's harmonic
basis is modal, like the basis of his 1976 fusion albums, full of
studio gimmicks such as stacked rock rhythms à la Hancock.
There are Eastern and Western instruments on these LPs,
and the latter-day fusion trio Codona (Cherry, Collin Walcott, Nana Vasconcelos) plays a variety of mostly exotic instruments, including Cherry's doussn'gouni, an African
guitar.

His playing on these modally based albums is a reversal of
his Free recordings. His lines formerly gathered much of
their freedom of motion from the free harmonic structures.
Within the static harmonic world of modes, a large element
of his ingenuity vanishes, and he plays cadences; the soothing
vamps of *Codona 3* bring a concomitant decline in his rhythmic vitality. One result is the currently fashionable pastoral
sentimentality; "Voice of the Silence" and "Travel by
Night," however well played, are by an almost impersonal
trumpeter.

Yet Cherry's Free style has remained vital over the years, if anything, growing in poise. His three mid-sixties Blue Note LPs show him as a prolific composer of adroit Coleman-inspired songs, with his short, crackling solos and the hard swinging rhythm team of Blackwell and bassist Henry Grimes. The wonderful *Crisis* is the first of several reunions with Coleman; it's Cherry's rhythmic animation that uplifts Johnny Dyani's *Song for Biko;* the light sound and melodism of tenorman Charles Brackeen are set off by Cherry, Blackwell, and bassist Charlie Haden to result in a fine Coleman-like quartet; then, in the popular touring group Old and New Dreams, Brackeen is replaced by a fourth ex-Coleman colleague, Dewey Redman. Each of these four, in fact, investigates non-Western musics, so the quartet's repertoire includes some exotic pieces as well as straight-ahead originals and Coleman songs. More than Coleman nowadays, Cherry exhibits a singular assurance and subtlety of rhythmic expansion and contraction. On the other hand, broken phrase solos like the ones in "Augmented" and his fast, nasty "Next to the Quiet Stream" propose that Cherry may be at his most creative when most tense and nervous.

He now lives in Sweden, and he exemplifies the all-embracing Free musician of today. The electrically amplified harmolodics idiom that Coleman brought into being is a more recent manifestation of not exactly cultural synthesis but at least culture straddling. Coleman himself plays alto in James "Blood" Ulmer's (James Blood's) *Tales of Coleman Black,* in which the rocking music emphasizes lines and contrasts: paranoid, threatening, low guitar calls against Coleman's rising responses ("Theme from Captain Black"); drums-bass chattering, sweet alto, and Ulmer's blues-drenched guitar ("Nothing to Say"); the motivic organization of Ulmer's accompaniments and solo in "See-Through." Ulmer is up-to-date with electric guitar gadgetry, but even though intensity is easy to simulate with these sound effects, rock patterns, and high-volume levels, he can be the hottest ("Time Out") as well as the best spontaneous organizer among harmolodic musicians. More than the others, he plays blues—"Nothing to Say" is pure Chicago fire—even though, as you'd expect, funky and disco rhythms frolic throughout his music.

His sophistication of design is a classic attitude; Coleman's Prime Time is ingeniously united collective playing. Composer-drummer Ronald Shannon Jackson's Decoding Society is the most extreme music in the harmolodic idiom and a denial of the others in that Jackson seeks to combine the most independent of elements. The largest portions of their performances are his elaborately detailed compositions, with long note values in Free tempos over throbbing multiple rhythm patterns; at all times one or more instruments is likely to be playing in Free, utterly unrelated tempos. Jackson's stated objective is to present rhythms and lines from many idioms and cultures at once, each maintaining its own identity while joining, however tenuously, with the others. One of his pieces, "Night Watch," was inspired by a Rembrandt painting, "a huge portrait, a street scene of all the night people—from the midget to the prostitutes to the barkeeps to the guards of the city to the prominent counts, even a little drummer boy, all the people who hung out. You look at the painting and vicariously you're there."[1] His composing is that highly populated with independent elements.

The clue to his objectives is in his own drumming, for he plays parade drums throughout his pieces. This is not to be confused with conventional or white marching band drumming. The parade drumming of African-American drum and bugle corps, for example, is an old tradition that's infinitely more swinging and varied in inception: All sorts of rhythms can be assimilated into its patterns; the patterns can change and even evolve. Indeed, parade drumming does synthesize all kinds of rhythms, but Jackson's Decoding Society is a pretty far-out drum and bugle corps. Its lead and accompaniment roles are divided like those in Coleman's Prime Time, but with much more disparity in the separate currents. The "melodic" players atop Jackson's ensembles (combinations of saxes and/or trumpet, violin, vibes, a guitarist) are often uncommonly Free among harmolodic musicians. Moreover, he writes some lovely melodies like "Nightwhistler" and the shimmering, trilling "Apache Love Cry."

Hyperstimulation characterizes harmolodic music in any case, but Jackson's and the Decoding Society's extremes of adrenaline bring about extraordinary juxtapositions of textures. His vision is simultaneously enticing (the rocking patterns) and alarming (the disparities). These pieces are highly detailed mixtures, rather than forms that evolve. Separate cultures coexist here; but their assent is temporary (his pieces are brief ones), and gatherings do not develop. Instead, the specter of chaos and disintegration is always lurking, and for all the high spirits of this band, its current popularity may be no accident, in an age when the human race is threatened with extinction.

In America, Free musicians must compete with fusion, bop, and swing players for bookings at nightclubs and the principal festivals. It's the alternative spaces where the music thrives, as it survived in the sixties—little theaters, art galleries, churches, sometimes the better colleges and universities. An entire art might have remained an underground secret for a quarter century without the concert-producing dedication of some hard-core music lovers and especially of musicians themselves. In New York "loft jazz' meant Free jazz in the seventies. Musicians owned and operated such places as Studio Rivbea, Ladies' Fort (singer Joe Lee Wilson), The Brook (Charles Tyler), Ali's Alley (Rashied Ali); disc jockey-singer Verna Gillis runs Soundscape, today s best-known music loft. Some of these are lofts in the upper floors of factory and warehouse buildings, with room for a couple of hundred listeners. The indefatigable Sam Rivers is aptly named, for music streams from him in rushing currents. Principally admired for his tenor sax mastery, he also moves to soprano, flute, piano, without pause, playing long solos on each, in the course of his sets. He founded Studio Rivbea in 1970, and year after year he presented concerts by one outside group after another, while maintaining his separate performing career, without any loss of his music's high energy. His was the most famous of the lofts; incidentally, the average life-span of the lofts is about the same as that of most jazz nightclubs.

Since the sixties a generation and more of outside musicians have emerged, to spend most of their careers in these alternative venues. Among the most vital or prominent younger players are trumpeters Bakaida Carroll and Olu Dara, trombonist Craig Harris, altoists Jemeel Moondoc and Jimmie Vass, the latter a frequent colleague of Rashied Ali's, violinist Billy Bang, tenorist Frank Lowe. Anthony Davis, from New Haven, is an all-purpose romantic pianist in modal and Free groups, and he's worked with distinction in Thelonious Monk's repertoire; one of his colleagues is James Newton, a romantic flute virtuoso with a classically clean sound and technique. There are many more valuable players, of course. Saxmen Byard Lancaster and (Black) Arthur Blythe are from a slightly older generation, and Blythe has become quite the most famous of all these musicians. The phrases he plays come from the most decorative material of essentially undecorative hard bop saxmen like Johnny Griffin, whose own musics refer to a fusion of the Lester Young and Coleman Hawkins schools. At fast tempos Blythe can be exciting, with a hot attack ("Voyage to Jericho"), but the severe discontinuity of his wholly ornamental style becomes increasingly obvious as his tempos become slower. Like Anthony Braxton, he recorded a popular *In the Tradition* album of pre-Free material.

Economically it's not feasible for a musician to lead concerts in New York more than a few times annually. Most of the city's outside musicians work with a variety of groups, which, musically, at least, is a healthy situation. To take an extreme example, Oliver Lake, one of the most active in Free Jazz, might play a solo concert, as a sideman, as a cooperative member of an *ad hoc* group, leading his own Jump Up reggae band, and with the World Saxophone Quartet, each gig on successive nights in different cities; I don't know if he's actually spent a week like this, but it is a real possibility. The World Saxophone Quartet is Lake, Julius Hemphill, Hamiet Bluiett, all St Louisians, and Californian David Murray, all doubling instruments. Hemphill's composing in particular is fine for this group, though on the whole, the quartet's music does not fulfill the promise of these four individuals' talents.

Since working big bands have gone the way of the passenger pigeon and the American eagle, a few composer-arrangers like David Murray and Henry Threadgill lead little big bands, the Murray Octet and Threadgill Sextet (actually a septet). These prove to be ideal-size groups, for what they lack of big bands' sonic weight is insignificant compared to the advantages in sonic richness, as each band member adds a personal sound to the ensembles. Through the seventies Murray played Ayler ecstasies on tenor sax; now, as a bandleader, he proves a natural successor to Charles Mingus, with a better collection of musicians than any Mingus led after 1960 Like Mingus, Murray loves counterpoint and rhythmic shifts, but instead of Mingus's brooding, Murray is a native optimist; that makes a real difference in Murray's mood pieces like "Home," with a line expressing simple sentiment and a mildly dissonant countermelody. Murray's own tenor solos are now in standard pitch more often than not, and the octet's best feature is its improvisers and interpreters of the composer's detailed scores.

For instance, in the ballad "Ming," trombonist George Lewis surely has the Jimmy Knepper sense of *rightness*. In place of the dynamism of Mingus and Dannie Richmond, Murray presents the sober bass playing of Wilbur Morris and the infinitely subtle and sensitive Steve McCall's drumming; he is also the most fiery of today's drummers. Cornetist Olu Dara and woodwind man Threadgill play with both the Murray and Threadgill groups. The Murray song that you hear everybody whistling is "Dewey's Circle"; the swinging performance features Dara's perfect Louis Armstrong phrases, including climactic high notes in Armstrong's classic vibrato. The elegant Dara possesses the most consistently opulent tone of any trumpeter since Roy Eldridge at least. He improvises finely balanced emotions with an especially acute ear for internal rhythmic contrasts. In Murray's "Jasvan" the beautiful (muted) Dara melodies modify crispness with pensive phrases; in a fast solo, "Last of the Hipmen," his internal flow makes high detail and contrast sound as natural as life.

It's Dara's sound that's the center of the Threadgill group. In contrast to Murray, this music is bathed in irony and curdled wit. Grand, vibrant-sounding horns intone the lines, which, as they're extended, subtly turn awry, ambiguous. Some of Threadgill's scores are darkly shadowed dirges and tone poems, like "Just B" and "Just the Facts and Pass the Bucket." A long anthem, "Soft Suicide at the Baths," slowly disintegrates with wayward tones by clarinet, cornet, trombone, over two drummers busy in unrelated velocities; for once, the assertion of a triadic final chord is ominous. The "Gateway" theme could be a violent climax in an Italian opera, before the devastation of Threadgill's alto solo; "Black Blues," which might have been a set piece, instead smolders with the players' rich sounds and hard attack. In the incendiary "When Was That?," theme fanfares fan blazes of incessant drums behind broken meteorite solo lines. There's an indescribable undertone of judgment and incipient eruption in this group. With three horns, two bass clef strings, and two percussionists, Threadgill has leeway to vary the instruments' roles; for example, "10 to 1" is structured in the way of a harmolodic band—but pre-Coleman, prerock, preelectricity.

There is, of course, exploratory jazz activity throughout America, away from the concentration of musicians in New York and the northeastern metropolises. It is quite varied activity, as different milieus are interested in different aspects of the art's development. The Chicagoans and Europeans have stimulated investigations of structures, sound, space, and completely Free improvisation by independent players who are usually multi-instrumentalists, like Milo Fine in Minneapolis; Henry Kuntz, Gerald Oshita, Greg Goodman (piano), Henry Kaiser (guitar) in the San Francisco Bay Area; the circle around *Coda* magazine and Onari records in Toronto, including altoist Maury Coles and soprano saxman Bill Smith. The early Free jazz styles may have been more influential throughout America. In New Orleans, trumpeter Clyde Kerr, Jr., altoist Edward "Kidd" Jordan, and drummer Alvin Fielder play a blistering post-Ornette Coleman jazz, while two of Coleman's very first colleagues (he lived in New Orleans in 1950) play a highly advanced kind of late bop: clarinetist Alvin Batiste and pianist Ellis Marsalis. (Marsalis's sons, trumpeter Wynton and tenorist Branford, have become the eighties' new young stars of hard bop.) Some gifted young musicians have appeared in Los Angeles, including saxman Vinny Golia, bassist Roberto Miguel Miranda, and drummer Alex Cline.

Occasionally there are older musicians in America's cities to encourage the rising generations the way John Carter, Bobby Bradford, and Horace Tapscott have worked with the young Los Angeles players. Back in 1961, four years before Chicago's AACM, the long-experienced Horace Tapscott founded the Union of God's Musicians and Artists Ascension (UGMAA) to produce concerts by his Pan Afrikan Peoples Arkestra. Tapscott himself is an impressive pianist. His solo *Song for the Unsung* is enveloped in expansive introductions, codas, and elaborate inner detail, yet his music does not become rhapsodic. On the contrary, he offers a disarming simplicity and directness despite his elaborate organization; the title piece is an ingenious flow of consonance and dissonance, he gives a winsome dignity to an acerbic Elmo Hope piece, and his forthright rhythmic resetting of "Bakai" is superior to Coltrane's version. The Arkestra deals in advanced modal areas and is a showcase for composers and improvisers; the UGMAA members also teach music to inner-city young people.

This kind of education in modern music is important because the days of jam sessions and informal music lessons have largely vanished. The explosion in high school and college jazz bands during the Free era is an illusion; these bands are the heritage of the cheap thrills of Stan Kenton and of mediocre eclectics like Woody Herman. There is some higher education available in Free music, most prominently at the Creative Music Studio in Woodstock, New York. It's run by vibist Karl Berger, and avant-garde musicians and composers from Don Cherry to Roscoe Mitchell teach intensive, specialized seminars. It was in a university town, East Lansing, Michigan, that AACM member Mitchell initiated the Creative Arts Collective, comprised of young Detroit musicians. CAC musicians include Spencer Barefield (guitar), Jaribu Shahid (bass), and Tani Tabbal (drums), the rhythm section of Mitchell's Sound Ensemble. In another university town, New Haven, Connecticut, Leo Smith of the AACM helped form the Creative Music Improvisers Forum (CMIF), which includes Dwight Andrews (woodwinds), Bobby

Naughton (vibes), Anthony Davis, and Wes Brown (bass). These activities have had no connections to the local academic institutions.

As far away as Austria, there is an outside musicians' cooperative centered on local players who recorded with the AACM's Fred Anderson. Back in the early sixties Rafael (Donald) Garrett helped begin the Experimental Band, precursor of the AACM, before he moved to San Francisco and played bass with (on records) Coltrane, Shepp, Redman, and drummer Smiley Winters. Garrett then lived in Europe, Africa, and Asia Minor, learning new musics and instruments wherever he went before once again becoming a source of inspiration and intensity in Chicago in the eighties. Garrett's intensity is matched by Hal Russell's NRG Ensemble, a quintet of prolific multi-instrumentalists who explode into delirious infernos of energy, ignited by the drumming of either Russell or Steve Hunt or sometimes both. The NRG Ensemble has a huge book of witty compositions, of which "Linda Jazz Princess" is a good example of their wild humor; it's a highly abstract version of a jazz radio show, with fast impressions of Dixieland, swing, bop, madness, and furious soloing. Out of the AACM school come drummers Reggie Nicholson and Kahil El'Zabar and a remarkable saxophonist, Edward Wilkerson. He takes the funky jump band tenor idiom into Free territory with infectious rhythms and a full, huge sound; on alto ("Seeker," "A Serious Pun") his forms show the care and sensitivity of a Jarman or a Mitchell.

These lists of prominent or valuable players who "arrived on the scene" after, say, 1975 are by no means exhaustive. There are no overwhelming mainstream movements and personalities in today's Free scene, a situation unique in jazz's history, even alarming to people accustomed to the presence of leading personalities like Armstrong or Parker. The proliferation of Free idioms today leaves jazz in the position of, let us say, painting and European classical music by World War I or poetry by the 1930s. By now the word "jazz" is an anachronism; the majority of today's Free musicians maintain that the jazz category is too narrowly defined to encompass their creative breadth. But no other satisfactory word has appeared to classify the Free exploration scene that has grown out of this African-American musical tradition.

More important than definitions is the experience of the music itself, given its power—and this is the great mystery—not merely to extend our emotions or decorate our lives but to transform them as we become participants in the artists' acts of communication. If art is the soul of an age, perhaps we moderns can discover our own souls in the course of the music. After the conflicts of Coltrane and the fury of energy music, do the joinings of the jazz and other national or native traditions, and Roscoe Mitchell's complete rebuilding of music's structure, beginning with the most basic elements, represent directions philosophically crucial to humanity as a whole? It's a characteristic theme in writing about twentieth-century music that the experiences of art can lead to a new human consciousness that will deter mankind from its present catastrophic course. This is an idea that is not to be dismissed. Surely everything else we've tried, from drugs to technology to thermonuclear threats, has failed us.

Appendix I
---•••---
Notes

Chapter 1: Steps in a Search for Freedom

1. Quoted in John B. Litweiler, "There's a Mingus Among Us," *Down Beat* (February 27, 1975).

Chapter 2: Ornette Coleman: The Birth of Freedom

1. Ornette Coleman interview by John Litweiler, September 24, 1981, transcribed by David Wild and Litweiler; parts of this interview will appear in *Disc'ribe*, No. 3. Unless otherwise indicated, all comments by Ornette Coleman in this chapter are taken from this interview.
2. Quoted in liner notes by Nat Hentoff to *Something Else! The Music of Ornette Coleman*, Contemporary 7551.
3. "Motivic evolution" is a term used in Terry Martin, "The Plastic Muse," *Jazz Monthly* (May, June, and August 1964). Martin's valuable essay inspired much of my discussion of *Change of the Century* and *This Is Our Music*.
4. Quoted in Nat Hentoff, "Jazz in Print," *Jazz Review* (February 1960).
5. Quoted in J. B. Figi, "Ornette Coleman, a Surviving Elder in the Universal Brotherhood of Those Who Make Music," (Chicago) *Reader* (June 22, 1973).
6. Quoted in Arthur Taylor, *Notes and Tones* (New York: G. P. Putnam's Sons, 1982 [reprint]).

Chapter 3: Eric Dolphy

1. Quoted in John B. Litweiler, "There's a Mingus Among Us," *Down Beat* (February 27, 1975).
2. Quoted in David Keller, "Eric Dolphy—The Los Angeles Years," *Jazz Times* (November 1981).
3. Quoted in Martin Williams, "Introducing Eric Dolphy," in Martin Williams, ed. *Jazz Panorama* (New York: Crowell-Collier Press, 1964).
4. Quoted in Vladimir Simosko and Barry Tepperman, *Eric Dolphy* (Washington, D.C.: Smithsonian Institution Press, 1974).
5. See Jack Cooke, "Eric Dolphy," *Jazz Monthly* (January 1966).
6. George Russell and Martin Williams, "Ornette Coleman and Tonality," *Jazz Review* (June 1960).
7. Booker Little, quoted in liner notes by Ben Sidran to Eric Dolphy, *Status,* Prestige 24070.
8. A composite of quotes from Simosko and Tepperman, *op. cit.,* and Mingus's introduction in Charles Mingus, *Portrait,* Prestige 24092.

Chapter 4: John Coltrane: The Passion for Freedom

1. Quoted in liner notes by Robert Levin to Cecil Taylor, *Hard Driving Jazz,* United Artists 4014.
2. John Coltrane in liner notes to *A Love Supreme,* Impulse 77.
3. John Coltrane as told to Don DeMicheal, "Coltrane on Coltrane," *Down Beat* (September 29, 1960).
4. Quoted in "John Coltrane, Finally Made," *Newsweek* (July 24, 1961); in Bill Cole, *John Coltrane* (New York: Schirmer Books, 1976).
5. Quoted in liner notes by Ralph J. Gleason to *Coltrane's Sound,* Atlantic 1419.
6. John Tynan, *Down Beat* (November 23, 1961); in Don DeMicheal, "John Coltrane and Eric Dolphy Answer the Jazz Critics," *Down Beat* (April 12, 1962).
7. Quoted in Frank Kofsky, *Black Nationalism and the Revolution in Music* (New York: Pathfinder Press, 1970).

8. Archie Shepp, "A View from the Inside," *Music '66/Down Beat Yearbook.*

Chapter 5: Transition: Miles Davis and Modal Jazz

1. Quoted in Bill Cole, *Miles Davis* (New York: William Morrow & Company, Inc., 1974); taken from Marc Crawford, "Evil Genius of Jazz," *Ebony* (January 1961).
2. Quoted in Nat Hentoff, "An Afternoon with Miles Davis," in Martin Williams, ed., *Jazz Panorama* (New York: Crowell-Collier Press, 1974).
3. Quoted in Leonard Feather liner notes to *Wayne Shorter*, GNP Crescendo 2-2075.
4. Quoted in liner notes by Nat Hentoff to Woody Shaw, *Blackstone Legacy*, Contemporary 7627/8.
5. Quoted in liner notes by Ira Gitler to Jackie McLean, *New Soil*, Blue Note 84013.
6. Jackie McLean in liner notes to *Let Freedom Ring*, Blue Note 84106.

Chapter 6: The Free Jazz Underground and Sun Ra

1. Archie Shepp, "A View from the Inside," *Music '66/Down Beat Yearbook.*
2. Quoted in John B. Litweiler, "Archie Shepp, an Old Schoolmaster in a Brown Suit," *Down Beat* (November 7, 1974).
3. Quoted in Tam Fiofori, "Sun Ra's Space Odyssey," *Down Beat* (May 14, 1970).
4. Quoted in Valerie Wilmer, Sun Ra interview, *Melody Maker* (October 29, 1966).
5. Quoted in the program booklet (compiled by Victor Schonfield) for the concert by Sun Ra and the Intergalactic Research Arkestra in Queen Elizabeth Hall, London, England, November 8, 1970, produced by Music Now.
6. Quoted in John B. Litweiler, "Von Freeman, Underrated but Undaunted," *Down Beat* (November 4, 1976).
7. Quoted by Bob Blumenthal in "The Sun Ra Show," *Boston Phoe-*

nix, May 6, 1975.

8. Sun Ra in program booklet to *Jazz by Sun Ra, Vol. I,* Transition 10.

9. Quoted in Mike Zwerin, Sun Ra interview, *Village Voice* (August 15, 1965).

10. Quoted in Ron Welburn, Ronnie Boykins interview, *The Grackle*, No. 4 (1977–78).

11. Quoted in Bob Rusch, Sun Ra interview, *Cadence* (June, 1978).

12. Quoted in Tam Fiofori, Sun Ra interview, *New York Free Press* (April 18, 1965).

Chapter 7: Albert Ayler

1. Quoted in Nat Hentoff, "The Truth Is Marching In," *Down Beat* (February 25, 1965).

2. Quoted in Valerie Wilmer, *As Serious as Your Life* (Westport, Conn.: Lawrence Hill & Co., 1980).

3. Quoted in Jacqueline and Daniel Caux, "My Name Is Albert Ayler" (Paris) *L'Art Vivant* (February 1971).

4. Quoted in liner notes by Frank Kofsky to Albert Ayler, *Love Cry,* Impulse 9165.

5. Quoted in Spencer Weston, "Sunny Murray" interview, *Cadence* (June 1979).

6. "Apple Cores Number 3," LeRoi Jones, *Black Music* (New York: William Morrow & Company, Inc., 1970).

7. Albert Ayler's replies to a questionnaire, in (Paris) *Jazz* (December 1965).

8. Quoted in liner notes by Nat Hentoff to *Albert Ayler in Greenwich Village,* Impulse 9155.

9. Albert Ayler, "To Mr. Jones—I Had a Vision," *The Cricket* (1969).

Chapter 8: Chicago, Sound in Space, and St. Louis

1. Read by Roscoe Mitchell in "Tutankhamen," Art Ensemble of Chicago, *The Paris Sessions,* Arista Freedom (1903).

2. Quoted in Terry Martin, "Roscoe Mitchell, Blowing Out from Chicago," *Down Beat* (April 6, 1967).

3. In the Art Ensemble of Chicago's résumé, circa 1969.
4. Quoted in John B. Litweiler, "There Won't Be Any More Music," *Music 72/Down Beat Yearbook.*
5. Interview with John Litweiler, Don DeMicheal Archives of the Jazz Institute of Chicago.
6. Quoted in John B. Litweiler, "Richard Abrams, a Man with an Idea," *Down Beat* (October 5, 1967).
7. Quoted in John Litweiler, "The Art Ensemble of Chicago, Adventures in the Urban Bush," *Down Beat* (June 1982).
8. Interview with John Litweiler (unpublished).
9. Interview with Ted Panken (unpublished).
10. Quoted in John B. Litweiler, "AACM's 20th Anniversary—An Interview with Muhal Richard Abrams" (Chicago) *Reader* (May 9, 1975).

Chapter 9: Cecil Taylor

1. Quoted in Bob Rusch, "Cecil Taylor" interview, *Cadence* (April 1978).
2. Quoted in J. B. Figi, "Cecil Taylor: African Code, Black Methodology," *Down Beat* (April 10, 1975).
3. Quoted in Nat Hentoff, "The Persistent Challenge of Cecil Taylor," *Down Beat* (February 25, 1965).
4. From "-Aqoueh R-Oyo" by Cecil Taylor; copyright 1973 by Cecil Taylor.
5. Quoted in John B. Litweiler, "Needs and Acts: Cecil Taylor in Wisconsin," *Down Beat* (October 14, 1971).

Chapter 10: Pop-Jazz, Fusion, and Romanticism

1. Keith Jarrett in program booklet to *Concerts,* ECM 3-1227.
2. Keith Jarrett in liner notes to *Death and the Flower,* Impulse 9301.
3 Quoted in Peter Danson, "McCoy Tyner" interview, *Coda,* No. 180 (1981).
4. Quoted in David Wild, "McCoy Tyner: The Jubilant Experience of the Classic Quartet," *Down Beat* (July 12, 1979).

Chapter 11: Free Jazz in Europe: American, National, International

1. Quoted in liner notes by Martin Davidson to Steve Lacy, *School Days*, Emanem 3316.
2. Quoted in Derek Bailey, *Improvisation* (Ashbourne, Derbyshire, England: Moorland Publishing Co. Ltd., 1980).
3. Quoted in Robert Terlizzi, "Steve Lacy" interview, *Coda* (February 1977).
4. Interview with John Litweiler (unpublished).
5. Bailey, *op. cit.*

Chapter 12: Leo Smith, Anthony Braxton, Joseph Jarman, and Roscoe Mitchell

1. Quoted in liner notes by Robert Palmer to Leo Smith, *Spirit Catcher*, Nessa 19.
2. Interview with John Litweiler (unpublished).
3. Leo Smith, *Notes (8 pieces)* (New Haven, Conn.: Leo Smith, no date).
4. Quoted in John Litweiler, "Anthony Braxton: Music for Interplanetary Travel" (Chicago) *Reader* (January 26, 1979).
5. Liner notes by Leo Smith to *The Complete Braxton 1971*, Arista/Freedom 1902.
6. Larry Kart, "Two Explosive Albums Emit Shattering Waves of Sound," *Chicago Tribune* (May 27, 1979).
7 Quoted in liner notes by Terry Martin to Roscoe Mitchell, *Nonaah*, Nessa 9/10.

Chapter 13: Free Jazz Today

1. Quoted in Charles Doherty, "Decoding the Society," *Down Beat* (August 1982).

Appendix II

Selected Discography

These records are essential documents of the growth and development of the Freedom principle, as described in the text. The record manufacturing business undergoes so many changes that some of these albums are presently unavailable from their original producers, though certain record labels are continually maintained in release in other countries, especially Japan. Moreover, some currently unavailable records will be rereleased by the time you read this, perhaps by new record companies, while others that are presently in release will be deleted. In this discography the most recent release to be widely available in America is the one listed.

Many records that are manufactured in Japan and by the smaller European labels are imported by jazz specialist stores in America. Here are some retailers who offer mail-order service, including difficult-to-find imported recordings. The supply of these albums is irregular; *Cadence* magazine (monthly) prints an extensive catalogue in each issue, and *Coda* also frequently lists its offerings.

Cadence Magazine Record Sale, Cadence Building, Redwood, New York 13679-9612.

Coda Magazine Record & Book Service, Box 87, Station J, Toronto M4J 4X8 Ontario, Canada.

Daybreak Express Records, P.O. Box 250, Van Brunt Station Brooklyn, New York 11215.

International Record Service, P.O. Box 717, Mentone, California 92359.

Jazz Record Mart, 11 West Grand Avenue, Chicago, Illinois 60610.

Mt. Fuji Imports, 1765 North Highland Avenue, #324D, Hollywood, California 90028.

Swingville Jazz Records, 3344 North Clark Street, Chicago, Illinois 60657.

Chapter 1: Steps in a Search for Freedom

Anthology, *Outstanding Jazz Compositions of the 20th Century*, Columbia C2L 31; includes works by John Lewis, Jimmy Giuffre, Charles Mingus, Harold Shapero, Milton Babbitt, Gunther Schuller, and "All About Rosie" by George Russell.

Stan Kenton, *City of Glass/This Modern World* (composed by Bob Graettinger), Creative World 1006.

Thelonious Monk, *The Complete Blue Note Recordings of Thelonious Monk*, Mosaic MR4-101; this includes the 1948–52 Monk recordings collected in *The Complete Genius*, Blue Note 579-H2, and his 1957 performances with Sonny Rollins.

————, *Pure Monk*, Milestone 47004.

Sonny Rollins, *Saxophone Colossus and More* (with Max Roach), Milestone 24050.

————, *A Night at the Village Vanguard* (with Wilbur Ware), Blue Note 81581.

Herbie Nichols, *The Third World* (1955–56), Blue Note LA 485-H2.

————, *The Bethlehem Years*, Bethlehem 6028.

Charles Mingus, *Passions of a Man*, Atlantic SD3-600 (three-LP set).

————, *East Coasting*, Affinity 86 (England).

————, *Tijuana Moods*, RCA (France) FXLI-7295.

————, *Mingus Ah Um*, Columbia CS 8171.

Lennie Tristano-Buddy De Franco, *Crosscurrents*, Capitol M-11060; includes "A Bird in Igor's Yard" by George Russell.

Chapter 2: Ornette Coleman: The Birth of Freedom

John Lewis Presents Gunther Schuller, Jazz Abstractions, Atlantic 1365.

Ornette Coleman, *Coleman Classics* (with Paul Bley, 1958), I.A.I. 37.38.52.

——, *Something Else!*, Contemporary 7551 (1958).

——, *Tomorrow Is the Question!*, Contemporary 7569 (1959)

——, *The Shape of Jazz to Come*, Atlantic 1317 (1959).

——, *Change of the Century*, Atlantic 1327 (1959).

——, *This Is Our Music*, Atlantic 1351 (1960).

——, *To Whom Who Keeps a Record*, Atlantic P-10085 (1960) (Japan).

—— Double Quartet, *Free Jazz*, Atlantic 1364 (1960).

——, *Ornette!*, Atlantic 1378 (1961).

——, *Ornette on Tenor*, Atlantic 1394 (1961).

——, *The Art of the Improvisers*, Atlantic 1572 (1959–61).

——, *Town Hall/December 1962*, ESP-Disk (Base) 1006 (Italy).

—— Trio, *The Great London Concert*, Arista/Freedom 1900 (1965).

—— *Trio at the Golden Circle, Stockholm*, Volume 1, Blue Note 4224, and Volume 2, Blue Note 4225.

——, *The Empty Foxhole*, Blue Note 4246 (1966).

——, *Crisis*, Impulse 9210 (1969).

——, *Broken Shadows*, Columbia FC 38029 (1971).

—— and the London Symphony Orchestra, David Measham, conductor, *Skies of America*, Columbia KC 31562.

——, *Dancing in Your Head*, A&M/Horizon SP722; includes the Master Musicians of Joujouka, Morocco (1972), and the early Prime Time band (1975).

—— and Prime Time, *Of Human Feelings*, Antilles 2001 (1979)

Chapter 3: Eric Dolphy

Charles Mingus Presents the Charles Mingus Quartet, Jazz Man
5048.
George Russell, *Outer Thoughts,* Milestone 47027.
Max Roach, *Percussion Bitter Sweet,* Impulse 8.
Eric Dolphy, Prestige 24008.
———, *The Great Concert of Eric Dolphy,* Prestige 34002 (a boxed
set of the Five Spot recordings, 1961).
——— *Music Matador,* Affinity 47 (England) (recorded by Alan
Douglas, 1963).
———, *Iron Man,* Douglas International 785 (recorded by Alan
Douglas, 1963).
———, *Out to Lunch,* Blue Note 84163.
———, *Last Date,* Limelight 86013.
Booker Little, *Out Front,* Barnaby Candid 5019 (with Dolphy).

Chapter 4: John Coltrane: The Passion for Freedom

Thelonious Monk & John Coltrane, Milestone 47011 (with Wilbur
Ware).
John Coltrane, Prestige 24003.
———, *Blue Train,* Blue Note 81577.
———, *Giant Steps,* Atlantic 1311.
———, *Africa/Brass,* Impulse 6.
———, *Impressions,* Impulse 42 (from the Village Vanguard, 1961,
with Eric Dolphy).
———, *The Other Village Vanguard Tapes,* Impulse 9325 (1961,
with Dolphy).
———, *Coltrane,* Impulse 21 (includes "Out of This World").
———, *Live at Birdland,* Impulse 50.
———, *A Love Supreme,* Impulse 77.
———, *Ascension,* Impulse 95.
———, *Meditations,* Impulse 9110.
———, *Interstellar Space,* Impulse 9277.

Chapter 5: Transition: Miles Davis and Modal Jazz

Miles Davis, *Birth of the Cool*, Capitol M-11026
————, *Tallest Trees*, Prestige 24012.
————, *Workin' and Steamin'*, Prestige 24034.
————, *Porgy and Bess*, Columbia PC 8085 (with Gil Evans).
————, *Kind of Blue*, Columbia PC-8163 (with Coltrane, Bill Evans).
Art Blakey and the Jazz Messengers, *Witch Doctor*, Blue Note 84258.
————, *Mosaic*, Blue Note 84090.
Wayne Shorter, *The All-Seeing Eye*, Blue Note 84219.
————, *Etcetera*, Blue Note LT-1056.
Grachan Moncur III, *Evolution*, Blue Note 84153 (with Jackie McLean, Bobby Hutcherson, Tony Williams).
Bobby Hutcherson, *Dialogue*, Blue Note 84198.
Andrew Hill, *Judgment*, Blue Note 84159.
Stanley Cowell, *Brilliant Circles*, Arista/Freedom 1009.
Woody Shaw, *Blackstone Legacy*, Contemporary 7627/8.
Jackie McLean, *New Soil*, Blue Note 84013.
————, *Let Freedom Ring*, Blue Note 84106.
————, *New and Old Gospel*, Blue Note 84262.
Miles Davis, *E.S.P.*, Columbia CS-9150.
———— *at the Plugged Nickel, Chicago*, Columbia C 21 38266.
————, *In a Silent Way*, Columbia PC-9875.
Sonny Rollins, *Our Man in Jazz*, RCA (France) 741091/092.
————, *There Will Never Be Another You*, Impulse IA-9349.
————, *Don't Stop the Carnival*, Milestone 55005.

Chapter 6: The Free Jazz Underground and Sun Ra

Archie Shepp, *In Europe*, Delmark 9409 (the New York Contemporary Five).
————, *Fire Music*, Impulse 86.
————, *Further Fire Music*, Impulse IA-9357/2.
New York Art Quartet, ESP-Disk (Base) 1004 (Italy).

Marion Brown, *Duets,* Arista/Freedom 1904 (with Leo Smith).
Bill Dixon, *Intents and Purposes,* RCA Victor LSP-3844.
Paul Bley, *Scorpio,* Milestone 9046.
Sun Ra, *Jazz in Silhouette,* Saturn 205 (also issued as Impulse 9265).
————, *The Nubians of Plutonia,* Saturn 406 (Impulse 9242).
————, *The Heliocentric Worlds,* Volume 1, ESP-Disk (Base) 1014, and Volume 2, ESP-Disk (Base) 1017 (Italy).
————, *The Magic City,* Saturn LPB-711 (Impulse 9243).
————, *Monorails and Satellites,* Volume 1 (Saturn SR-509).
New Art Jazz Ensemble, *Seeking,* Revelation 9 (John Carter-Bobby Bradford).

Chapter 7: Albert Ayler

My Name is Albert Ayler, Fantasy 86016.
Albert Ayler, *Witches and Devils,* Arista/Freedom 1018.
———— Trio, *Spiritual Unity,* ESP-Disk (Base) 1002 (Italy).
————, *Vibrations,* Arista/Freedom 1000.
————, *The Hilversum Session,* Osmosis 6001 (Holland).
————, *Spirits Rejoice,* ESP-Disk (Base) 1020 (Italy).
————, *Lörrach/Paris 1966,* Hat Musics 3500.
————, *New Grass,* Impulse 9175.
New York Eye and Ear Control, ESP-Disk (Base) 1016 (Italy).
Charles Tyler, *Saga of the Outlaws,* Nessa 16.
————, *The Definite,* Storyville 4098.

Chapter 8: Chicago, Sound in Space, and St. Louis

Roscoe Mitchell, *Sound,* Delmark 408.
———— *Old/Quartet,* Nessa 5.
————, *Congliptious,* Nessa 2.
Joseph Jarman, *Song For,* Delmark 410.
Art Ensemble of Chicago, *People in Sorrow,* Nessa 3.
————, *A Jackson in Your House,* BYG Actuel 2 (France).
————, *Urban Bushmen,* ECM 2-1211.
Lester Bowie, *Numbers 1 & 2,* Nessa 1.

——, *The Great Pretender,* ECM 1-1209.
Oliver Lake, *Heavy Spirits,* Arista/Freedom 1008.
Julius Hemphill, *Blue Boyé,* Mbari MPC 1000X.
Kalaparush Maurice McIntyre, *Humility,* Delmark 419.
Von Freeman, *Have No Fear,* Nessa 8.
Creative Construction Company, Volume 1, Muse 5071.
Air Song, India Navigation 1057.
Air Time, Nessa 12.
Muhal Richard Abrams, *Levels and Degrees of Light,* Delmark 413
——, *Mama and Daddy,* Black Saint 0041.
Julius Hemphill and Oliver Lake, *Buster Bee,* Sackville 3018.

Chapter 9: Cecil Taylor

The World of Cecil Taylor, Jazz Man 5026.
Cecil Taylor, *Looking Ahead,* Contemporary 7562.
——, *Unit Structures,* Blue Note 84237.
——, *In Transition,* Blue Note LA458-H2 (1955, 1959).
——, *Conquistador,* Blue Note 84260.
——, *Silent Tongues,* Arista/Freedom 1005.
——, *Indent,* Arista/Freedom 1038.
——, *Air Above Mountains (Buildings Within),* Inner City 3021.
——, *Spring of 2 Blue-Js,* Unit Core 30551.
——, *3 Phasis,* New World 303
—— *Unit,* New World 201.
Gil Evans, *Into the Hot,* Impulse 9 (with Cecil Taylor, Johnny Carisi).

Chapter 10: Pop-Jazz, Fusion, and Romanticism

Miles Davis, *Bitches Brew,* Columbia PG-26.
Wayne Shorter, *Super Nova,* Blue Note 84332.
Weather Report, Columbia KC-30661.
George Russell, *Othello Ballet Suite,* Flying Dutchman 122.
Charlie Haden, *Liberation Music Orchestra,* Impulse 9183.
Carla Bley Band, *European Tour 1977,* Watt 8.
Bill Evans Trio, *Spring Leaves,* Milestone 47034.

Gary Burton-Chick Corea, *Crystal Silence*, ECM 1-1024.

Keith Jarrett, *Concerts*, ECM 3-1227.

McCoy Tyner, *Expansions*, Blue Note 84338.

———, *Echoes of a Friend*, Milestone 9055.

———, *Song for My Lady*, Milestone 9044.

Chapter 11: Free Jazz in Europe: American, National, International

Steve Lacy, *School Days*, Emanem 3510.

———, *Threads*, Horo HZ 05 (Italy).

———, *Trickles*, Black Saint 0008.

Mal Waldron, *Hard Talk*, Enja 2050.

Giorgio Gaslini, *Nuovi Sentimenti*, EMI QELP 8154 (Italy).

Chris McGregor's Brotherhood of Breath, RCA Neon NE2.

Willem Breuker Kollektief, *In Holland*, BVHaast 041/042 (Holland).

Peter Brötzmann/Fred Van Hove/Han Bennink/Albert Mangelsdorff, *Elements*, FMP 0030 (West Germany).

Albert Mangelsdorff, *Tromboneliness*, Sackville 2011.

Conrad Bauer, Amiga 8 55 783 (East Germany).

Paul Rutherford, *The Gentle Harm of the Bourgeoisie*, Emanem 3305.

Tristan Honsinger-Günter Christmann, *Earmeals*, Moers Music 01040.

Globe Unity Orchestra, *Pearls*, FMP 0380 (West Germany).

Evan Parker at the Finger Palace, The Beak Doctor 3/Metalanguage 110.

Derek Bailey, *Aida*, Incus 40 (England).

————-David Holland-George Lewis-Evan Parker, *Fables by Company*, Incus 36 (England).

————-Han Bennink, *Company 3*, Incus 25 (England).

Chapter 12: Leo Smith, Anthony Braxton, Joseph Jarman, and Roscoe Mitchell

Leo Smith, *Creative Music—1*, Kabell 1.
————/New Dalta Akhri, *Song of Humanity*, Kabell 2.
————/New Dalta Akhri, *Reflectativity*, Kabell 3.
————, *Spirit Catcher*, Nessa 19.
Anthony Braxton, *For Alto*, Delmark 420/421.
————, *Five Pieces 1975*, Arista 4064.
————, *In the Tradition*, Volume 1, SteepleChase 1015.
————, *The Montreux/Berlin Concerts*, Arista 5022.
————, *Creative Orchestra Music 1976*, Arista 4080.
————, *Alto Saxophone Improvisations 1979*, Arista 8602.
————, *Composition No. 95, for Two Pianos*, Arista 9559.
Roscoe Mitchell, *Solo Saxophone Concerts*, Sackville 2006.
————, *Nonaah*, Nessa 9/10.
————, *More Cutouts*, Cecma 1003.
————, *L-R-G/The Maze/S II Examples*, Nessa 14/15.
———— Sound Ensemble, *Snurdy McGurdy and Her Dancin' Shoes*, Nessa 20.

Chapter 13: Free Jazz Today

Don Cherry, *Complete Communion*, Blue Note 84226.
Old and New Dreams, Black Saint 0003.
James Blood (Ulmer), *Tales of Captain Black*, Artists House 9407.
Ronald Shannon Jackson and the Decoding Society, *Eye on You*, About Time 1003.
David Murray Octet, *Ming*, Black Saint 0045.
Henry Threadgill Sextet, *When Was That?*, About Time 1004.
Horace Tapscott, *Songs of the Unsung*, Interplay 7714.

Index

Abercrombie, John, 233
Abrams, Muhal Richard, 120, 173,
    177, 181–82, 192, 196–99, 253,
    275, 278
Adderley, Julian "Cannonball," 87,
    112, 226
Aebi, Irene, 243
Ajaramu, 190
Ali, Rashied, 101, 102, 103, 158
Allen, Henry "Red," 81
Allen, Marshall, 145, 146–47
Altschul, Barry, 136, 232, 273
Ameen, Ramsey, 218
Ammons, Gene, 84, 105
Anderson, Fred, 172, 189–90, 298
Anderson, Ray, 192, 275, 276
Andrews, Dwight, 297
Armstrong, Louis, 14, 20, 81, 152,
    176–77, 287, 295, 298
Association for the Advancement of
    Creative Musicians (AACM),
    172–99
Ayler, Albert, 37, 50, 99, 100, 103,
    118, 137, 138, 147, 151–71,
    175, 210, 241, 248, 256,
    259–60, 280, 287, 288
Ayler, Donald, 159, 163, 164, 166,
    168, 169

Babbitt, Milton, 16, 17
Bailey, Derek, 257–63, 269, 275
Baker, David, 68
Bang, Billy, 293
Baraka, Imamu Amiri, 167
    See also Jones, LeRoi
Barbieri, Gato, 229, 230
Barefield, Spencer, 297
Barker, Thurman, 180
Bartók, Béla, 133, 201
Bartz, Gary, 119
Basie, Count, 14, 18, 201
Bass, Fontella, 177
Batiste, Alvin, 296
Bauer, Conrad, 254
Bechet, Sidney, 159, 241
Bennink, Han, 246, 247, 248, 262, 263
Berger, Karl, 297
Bernstein, Leonard, 40
Black Artists Group (BAG), 187–99
Blackwell, Edward, 41, 44, 47, 48, 52,
    53, 57, 70, 157, 170, 289, 290
Blake, Ran, 288–89
Blakey, Art, 18, 19, 112, 113, 114,
    116, 142
Blanton, Jimmy, 29
Bley, Carla, 138, 139, 228, 229–31
Bley, Paul, 34, 37, 136, 138, 140, 229,
    258

Bloch, Ernest, 264
Blood, James, 57
    See also Ulmer, James "Blood"
Blount, Herman. *See* Sun Ra
Bluiett, Hamiet, 189, 294
Blythe, Arthur, 293–94
Bostic, Earl, 82
Boulez, Pierre, 256
Bowden, Mwata, 191
Bowie, Lester, 175, 176–79, 181, 183,
    185–86, 189, 246, 260, 268
Boykins, Ronnie, 135, 143, 145–46
Brackeen, Charles, 290
Bradford, Bobby, 32, 48, 52, 54,
    149–50, 155, 259, 296
Bradshaw, Tiny, 106
Brand, Dollar, 248
Braxton, Anthony, 120, 173, 180, 181,
    182, 183, 193, 197, 232, 244,
    247, 252, 256, 261, 265, 267,
    269, 271–78, 283, 284, 294
Brecht, Bertolt, 251
Breuker, Willem, 246, 247, 250–52
Brotherhood of Breath, 248–52
Brötzmann, Peter, 247, 248, 253
Brown, Clifford, 18, 61, 112
Brown, Marion, 133, 136–37, 190, 267
Brown, Wes, 270, 298
Brubeck, Dave, 201, 222, 275
Buckner, Tom, 284
Buñuel, Luis, 133
Burroughs, William, 70
Burton, Gary, 229, 232–33
Byard, Jaki, 229
Byas, Don, 105, 153

Cage, John, 51, 272
Campbell, Wilbur, 191, 196
Carisi, Johnny, 107, 198, 207–08
Carroll, Bakaida, 189, 197, 293
Carter, Benny, 66, 133
Carter, Jimmy, 220
Carter, John, 32, 54, 149–50, 296
Carter, Kent, 245
Carter, Ron, 123, 124, 125

Carvin, Michael, 123
Casals, Pablo, 264
Chadbourne, Eugene, 264
Chambers, Joe, 116
Chambers, Paul, 109
Chancey, Vincent, 197–98
Charles, Dennis, 170, 203, 208
Chekasin, Vladimir, 254
Cherry, Don, 33, 34, 37, 40, 41, 42,
    43, 45, 46–48, 51, 52, 55, 57,
    90, 125, 127–28, 132, 138, 139,
    153, 155, 161–63, 170, 229,
    242, 246, 250, 267, 275,
    289–91, 297
Christian, Charlie, 35
Christian, Jodie, 173
Christmann, Günter, 253, 254–55,
    256, 257, 264
Clark, Charles, 180, 183
Clay, James, 45
Cline, Alex, 296
Cobbs, Call, 164, 168
Coe, Tony, 262
Cohran, Phil, 173
Coleman, George, 123
Coleman, Ornette, 13, 30, 31–58,
    62–63, 64, 65, 66, 67, 79, 80,
    90, 92, 100, 103, 105, 111, 122,
    123, 125, 129, 130, 131,
    132, 135, 149, 153, 161, 169,
    171, 174, 180, 191, 200, 227,
    239, 241, 242, 245, 246, 256,
    262, 265, 267, 287, 289, 290,
    296
Coles, Maury, 296
Colson, Andegoke Steve and Iqua, 192
Coltrane, Alice, 101, 103, 237
Coltrane, John, 18, 20, 59, 61, 63,
    71–73, 76, 78, 80–104, 105,
    109, 114, 118, 119, 133, 135,
    136, 137, 147, 161, 165, 166,
    169, 174, 179, 191, 200, 210,
    220, 235–36, 256, 272, 273,
    274, 281, 287, 297, 299
Coltrane, Naima, 82

Connors, Red, 32
Cooke, Jack, 21, 63
Corea, Chick, 119, 227, 231–32, 273
Coryell, Larry, 233
Cosey, Pete, 192
Cowell, Stanley, 118
Cranshaw, Bob, 127
Crispell, Marilyn, 276
Curran, Alvin, 261
Curson, Ted, 133, 136, 204, 208
Cyrille, Andrew, 210, 212, 214, 217

Dabney, Ford, 123
Daley, Joe, 173
Dameron, Tadd, 85
Dara, Olu, 293, 295
Davis, Anthony, 293, 298
Davis, Art, 48
Davis, Charles, 142
Davis, Danny, 146, 147
Davis, Miles, 15, 80, 81, 82–84, 85,
        87–90, 92, 105–28, 132, 153,
        200, 201, 207, 223–25, 226,
        227, 231, 233, 236, 267
Davis, Richard, 70, 73, 74, 76, 79,
        116, 117, 193
De Franco, Buddy, 66
DeJohnette, Jack, 173, 227
DeMicheal, Don, 88
Dixon, Bill, 131, 138, 155, 211, 212
Dodds, Baby, 41
Dodds, Johnny, 270
Dolphy, Eric, 29, 47, 59–79, 80, 82,
        92–93, 94, 96, 102, 105, 116,
        117, 119, 179, 187–88, 200,
        241, 274
Donald, Barbara, 149
Donovan, Jerol, 190
Dørge, Pierre, 255
Dorsey, Tommy, 222
Dotson, Hobart, 142
Douglas, Alan, 73, 75
Dudziak, Urszula, 233
Dufay, Guillaume, 281
Dyani, Johnny, 249, 290
Dyett, Walter, 179

Eckstine, Billy, 106, 107
Eldridge, Roy, 81, 295
Ellington, Duke, 18, 22, 24, 28, 97,
        134, 147, 149, 201, 202, 228,
        287–88
Ellis, Don, 68, 228–29
El'Zabar, Kahil, 298
Estes, Sleepy John, 39
Europe, James Reese, 123
Evans, Bill, 231–32, 289
Evans, Gil, 107, 110–11, 206, 207
Evers, Medgar, 133
Ewart, Douglas, 191–92, 197

Fahey, John, 233
Farmer, Art, 61
Farrell, Joe, 119
Favors, Malachi, 173, 175, 176, 179,
        181, 183, 184, 185, 281
Fela, Anikilapo Kuti, 186
Ferguson, Maynard, 17
Feza, Mongezi, 249
Fielder, Alvin, 176, 183, 296
Fine, Milo, 296
Fortune, Sonny, 119, 256
Foster, Stephen, 163
Francis, Al, 229
Freedman, Joel, 166
Freeman, Chico, 191–92, 197
Freeman, Von, 141, 191, 192

Gaddy, Christopher, 180
Ganelin, Vyacheslav, 254
Garbarek, Jan, 228
Garland, Red, 86, 109, 236
Garner, Errol, 153
Garrett, Rafael (Donald), 101, 173,
        182, 298
Garrison, Jimmy, 44–45, 48, 101
Garvey, Marcus, 130
Gaslini, Giorgio, 246
Gillespie, Dizzy, 14, 15, 21, 32, 62,
        66, 82, 83, 106–07, 241, 287
Gillis, Verna, 292
Gilmore, John, 146
Ginsberg, Allen, 180

Giuffre, Jimmy, 16, 136
Glass, Philip, 273, 280
Globe Unity Orchestra, 252–55
Globokar, Vinko, 256
Golia, Vinny, 296
Goodman, Benny, 256
Goodman, Greg, 261, 296
Gordon, Dexter, 61, 82, 83, 105
Graettinger, Bob, 17–18
Gravenites, Nick the Greek, 174
Graves, Milford, 136, 137, 139, 158,
    165
Greene, Burton, 138
Griffin, Johnny, 84, 293
Griffith, Earl, 203
Griffiths, Malcolm, 250
Grimes, Henry, 135, 153, 155, 165,
    210–11, 290

Haden, Charlie, 21, 33, 37–38, 40, 44,
    45, 46, 53, 57, 229, 234, 258,
    290
Hadi, Shafi (Curtis Porter), 26
Haines, Paul, 230
Hamilton, Chico, 62
Hampel, Günter, 246, 247
Hancock, Herbie, 123, 124, 125,
    231–32
Handel, George Friedrich, 60
Handy, John III, 119
Harden, Wilbur, 89
Hardman, Billy, 45
Harriott, Joe, 246
Harris, Beaver, 134, 136, 165, 245
Harris, Craig, 293
Harrison, Max, 51
Hawes, Hampton, 60
Hawkins, Coleman, 20, 65, 84, 191,
    268
Hawkins, Screamin' Jay, 220
Heath, Percy, 35
Hemphill, Julius, 187, 188–89, 191,
    294
Henderson, Earle, 155
Henderson, Fletcher, 140, 149, 222
Henderson, Joe, 114, 119

Hendrix, Jimi, 233
Hentoff, Nat, 62
Herman, Woody, 297
Herndon, Jim, 143
Higgins, Billy, 33, 34, 37, 41, 45, 47,
    52, 127
Hill, Andrew, 76, 116, 117–18
Hines, Earl, 66, 201, 203
Hodges, Johnny, 82, 202
Holiday, Billie, 22
Holland, David, 232, 259, 263,
    273–74, 275
Honsinger, Tristan, 255, 264
Hooker, John Lee, 266
Hope, Elmo, 297
Hopkins, Fred, 194, 195–96
Howard, Norman, 155
Howling Wolf, 266
Hubbard, Freddie, 47, 63, 74, 119
Hunt, Steve, 298
Hutcherson, Bobby, 73, 74, 116, 117,
    118, 122, 134, 229, 237

Izenzon, David, 48, 49–50, 57, 115,
    134

Jackson, Milt, 201
Jackson, Ronald Shannon, 165, 218,
    219, 291–92
James, Elmore, 266
Jarman, Joseph, 173, 174, 178,
    179–81, 183, 184, 186, 190,
    192, 197, 265, 271, 272, 274,
    275, 278–79, 281–82, 285
Jarrett, Keith, 227, 233–35
Jenkins, Leroy, 183, 193, 272, 273
Johnson, J.J., 108
Johnson, James P., 22, 24
Jones, Elvin, 52, 72, 91, 93, 95–96, 97,
    98, 101, 103, 114, 116, 118,
    157, 158, 183, 239
Jones, Jo, 65
Jones, LeRoi, 138, 163, 167, 180
Jones, Norris, 217, 218
Jones, Philly Joe, 95, 109, 116, 123

Joplin, Scott, 194
Jordan, Edward "Kidd," 296
Jost, Ekkehard, 211

Kaiser, Henry, 264, 296
Kalaparush(a). *See* Maurice McIntyre
Kart, Larry, 281
Keane, Shake, 246
Kenton, Stan, 18, 33, 297
Kenyatta, Robin, 119
Kerr, Clyde, Jr., 296
Khan, Eddie, 73
Kilgallen, Dorothy, 40
King, Albert, 266
King, B.B., 266
King, Martin Luther, Jr., 141
Kirk, Rahsaan Roland, 27, 78, 251
Knepper, Jimmy, 26, 28, 61, 295
Konitz, Lee, 29, 118, 181
Kowald, Peter, 252–53, 270
Krupa, Gene, 251
Kuryokhin, Sergey, 254

Lacy, Steve, 48, 184, 200, 203,
    241–45, 246, 247, 253, 262,
    263
LaFaro, Scott, 44–45, 47, 49, 65, 115
Lake, Oliver, 186, 187–88, 270, 294
Lancaster, Byard, 293
Land, Harold, 60, 61
Lasha, Prince, 32, 149
Lashley, Lester, 175, 183, 192, 255
Lee, Jeanne, 247, 259
LeFlore, Floyd, 187
Lewis, George, 190, 192, 197, 260,
    263, 275, 277, 283, 295
Lewis, Herbie, 237
Lewis, John, 16, 35, 65, 72, 107, 111
Lincoln, Abbey, 70
Little, Booker, 46, 63, 69, 70, 71, 119,
    268
Little Walter, 152
Lloyd, Charles, 119
Lowe, Frank, 293
Lunceford, Jimmy, 18
Lyons, Jimmy, 207, 208, 212, 214,
    217–18, 220

McCall, Steve, 170–71, 173, 183, 193,
    194, 196, 295
McGregor, Chris, 248
McIntyre, Maurice, 173, 175, 182,
    197, 248, 273, 274
McLaughlin, John, 227, 233
McLean, Jackie, 25, 27, 51, 116, 117,
    120–23, 187
McLean, Rene, 122
McMillan, Wallace, 193, 197
Malik, Raphe, 218
Manen, Willem van, 251
Mangelsdorff, Albert, 247, 248, 253,
    254
Mantler, Mike, 138, 139, 213
Marsalis, Branford, 296
Marsalis, Ellis, 296
Marsalis, Wynton, 296
Marsh, Warne, 274
Mary Maria (Parks), 167, 168
Masekela, Hugh, 248
Massey, Cal, 91, 93, 135, 235
Measham, David, 54
Mengelberg, Misha, 246
Metheny, Pat, 233
Mingus, Charles, 16, 21, 24–29, 44,
    49, 59, 60, 62, 63, 64–65, 66,
    67, 72, 76–77, 111, 122, 133,
    136, 139, 170, 183, 231, 294,
    295
Miranda, Roberto Miguel, 296
Mitchell, George, 270
Mitchell, Louis, 240
Mitchell, Red, 37
Mitchell, Roscoe, 170, 173, 174–75,
    177, 178, 179, 180, 181, 183,
    189, 190, 192, 197, 256, 260,
    265, 271, 272, 274, 275, 278,
    279–86, 297, 299
Mobley, Hank, 19, 84, 112, 247
Modern Jazz Quartet, 15
Moffett, Charles, 32, 48, 51
Moncur, Grachan III, 117, 122
Monk, Thelonious, 19–20, 21, 23, 65,
    68, 85, 86–87, 107, 109, 117,
    120, 132, 149, 201, 204, 205,
    232, 241–42, 243, 293

Montrose, J.R., 25
Moondoc, Jemeel, 293
Moore, Brew, 207
Moreira, Airto, 227
Morgan, Lee, 18, 45, 46, 112, 113,
    119, 120–23, 135, 204, 247
Morris, Wilbur, 295
Morton, Jelly Roll, 288
Moses, J.C., 73, 74, 134, 136
Motian, Paul, 230, 234
Moye, Don, 184, 185
Mulligan, Gerry, 107, 109
Murray, David, 294, 295, 296
Murray, Sunny, 96, 116, 136, 137,
    138, 155, 156, 157–59, 163,
    165, 170, 200, 208, 210
Myers, Amina Claudine, 190

Nancarrow, Conlon, 254
Naughton, Bobby, 297–98
Navarro, Fats, 14, 18, 107
Neidlinger, Buell, 203, 204, 206
Nelson, Oliver, 71
Newton, James, 293
Nichols, Herbie, 21–24, 147, 200, 201,
    217
Nicholson, Reggie, 298
Norvo, Red, 24
Ntshoko, Makaya, 249

Oliver, King, 176, 222
Original Memphis Five, 222
Ory, Kid, 19
Oshita, Gerald, 284, 296

Page, Hot Lips, 202
Parker, Charlie, 14, 18, 20, 27, 35, 42,
    61, 66, 70, 71, 75, 81, 83,
    106–07, 120–21, 145, 146–47,
    152, 189, 217, 241, 275, 287,
    298
Parker, Evan, 249, 253, 257, 260, 261,
    263
Parlan, Horace, 135
Patrick, Pat, 142, 146, 147
Payne, Don, 45

Peacock, Gary, 135, 156, 157, 165
Pepper, Art, 36
Peterson, Oscar, 206
Pettiford, Oscar, 29
Ponty, Jean-Luc, 233
Portal, Michel, 256
Porter, Roy, 61
Potts, Steve, 244
Powell, Bud, 14, 18, 120, 201
Pozo, Chano, 66
Pukwana, Dudu, 249
Pullen, Don, 136, 139
Purim, Flora, 233

Ragin, Hugh, 275, 276, 284, 285
Redd, Freddie, 204
Redman, Dewey, 32, 52, 53, 57, 149,
    234, 290
Reich, Steve, 280
Reinhardt, Django, 240
Rexroth, Kenneth, 39
Richmond, Dannie, 26, 295
Rivers, Sam, 114, 119, 123
Roach, Max, 18, 20, 23, 24, 25, 26, 61,
    65, 70, 95, 130, 133, 135, 139,
    196, 275
Robeson, Paul, 133, 135
Robinson, Leroy "Sweetpea," 61
Robinson, Troy, 173, 174
Rollins, Sonny, 20, 38, 42, 45, 81, 84,
    95, 103, 108, 113, 127, 128,
    132, 133, 134, 153, 162, 171,
    181, 210, 261, 267, 289
Rova Saxophone Quartet, 285–86
Rudd, Roswell, 134, 137–38, 139, 162,
    193, 230, 242, 245
Russell, George, 16, 64, 66–69, 71,
    110, 198, 227–28, 229, 232
Russell, Hal, 298
Rutherford, Paul, 250, 253, 254–55,
    256, 257

Sampson, Michel, 165
Sanders, Pharoah, 101, 102, 103, 136,
    139

Schlippenbach, Alexander von, 246, 252–53

Schuller, Gunther, 16, 47, 65, 72, 76, 203, 204, 288

Shahid, Jaribu, 297

Shapero, Harold, 16

Shaw, Charles Bobo, 187, 189

Shaw, Gene (Clarence), 26

Shaw, Woody, 73, 118, 119–20

Shepp, Archie, 99, 100, 101, 130, 131–35, 136, 137, 170, 200, 204–05, 207, 208, 248

Shorter, Alan, 114

Shorter, Wayne, 112–15, 116, 120, 124, 126, 223, 224, 225–27

Silva, Alan, 165, 166, 211, 212

Silver, Horace, 18, 112, 117, 119, 142, 201

Simmons, Sonny, 149

Sims, Zoot, 109

Sirone (Norris Jones), 217, 218

Smith, Bessie, 270

Smith, Bill, 296

Smith, Joe, 270

Smith, Leo, 69, 183, 265–71, 273, 275, 277, 278, 280, 283, 297

Smith, Leonard, 178

Spellman, A.B., 21, 40, 120

Spencer, Harry, 147

Stamm, Marvin, 208

Stevens, John, 259–60

Stitt, Sonny, 20, 106

Stravinsky, Igor, 66, 201

Subramaniam, L., 233

Sun Ra, 138, 139, 140–49, 172, 177

Tabbal, Tani, 285, 297

Tapscott, Horace, 296–97

Tarasov, Vladimir, 254

Tatum, Art, 15, 117, 181, 201

Taylor, Cecil, 17, 59, 63, 80, 105, 117, 131, 136, 138, 139, 147, 153, 155, 157, 158, 175, 182, 200–221, 238, 241, 246, 253, 287

Tchicai, John, 132, 137, 138, 161, 249, 255

Teitelbaum, Richard, 275

Tex, Joe, 186

Theile, Bob, 99, 133

Thompson, Danny, 147

Threadgill, Henry, 173, 193–95, 197, 272, 284, 294, 295, 296

Toomer, Jean, 136

Towner, Ralph, 233

Tristano, Lennie, 15, 29–30, 108, 201, 255, 274

Turrentine, Stanley, 227

Tyler, Charles, 40, 161, 163, 164, 165, 169, 171, 292

Tyner, McCoy, 91, 93, 97, 99, 101, 103–04, 235–39

Ulmer, James "Blood," 57, 227, 290

Urbanick, Michal, 233

Varèse, Edgard, 72

Vasconcelos, Nana, 289

Vinson, Eddie, 82

Voigt, Andrew, 286

Von Hove, Fred, 247, 248

Waits, Freddie, 237

Walcott, Collin, 289

Waldron, Mal, 25, 70, 71, 85, 244–45

Wallace, Bill, 266

Waller, Fats, 201

Ware, Wilbur, 20–21, 24, 37, 65, 87

Washington, Tyrone, 118, 119

Watts, Trevor, 259

Weather Report, 225–27

Webster, Ben, 132

Westbrook, Mike, 250

Wheeler, Kenny, 259, 275

Wilkerson, Edward, 298

Williams, Mary Lou, 217, 219

Williams, Tony, 74–75, 116–17, 118, 122, 123–24, 126, 157, 227, 273

Wilson, Joe Lee, 292

Wilson, Phillip, 177–79, 186–87, 189

Winters, Smiley, 298
Wolpe, Stefan, 207
Worrell, Lewis, 135, 137, 165

Yakub, Abdullah, 178, 186, 187
Yancey, Jimmy, 40, 201

Young, Larry, 227
Young, Lester, 21, 39, 84, 105, 120,
    191, 269

Zawinul, Joe, 225–27

Other DA CAPO titles of interest

JOHN COLTRANE
Bill Cole
278 pp., 25 photos
80530-8 $13.95

ERIC DOLPHY
A Musical Biography and
Discography
Revised Edition
Vladimir Simosko and
Barry Tepperman
156 pp., 17 photos
80524-3 $10.95

MILES DAVIS
The Early Years
Bill Cole
256 pp.
80554-5 $13.95

FORCES IN MOTION
The Music and Thoughts
of Anthony Braxton
Graham Lock
412 pp., 16 photos, numerous illus.
80342-9 $13.95

FREE JAZZ
by Ekkehard Jost
214 pp., 70 musical examples
80556-1 $13.95

CHASIN' THE TRANE
The Music and Mystique
of John Coltrane
J. C. Thomas
256 pp., 16 pp. of photos
80043-8 $10.95

IMPROVISATION
Its Nature and Practice in Music
Derek Bailey
172 pp., 12 photos
80528-6 $12.95

NOTES AND TONES
Musician-to-Musician Interviews
Expanded Edition
Arthur Taylor
318 pp., 20 photos
80526-X $13.95

Available at your bookstore

OR ORDER DIRECTLY FROM

DA CAPO PRESS, INC.

1-800-321-0050